DATE DUE

BRODART, CO. Cat. No. 23-221

KILLING AS PUNISHMENT

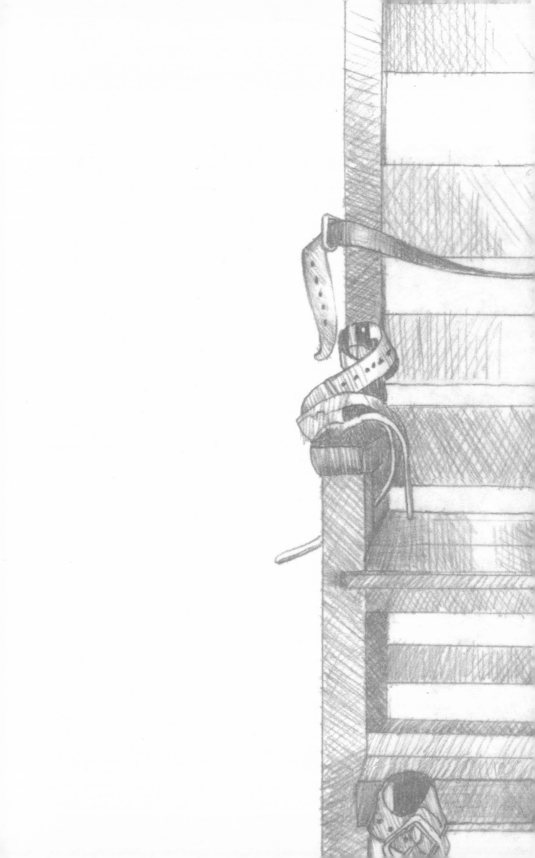

KILLING AS PUNISHMENT

REFLECTIONS ON THE DEATH PENALTY IN AMERICA

HUGO ADAM BEDAU

NORTHEASTERN UNIVERSITY PRESS   BOSTON

Northeastern University Press

Library of Congress Cataloging-in-Publication Data
Bedau, Hugo Adam.
   Killing as punishment : reflection on the death penalty
in America / Hugo Adam Bedau.
       p.   cm.
Includes bibliographical references and index.
   ISBN 1-55553-595-x (cloth : alk. paper)
   1. Capital punishment—United States. 2. Capital punishment—
Political aspects—United States. 3. Capital punishment—Moral
and ethical aspects—United States. I. Title.
   HV8699.U5.B43 2004
   364.66'0973—dc22   2003018649

Designed by Steve Kress

Composed in Janson by Creative Graphics, Inc., Allentown,
Pennsylvania. Printed and bound by Maple Press, York,
Pennsylvania. The paper is Maple Tradebook Antique,
an acid-free stock.

MANUFACTURED IN THE UNITED STATES OF AMERICA
08 07 06 05 04   5 4 3 2 1

For Constance, again

CONTENTS

An examination of the death penalty might conveniently be divided along two major axes: one factual or descriptive, the other critical or analytical. Whatever may be true of other volumes on this subject, the chapters in this book fall rather neatly under these two rubrics.

The first five chapters explore in detail a variety of factual issues raised by the controversy over the death penalty. Chapter 1 sketches a comparison of the situation at the beginning of the twenty-first century with that of the late 1950s, providing an overview of the entire subject and an opportunity to measure progress and shortfall as seen from the standpoint of an ardent opponent of the death penalty. Despite the fact that as of this writing killing as a lawful punishment in American is far from being abolished, a variety of reforms have been introduced during the past half century that can best be interpreted as moving in that direction. Chapter 2 introduces the reader to three of the important populist aspects of our current death penalty culture: the influence on the sentencing jury of so-called victim-impact statements offered by surviving family members; personal witness by such family members at the actual execution of the murderer of their loved one; and the debate over broadcasting executions "live" on television. Chapter 3 is devoted to examining the most troublesome feature of any death penalty system: the sources and extent of wrongful convictions, sentences, and executions. As the evidence shows, this worry is not confined to the remote past. Rather, a new case of this sort has been uncovered virtually every month during the past decade. Chapter 4 tracks the vanishing act of executive clemency in capital cases. What was once a fairly widespread practice by governors in response to excessive reliance on the death penalty by trial juries—unavoidable in the era of mandatory capital punishment—has now become an endangered species. With more than 3,700 persons on death row, not one condemned person has received executive clemency in the most recent four years for which we have records (1997–2000); Governor George Ryan's mass clemency grant to Illinois's 171 death row prisoners in early 2003 was a dramatic departure from that pattern. Chapter 5 brings the first half of the book to an end with an evaluation of the merits of the death penalty versus the usual alternative punishment of life imprisonment without the possibility of parole (LWOP, as it is now commonly called). Each chapter in this half of the book sheds light from a different direction on the actual administration of the death penalty in the United States today and in the recent past.

The second half of the book undertakes a critical evaluation of the death penalty from a constitutional and an ethical point of view. Chapters 6 and 7 consider the death penalty in light of relevant constitutional principles. Many readers of the Supreme Court's ruling in *Gregg v. Georgia* (1976), which protected the constitutional status of the death penalty, have not been persuaded by the Court's arguments. These two chapters offer reasons why one ought to agree with these dissenters. Chapter 8 offers an argument against the death penalty and searches for common ground between the friends and opponents of this mode of punishment, relying mainly on general principles governing punishments of every sort. This is but one of many different kinds of anti–death penalty arguments that need careful formulation and examination. In chapter 9 the constitutional arguments are again set aside in order to address the death penalty again from the moral point of view. Here I attempt to show principally two things: First, that many of the moral arguments used by opponents of the death penalty are less conclusive than their users believe; and second, that there are nevertheless reasons favoring abolition of the death penalty even for the worst murderers (however one proposes to define "worst"). The book closes with an epilogue devoted to reviewing some of the extensive current literature on a variety of issues raised by the death penalty. Special attention is given to the many procedural reforms now under discussion in Congress and in several state legislatures that fall short of outright abolition but move in that direction.

Perhaps the best, and certainly the briefest, way to describe this book as a whole is as an exercise in applied ethics. (I have explained my ideas about applied ethics elsewhere, in *Making Mortal Choices: Three Exercises in Moral Casuistry* [1997].) Taken together, these chapters constitute an interdisciplinary inquiry. Sociologists, criminologists, lawyers (practicing and academic), historians and other students of American politics and contemporary culture, and of course philosophers should find suggestive material here for their reflection. The reader should be forewarned, however: I do not attempt in this volume to review comprehensively all aspects of the death penalty controversy. For example, I say little or nothing about deterrence, the deplorable conditions on death row, the racial and class biases in the actual administration of capital punishment, or the inconsistencies of our death penalty practices with international human rights law. Such omissions ought to be excusable because at irregular intervals I have undertaken to provide just such a comprehensive account in the successive editions of my book *The Death Penalty in America* (1964, 1967, 1982, 1997). In this volume my aim is limited to offering the reader an intensive education on several of the major empirical and normative issues raised by the death penalty.

As I said at the outset, I do not write from a neutral perspective on the death penalty. I have long been an opponent of this form of punishment, and my interest as a philosopher in the theory of punishment has been much influenced by my efforts to understand and resist the attractions of killing as a punishment in our society. There was a brief period during the summer of 1972, in the immediate aftermath of the Supreme Court's decision on *Furman v. Georgia*, when I thought that the struggle to abolish executions in this country was on the verge of a successful and long overdue end. The subsequent three decades have shown that I could not have been more in error. Progress in abolishing the death penalty has proved to be very slow, intermittent, and fragmentary. This book provides no remedy for that delay, but it does provide some benchmarks along the road traveled so far.

KILLING AS PUNISHMENT

1 THE DEATH PENALTY IN AMERICA, YESTERDAY AND TODAY

Where does our society now stand on the matter of abolishing capital punishment? To answer that question, I propose to contrast our current situation with the recent past, and to take as my baseline the late 1950s, when I first became concerned about the death penalty. To tally the relevant facts, let us start by identifying those developments that have tended to entrench the death penalty in our society.

I

Fifty years ago the American public was almost evenly divided over the death penalty, according to survey research of that day, with perhaps fifteen percent of the public undecided. In the 1980s, public support for the death penalty increased to about three or four to one, with barely 10 percent undecided. It may be, as some have remarked, that current national support for the death penalty is indeed a mile wide, but only an inch deep, and that given an effective alternative punishment, a majority of Americans would be willing to end executions. Yet popular support for the death penalty today is widespread and occasionally reaches strident proportions, as the circus atmosphere surrounding the execution of Ted Bundy in Florida in January 1989 illustrates. This apparently overwhelming public support for the death penalty (even though it has recently declined from around 80 percent to around 70 percent) is no doubt the greatest single obstacle—directly or indirectly—at the present time to total nationwide abolition.

Five decades ago the nation's major political parties ignored the death penalty; the issue played no visible role in electoral politics at the local, state, or federal levels. Today, the national Republican Party has a standing platform plank favoring the death penalty, and five Republican presidents have used the "bully pulpit" of the White House to cultivate public support for executions. Two of them, Richard Nixon and Ronald Reagan, went even further. They openly criticized Supreme Court decisions that introduced some measure of justice into the law on capital punishment. During 1988, the world witnessed an unprecedented spectacle as our presidential election campaigns were polarized around this issue. In 2000 the nation elected a president (George W. Bush) who had presided over dozens of executions in his capacity as the governor of Texas.

Fifty years ago, any prospective juror in a capital case who voiced opposition to the death penalty was summarily dismissed "for cause" by the trial judge. Today, despite the *Witherspoon* ruling in 1968, little has changed. Every prosecutor in a capital case begins the trial knowing he or she has a death-scrupled jury, and knowing that such juries are more willing to convict on a given body of evidence than a jury chosen at random, a true jury of the defendant's (and the victim's) peers in the community.

In the late 1950s, it was not uncommon for a governor to commute a death sentence, especially if it had been imposed under a mandatory death statute, or on someone other than the "triggerman," or on a juvenile or a woman, or for other reasons of mercy. Today, excepting Governor Ryan's recent extraordinary mass commutation, commutation of the death sentence has virtually ceased. (See the discussion in Chapter 4.) The reasons for this change are not fully understood, but substantial public support for the death penalty and the unwillingness of governors to commit what they view as political suicide are no doubt the principal factors. The result is a curious and unbalanced struggle: The populist trial court tries to wrestle the offender into the execution chamber; the elitist appellate court is on the lookout for the grosser fouls; and the chief executive stands passively to one side.

Five decades ago the racial impact of the death penalty was a troubling matter, but it was neither carefully studied nor widely lamented—hardly surprising in a day when the white threat to lynch blacks was still quite real and Jim Crow governed the relations between the races. For the past thirty years, we have known that the death penalty for rape was virtually reserved for black males found guilty of raping white females. We also know that among those executed for murder, the race of the victim is still decisive. In eighty percent of the executions during the past decade (1993–2002), the offender's victim was white. Rarely has a white offender been executed for the murder of a nonwhite victim. In 1987, the Supreme Court acknowledged in *McCleskey v. Kemp* that the racial pattern of capital indictments, sentences, and executions cannot plausibly be explained except by assuming some form of bias against offenders whose victims are white. Even so, the Court could find no constitutional ground for overturning the death sentences that were the product of such systemic bias.

In the late 1970s in *Gregg v. Georgia* and related cases, the Supreme Court rejected the argument that the death penalty in principle is a "cruel and unusual punishment." The Court had earlier upheld the death penalty in *McGautha v. California* against the criticism that it was in violation of "equal protection of the laws." Not only has the Court held that the death penalty is not per se unconstitutional, the current Court has apparently brought to a halt most efforts to introduce procedural reforms in capital cases. Such reforms during the 1970s were the product of the belief shared by most members of the Burger Court that "death"—that is, the punishment of death—"is different," and so of course more stringent procedures are required when someone is sentenced to death. Today, however the conservatives on the Rehnquist Court would roll back these reforms. They have been under steady criticism by the Chief Justice himself. Two areas of concern above all others have marked the Court's retrograde practices when measured by the standards of international human rights law. One is the toleration of death sentences for the mentally retarded. The other is allowing persons who were under eighteen at the time of their crime to be sentenced to death. The Court has yet to muster a majority against the latter issue. On the former, however, in 2002 by a vote of six to three in *Atkins v. Virginia* the Court ruled—in the words of Justice Stevens—that "Death is not a suitable punishment for a mentally retarded individual."

In earlier decades, legislatures would respond to public outcry over "the crime of the hour" by increasing the severity of the punishment from imprisonment to death. In the 1930s, this happened with the crime of kidnapping; in the 1960s the crime was aircraft hijacking; today, the crime is drug-related homicide. During the presidential campaign of 1988, Congress passed by an overwhelming vote the Anti-Drug Abuse Act. One of its provisions treats as a federal crime any homicide that occurs during drug-related activities. The provision also authorizes the trial court to sentence to death anyone so convicted. This law effectively introduces capital punishment into every jurisdiction in the nation, whether abolitionist under its own laws or not; the law in effect threatens for the first time to nationalize the death penalty.

Finally, on this side of the debate, we must look squarely at the worst development of all. In the 1950s, on any given day, there were about 200 prisoners awaiting execution. Rarely did anyone remain on death row for more than a few years. Today, in two dozen American prisons there are over 3,700 condemned convicts, most of whom have been under a death sentence for more than a decade. Apart from the Hitler and Stalin eras in Europe, this is the greatest concentration of prisoners on the altar of Moloch in the modern history of western civilization.

II

Now let us turn to the other side of the debate. The set of developments over the past five decades favoring abolition are many and diverse. Five decades ago, only six states were completely without the death penalty. Delaware's decision to abolish executions in 1958 was the first in many years where a state legislature voted to end executions. Today, abolition jurisdictions number a baker's dozen.

Fifty years ago persons could be and were sentenced to death and executed not only for murder but also for rape; indeed, ten percent of all executions were for that crime. From time to time executions also occurred for armed robbery, burglary, and kidnapping. The most famous execution of the 1950s—Julius and Ethel Rosenberg in New York—and of the 1960s—Caryl Chessman in California—were for non-homicidal crimes. Dozens of different offenses were punishable by death; my favorite was the death penalty in Georgia for kicking over a tombstone ("desecrating a grave," in the sober language of the statute). Today, using the death penalty to punish crime has survived Supreme Court scrutiny only when the crime is some form of homicide.

In the 1950s, death was the mandatory punishment for at least one crime in many capital jurisdictions. Today, the death penalty is not a mandatory punishment for any crime.

Fifty years ago, the trial courts that did have sentencing discretion in capital cases were free to exercise that discretion unfettered by any pretense of fairness. The law did not even attempt to curb arbitrariness or discrimination in the choice of sentence for a capital crime. Today, judges and jurors must at least profess to have well-grounded reasons for a death sentence rather than a prison sentence, based on evidence presented during the post-conviction, pre-sentencing phase of the trial. Furthermore, the trial jury is entitled to hear anything of a mitigating nature that might serve as a reasonable ground for a prison sentence rather than a death sentence, and defense counsel is free to present a complete personality profile on the defendant to the sentencing court.

Five decades ago persons were sentenced to death and executed without assurance of review by the highest state appellate court, much less review in the federal courts, of constitutional issues. Today, review of every death sentence by the relevant state court is required by law in most jurisdictions and further review in the federal courts is a virtual certainty. These reviews are significant if one judges by their effects. The research by Professor James Liebman and his associates at Columbia University Law School has shown in their report, *A Broken System* (2000, 2002), that two-thirds of all death sentences in recent years meted out by trial courts have been reversed on appeal in state or federal courts.

In the late 1950s, the Supreme Court had expressed no views on the constitutionality of the death penalty. Since that time, the Court has rejected on constitutional grounds mandatory death sentences and death sentences for nonhomicidal crimes such as rape and kidnapping.

Five decades ago, two or three executions were carried out each week in any of three dozen states across the nation. During the 1990s, very few executions occurred each month, and they were confined to a dozen jurisdictions. The only places where death sentence prisoners have been regularly executed are in the deep South.

In the 1950s, executions were carried out by hanging, shooting, electrocuting, or asphyxiating the prisoner. These methods are still in use, but in the latest phase of the continuing search for the ideal form of execution, legislatures have increasingly favored death by lethal injection. This procedure is relatively painless, clean, reliable, and quick, at least when compared with neck-breaking, high-voltage frying, choking by gas, or the trauma of multiple bullet wounds. Nevertheless, lethal injection illustrates Schwarzschild's Paradox, named after the late Henry Schwarzschild, who first formulated it: Some methods of carrying out the death penalty are worse than others, but none is better than any (for a fuller discussion, see Chapter 5.)

In the late 1950s, social scientists, lawyers, and humanists in this country rarely studied the death penalty, and even more rarely published the results of their investigations and reflections. Ignorance about the actual status, effects, and functions of the death penalty in the United States was widespread. Today, two or three articles on one or another aspect of the death penalty appear in professional journals every month, and books on the subject are published every year. With a whole library of current materials to consult (see the Epilogue), there is no excuse for anyone not to be fully informed about our lawful lethal practices.

Five decades ago, pioneering research had just been published that cast doubt on the special deterrent effect of the death penalty. Now, after three decades of increasingly sophisticated inquiry, the results are reasonably clear. Either we can infer nothing from the data on the question because the statistical methods are too crude given the infrequency of executions and the importance of unquantifiable variables, or we can conclude that the two penalties—death vs. long-term imprisonment—are about equally (in)effective as deterrents.

Finally, in 1959, only one frail voice was raised against the death penalty nationwide; it issued from the American League to Abolish Capital Punishment, founded in the 1920s. But by the mid-1960s, the American Civil Liberties Union and the NAACP Legal Defense and Educational Fund had joined the cause. In the 1970s, Amnesty International focused the efforts of its worldwide organization to attack the problem. Today, the National Coalition to Abolish the Death Penalty supports a fully staffed office in Washington, D.C., national and regional conferences, and the participation of more than one hundred multi-issue organizations concerned with civil liberties, human rights, and legal aid. Foremost among these organizations is the Death Penalty Information Center, founded in 1990 and located in the nation's capital. Its regular reports on all the major empirical and legal issues surrounding the death penalty offer assistance to journalists and others who wish to keep informed.

In the 1950s, no one thought that a nationwide moratorium on executions was desirable or possible. Today, thanks to the leadership of the American Bar Association, such a moratorium is openly advocated in many quarters and as of this writing has found favor in two states, Illinois and Maryland.

In the 1950s, many Protestant and Jewish denominations opposed the death penalty on religious grounds. In recent years they have been joined by the powerful voices of the American Catholic Bishops and the Vatican. If the Catholic laity were to join the clergy, the end of the death penalty would be within reach.

III

It is apparent that awareness of and opposition to the death penalty is growing. But rather than dwelling on that point, I want to offer a few cautionary observations suggested by the foregoing survey.

First, despite evidence to the contrary, the reforms enacted during the past several decades have brought greater fairness into a death sentence system hitherto shot through with arbitrary and discriminatory use of authority. To that extent, these reforms rationalize every death sentence and every execution; they have made what remains of capital punishment in the United States more, not less, acceptable. This is but the latest irony in the whole history of the struggle against the death penalty in this nation, a history that began two centuries ago in Pennsylvania when the reach of the death penalty was limited by the distinction between first- and second-degree murder.

Second, defense of the death penalty publicly, jurisprudentially, and philosophically has become increasingly and openly grounded on retributive feelings and principles. By retribution I do not mean that potent combination of anger, fear, and frustration that in fact seems to characterize the prevailing national desire to "get tough with crime." This retaliatory syndrome should be kept distinct from retribution. Retaliation knows no limits imposed by respect for justice, whereas legitimate retributive punishment does acknowledge a constraint of that sort.

The chief consequences of resting the defense of the death penalty on retribution is that it makes criticism of executions on grounds of justice, or reason, or experience, increasingly difficult. In the days when many different crimes were punishable by death, the simple retributive maxim, "A Life for a Life," obviously was insufficient. Something more was needed to defend the death penalty for rape, armed robbery, espionage, and the like. So defense of executions rested primarily on claims of special deterrence and incapacitation; these purposes, not retribution, provided the necessary rationale. Today, however, deterrence and incapacitation seem less important than they used to be. Instead, the laws and prevailing attitudes rest on the appeal to "just deserts," and as Mother Wit long ago taught us, the murderer deserves to die, period. As a result, argument over the death penalty has become correspondingly more complex and abstract (see Chapters 6 to 9).

Finally, the current system of capital punishment entrenches our national obsession with killing people. It teaches the lesson that some may kill others willfully, deliberately, and with premeditation as long as they are the right people doing it for the right reasons in the right manner. The fact that such killings as punishment are not necessary, that there is a well-established alternative method of punishment—long-term imprisonment—now used throughout Europe and in many American jurisdictions for over a century, does not matter. Defenders of the death penalty insist that the killings they favor are justified, desirable, authorized—and therefore *are* "necessary." Besides, we are told, those who are condemned to die by the death penalty are less than human. Their conduct and their histories prove that they are not like us, and they have done unspeakable things for which there is no forgiveness or repentance; they deserve our righteous indignation. Any refusal on our part to put them to death is proof of our own failure of nerve. Thus do we extend the reign of Thanatos, the god of death.

Writing some years ago, Dr. Louis Gold, a New York psychiatrist, observed that in his experience, discussion of capital punishment inevitably provoked "a great deal of blind and highly personalized affect . . . , identification and projection, repressed hostility and aggression, rejection, passivity and guilt." My remarks verge on illustrating Dr. Gold's observation. Even a philosopher cannot pretend to suppress indefinitely all affect on this subject.

I digress, and I must return to my main theme. This year in the United States, there will be 16,000 or more criminal homicides. At most, half of these crimes will result in a conviction of murder or manslaughter. Of the 8,000 or so persons convicted, a small number, perhaps as many as 250, will be sentenced to death. Of these few, an unknown number will eventually be executed sometime during the next decade. This year perhaps two or three a month will enter the execution chamber. With more than 15,000 murders, there will be fewer than 100 executions.

These facts strongly suggest that we abolitionists have virtually won our struggle no matter what the courts decree or public opinion declares. Perhaps it is only a question of time before advocates of judicially authorized executions throw in the towel. I am sure these figures prove beyond question that it is no longer possible to defend the death penalty in our society on a retributive, utilitarian, or any other rationale.

Nevertheless, the position of many abolitionists deviates from the typical and prevailing position of most Americans on several important questions of morality. This difference is crucially relevant to the likelihood of any early success of our efforts in the future. I do not suggest merely that the public opinion polls show how abolitionists would be outvoted. Rather, I suggest two things.

First, abolitionists take an *absolute* position (categorically opposing all executions) at a time when our society is afloat on a sea of moral relativity in which there are few if any absolute prohibitions at all. Second, we fight against one kind of homicide—the kind done by the state as punishment—while tolerating many other forms of homicide. No wonder we appear deviant and even inconsistent to our opponents! Bear with me for a few moments as I explore these ideas.

The bulk of the American public agrees with us that hardly any criminals really deserve the death penalty. Thanks to the dispersal of judicial power among the prosecution, trial judges, and appellate courts, only 250 or so persons were sentenced to death annually in the 1990s out of a possible 8,000 or so convicted annually of criminal homicide. What most of our fellow Americans do not understand is why we oppose *all* executions, even of the worst offenders, and especially of recidivist murderers. We know, of course, that the 250 out of the 8,000 who are sentenced to death are the losers in a crude and arbitrary lottery, and that they go to their deaths not because they are the worst among the bad, and thus the most deserving, but for a variety of other reasons that make a mockery of the rule of law and equal justice for all. Even so, if all arbitrariness was magically ended tomorrow, and only the 250 of the very worst, most dangerous, least manageable or reformable murderers were sentenced to death, we would *still* oppose their execution. However much our opponents may respect us for our sincere convictions, they are bewildered by our moral absolutism.

And the truth is, most of us do not take a position of moral absolutism against killing human beings in every circumstance. We do not universally oppose all abortions. We do not unequivocally condemn all killings in self-defense or in the aid of helpless third parties. We do not universally oppose all use of lethal force by the police. We do not absolutely condemn all mercy killings and all suicides. We do not denounce as immoral the conduct of a death sentence convict who refuses any further legal assistance to fight his death sentence and who, to that extent, "volunteers" to die.

As I contemplate my own answers to these questions and the profile of my attitude toward the value of human life, I confess that I cannot take any easy refuge behind such bulwarks as the sanctity of human life or the absolute right to life. These principles are simultaneously too rigid and too vague to do justice to my reflective convictions on matters of human life and death (see Chapter 9). And I suspect I am not the only one who opposes the death penalty in a setting of relative approval, toleration, or permission regarding some of these other kinds of human killings.

In admitting the above, I do not believe that I am guilty of any moral inconsistency. I do not think that logic requires anyone who is absolutely opposed to the death penalty to oppose as well all abortions, suicides, mercy killings, lethal force, and so on. In fact it is quite easy to defend hostility toward capital punishment and toleration toward other kinds of homicide in certain circumstances. All one must do is notice the distinctive things about the kind of killing that capital punishment always involves:

1. When the state kills a prisoner, no one else's life, limb, or liberty is therewith preserved, saved, or restored; nor is anyone's death or harm prevented.
2. When the state kills a prisoner, it kills a human being whose abilities, moral development, and capacities for autonomous conduct are not significantly different from those of all other prisoners and most other persons.
3. When the state kills a prisoner, an alternative was available—incarceration, isolation, temporary sedation—that would effectively reduce the risk of harm to others.
4. When the state kills a prisoner, it does not care what the prisoner desires or prefers or what the likely future life of that prisoner would have been if he had not been killed.

No homicide except capital punishment presents these four features. All other types of homicide lack one or more, and that is enough to make capital punishment homicide different from other homicides in morally relevant respects. But it is far from clear that these differences make it reasonable to oppose *all* cases of capital punishment and only some or most of the other types of homicide.

Why then do abolitionists oppose the death penalty in all cases? Is it in fact reasonable to do so? I cannot answer for anyone but myself, and I am not entirely sure even now, after more than forty years, that I can do so adequately. But I shall try.

First, I shrink from the whole idea of killing anyone, especially without the fully rational consent and knowledge of the one who is to die, and I oppose hiring or in any way supporting others to do a job I am morally unwilling to do myself. I do not believe that I could kill any prisoner (or, if I had done so, believe that I was fully justified) and I do not want to hire anyone else to do it for me.

Second, the reasons that public officials and the general public give for their support of any execution, or for capital punishment in general, seem to me to spread across a spectrum the ends of which are marked by ignorance, inconsistency, and insincerity.

Third, killing by the government of one of its own citizens as punishment symbolizes for me everything that is wrong about coercion, power, bureaucratic institutions, and lawful authority. The death penalty system has its chief effects not on crime but on the criminal justice system. There its effects are two. The death penalty increases costs by way of tax dollars, judicial time and effort, and human stress. The death penalty also decreases understanding of and accommodation to the facts of modern life.

Beyond these effects lies the symbolic significance of capital punishment, and this for me is a crucial consideration. This symbolic significance explains the role of capital punishment in the public forum and the grip it continues to have on our imagination. The three reasons mentioned above which explain my own opposition to the death penalty are evidence of the symbolic significance this form of punishment has for me.

Let me end by drawing attention to a wise comment of seventy years ago that has relevance to the death penalty, even though it was offered originally in a completely different context. As Sigmund Freud reached the conclusion of his sobering little book *Civilization and Its Discontents*, he observed that "the question is how to dislodge the greatest obstacle to civilization, the constitutional tendency in men to aggressions against one another. . . ." Who can disagree? But if we do agree with Freud, then surely our opposition to the death penalty must be seen as part of the progressive effort to civilize the aggressive tendencies in our society, thus vindicating our unremitting efforts to see the death penalty abolished once and for all. Capital punishment, as a foremost example of the dysfunctional use of violence and of the ritualization of the tendency toward aggression in one of its most seductive forms, the expression of righteous indignation, deserves our condemnation and all the resistance we can muster.

AMERICAN POPULISM: WITNESSES TO AN EXECUTION

As we move through the early years of this century, the death penalty in the United States seems firmly entrenched in the nation's laws and practices, and in the attitudes of the people. More than 3,700 persons are under sentence of death. About 250 more will be sentenced to death this year. In 2002 an execution occurred somewhere in the nation roughly every five days. Legislative repeal of any death penalty statutes is highly unlikely. State governors or pardon boards—with rare exceptions—will commute few death sentences to terms of life imprisonment, even in cases where there is considerable doubt over the guilt of the prisoner (see Chapter 4). Members of both political parties in Congress support legislation to extend the federal death penalty as the punishment for crimes not involving homicide. The majority of the Supreme Court remains content to see the states carry out death sentences under laws that cry out for nullification on federal constitutional grounds. The nation's president, in his former capacity as governor of Texas, presided over dozens of executions.

Against this background I want to review some aspects of the popular standing of the death penalty in the United States.

Such a review might well start with an evaluation of the survey research purportedly showing that public attitudes until quite recently favored the death penalty for the punishment of murder by an overwhelming majority. It certainly ought to include examination of the way electoral politics have been apparently increasingly influenced by a candidate's announced position on the death penalty. However, both these themes have been relatively well publicized; I will touch on them only in passing, and will concentrate on three other aspects of the topic that attest to the populist character of the death penalty in the United States today: the way persons, including surviving family members of a murder victim, seek to be present at executions; the controversy over whether executions ought to be shown on television; and the use of so-called victim-impact statements in the sentencing phase of a capital trial.

I

Who really supports the death penalty in the United States? In particular, who supports actually imposing death sentences and then executing the prisoner according to the sentence? Let us put aside criminal justice officials and employees in death penalty jurisdictions, since they are acting in their official capacities and thus could be said to be "only doing their jobs." Let us also put aside elected politicians, since if most of them believed the public strongly opposed the death penalty, they would probably oppose it too. If we move nearer to the actual capital crime and the punishment for it, we encounter representative citizens in one or the other of two capacities: as members of a capital trial jury, or as the surviving family members of a murder victim. The attitudes and behavior of the persons in these roles deserve a closer look.

Capital trial juries, as it turns out, are not very enthusiastic supporters of the death penalty, even though each juror is screened during the *voir dire* to ferret out and reject any who have a principled objection to the death penalty. This reluctance is an important factor in explaining the remarkable attrition that occurs between potentially capital crimes and actual death sentences. Although exact figures are not available, this attrition appears to be roughly as follows: In recent years about 16,000 criminal homicides were committed annually in the three dozen capital jurisdictions in the United States; some 11,000 persons were arrested for these crimes; about 7,000 were convicted of some form of criminal homicide; but only some 250 were actually sentenced to death. Several factors help cause this extraordinary reduction; one of the most important is the readiness of prosecutors themselves to trade a guilty plea for a sentence other than death. But the reluctance of so-called death-qualified juries to mete out a death sentence to the person they have just convicted is surely one of them. That brings us to the surviving family members of murder victims.

In January 1993, Westley Allan Dodd was put to death by hanging in Walla Walla, Washington, the first such execution anywhere in the nation since 1965. Dodd had been convicted of mutilating and killing three young boys. Present at the execution were the father of two of the victims and the mother of the third. The reaction of these parents to the hanging of the murderer of their sons is not recorded; as soon as the execution was over, they left the prison and avoided reporters on their way out.[1] Outside the prison, "about 150 people in favor of the execution . . . cheered [Dodd's] hanging. Some set off firecrackers and sparklers."[2] "[T]he raucous crowd . . . counted down the seconds to the hanging and treated it like a New Year's celebration. . . . [They] jeered, whooped, threw snowballs and tried to incite a confrontation" with the few dozen also present who quietly protested the execution.[3] Scenes of this sort have become commonplace across the United States when an execution is held.

What draws spectators to the scene of the execution? Above all, why do family members want to watch the killer of their loved one die? In her book *Dead Man Walking* (1993), Sister Helen Prejean, a Roman Catholic nun, tells about her sustained encounter with Vernon and Lizabeth Harvey, husband and wife, who waited six years to witness the death in Louisiana's electric chair of the man convicted of murdering their daughter, Faith. Sister Helen writes that in the immediate aftermath of Robert Willie's execution, the Harveys spoke to a national television audience about their feelings. Here is how she recounts what transpired on network television news:

Vernon says he wishes every victim could have the opportunity he had tonight. Lizabeth says that since Robert Willie saw Faith die, her parents should see him die. . . . Vernon says he feels it was too easy and quick for Willie [because] "he didn't suffer no pain, and my daughter had to."[4]

Because she is a caring person, and wanted to try to understand better the grief and anger of these survivors, Sister Helen befriended the Harveys and watched sympathetically their struggle to cope with the death of their beloved child. After the execution, when Vernon broke down in tears, she writes:

I realize that now, with Robert Willie dead, [Vernon] doesn't have an object for his rage. He's been deprived of that, too. I know that he could watch Robert killed a thousand, thousand times and it could never assuage his grief. He had walked away from the execution chamber with his rage satisfied but his heart empty.[5]

A few months later, Sister Helen encountered Vernon Harvey again, outside the Louisiana state prison on the occasion of another execution. The sign he carried read: "TELL THEM ABOUT JESUS, THEN PUT THEM IN THE ELECTRIC CHAIR." On another occasion, when Sister Helen visited him in the hospital, he told her:

Know what they should've done with Willie? . . . They should've strapped him in that chair, counted to ten, then at the count of nine taken him out of the chair and let him sit in his cell for a day or two and then strapped him in the chair again. It was too easy for him. He went too quick. . . . What we ought to do is fry the bastards on prime-time t.v., that's what we oughta do. Show them dying in the electric chair, say, at eight at night.[6]

These remarks from Vernon Harvey can be matched, indeed, exceeded in their anger and vituperation, by the remarks of many others who have survived the murder of a loved one and sought opportunities on television to remind the public of their anger and grief to prod the authorities to sentence and execute the person who caused it all— the murderer. I do not wish to argue that the attitudes expressed by the Harveys are universal among murder victims' families, however, or even typical. I do want to argue that attitudes and behavior like the Harveys' are not uncommon, that they are regularly reported in the press and on television, and that bit by bit these behaviors and attitudes are increasingly portrayed by the media (intentionally or not) as the appropriate ones for survivors.

In fact, the Harveys and others like them are now familiar figures at executions around the country. Along with hundreds of others similarly situated, the Harveys belong to a new national organization, Parents of Murdered Children, Inc., with headquarters in Cincinnati, Ohio. To judge from its newsletter, *Survivor*, most of its members are strong supporters of the death penalty, as are the Harveys. The organization, however, has no official position on the issue. In the 1980s alone, roughly 200,000 persons were victims of criminal homicide, leaving behind a million or so immediate family members. Perhaps what is amazing is not that some of these folks support the death penalty loudly and angrily, but that far more do not.

Just how costly it can be to deviate from this norm was taught to the whole nation in the presidential campaign of 1988. The second debate between the two main candidates on national television opened with this question to Michael Dukakis, the Democratic candidate: "Governor, you're an opponent of the death penalty, but what would you say if you arrived home one evening only to find [your wife] Kitty raped and murdered?" Dukakis fumbled for the right words, failed to find them, and lost the votes of the viewers. His opponent, Vice President George Bush, unhesitatingly embraced the death penalty as the only suitable response to such a ghastly crime.[7]

Not all the survivors of a murder in the family, however, react as did the Harveys. Some oppose the death penalty and have banded together to form their own organization, Murder Victims Families for Reconciliation, with headquarters in Cambridge, Massachusetts. One of their organizers is Sam Reese Sheppard; his father was wrongly convicted of the murder of his own wife, young Sam's mother, in Ohio in 1954, in one of the nation's most publicized murder trials of the twentieth century. Another is Theresa Mathis, whose brother was murdered in 1983. After visiting with her family the open casket of her deceased brother, she said: "I had opposed the death penalty before my brother's murder. Afterwards my opposition grew stronger. I knew what killing looked like. And I felt, with my mother, that enough was enough."[8]

II

Public hangings were carried out in England well into the nineteenth century; the last was held at Newgate Prison in London on May 29, 1868. In the United States, the movement to abolish public executions is as old as the nation itself; it dates from the gathering in the Philadelphia residence of Benjamin Franklin in 1787 to hear Dr. Benjamin Rush's address "The effects of public punishments upon criminals and upon society." Some five decades later, in 1835, New York State became the first jurisdiction in the nation to require that lawful hanging be carried out behind closed doors. Elsewhere, however, public executions continued into this century. The last in the nation were well within living memory—a hanging in Owensboro, Kentucky, on August 14, 1936, followed nine months later, on May 21, 1937, by another in Galena, Missouri. A newspaper photograph of the Kentucky hanging shows some 20,000 people packed around the gallows, with the dead man dangling at the end of his rope. Several spectators are atop a nearby utility pole, and others are leaning out of windows a block away. The platform is jammed with official witnesses. In the Missouri hanging, some 500 persons, mostly men, watched. Those who could afford the price of admission were allowed to enter the forty-foot-square stockade that surrounded the gallows in front of the county courthouse; for the throng outside, the view was hampered by the twenty-foot-high walls. Many of those present took away a souvenir piece of the rope used in the hanging.

After these two public executions in the mid-1930s, little or no further attention seems to have been given to the issue for the next forty years. Executions were typically carried out in relative privacy; practices differed from state to state but the prevailing pattern was like this: witnesses attended the event by invitation only (some came from the state department of corrections, others were selected from the law enforcement community); interested print news media and wire service representatives were always present, but photographers were typically prohibited from taking any pictures of the condemned man (or, rarely, woman) before, during, or after the execution; reporters in attendance published whatever graphic and detailed eye-witness accounts their editors saw fit to print. The general public was thus kept entirely at one remove from the scene.

With the advent of television in the 1950s and the increasing public support for the death penalty beginning in the late 1960s, it was all but inevitable that some would begin to agitate to show an execution live on television. The move to do so was made initially in Texas, in December 1976, when the state's first execution in twelve years seemed imminent. A Dallas reporter with television station KERA went to federal court, arguing that barring local public television coverage was unfair and unconstitutional, since the newspapers were allowed by Texas law to cover executions and favoritism of print over electronic media was arbitrary and indefensible. The reporter appealed both to the "free press" clause of the First Amendment to the federal constitution, and to the "equal protection" clause of the Fourteenth Amendment.[9] The local chapter of the American Civil Liberties Union filed an amicus brief in support of the reporter's motion. The reporter's argument persuaded the federal district court, as well it might have.[10]

The state of Texas challenged the decision before the circuit court of appeals, however, and the appellate court ruled against the reporter (*Garrett v. Estelle*, 556 F.2d 1274 [1977]), arguing that neither of the constitutional protections he cited required Texas to revise its execution regulations. If Texas law permitted only newspapers reporters without cameras to have direct access to an execution, then such a law might stand until the Texas legislature chose to repeal it—however arbitrary it might appear to be to exclude the other media. Before further appeal to the Supreme Court could be adequately considered, the controversy was mooted when the execution itself was indefinitely postponed. Since that date, Texas has carried out nearly 300 executions, none of which has been televised.

One might well be somewhat skeptical of the motives of those who seek to televise executions. Market share is the name of the game, and the pornography of death and dying might well be calculated to capture the public's interest and for that reason alone be deemed worthy of broadcast. Presumably not every station would yield to the temptation to intersperse scenes of the impending death in the electric chair with, say, commercials for beer, cosmetics, or dog food framing the climactic moments before and after the poison flows through the body of the condemned prisoner. Good taste might well be expected to confine such morbid details to a small segment of the regular newscasts at 6 P.M. or 11 P.M., just before dinner or before bed. Still, motives apart, vigorous and untrammeled press coverage by print, radio, and television media is a characteristic feature of American public life; the umbrella afforded by the "free press" clause of the First Amendment is jealously guarded by all Americans who love democracy. Two centuries ago Thomas Jefferson observed that if he had to choose between having a free press and no government, or a government but no free press, he would unhesitatingly choose the press and do without the government. Many Americans would echo his sentiments today. Nevertheless, a corollary of Gresham's Law in economics assures us that if executions were permitted on television, stations would vie with each other in showing the grisly realities of the events as captured on camera.

Would the American public watch executions on television if they had the chance, and if they did, what effect would such experiences have on public attitudes toward the death penalty? The first question is partially answered by a survey in Texas in 1977, which reported that 37 percent of the men and 17 percent of the women interviewed said they would watch an execution on television if they could.[11] If these figures are reliable, they show that a televised execution (suitably announced in advance, one assumes, and shown during normal viewing hours) would attract an audience only slightly smaller than what the most popular television shows on prime time can expect to get. The second question was partly answered in 1984, when Texas death row convict James Autry persuaded his lawyers to try to get the prison authorities to permit television to film his execution by lethal injection. The Texas Board of Corrections decided unanimously not to grant Autry's request. By way of explanation, Board chairman Robert Gunn said: "I have many concerns, not only in the propriety and decency of such an act, but in the possibility of televising this thing having an eventual effect on the death penalty itself."[12] What "effect on the death penalty itself" could he have been referring to? Perhaps Gunn had read W. M. Thackeray's remarks a century and a half ago, in which he described the "feeling of terror and shame" he experienced when he witnessed a hanging at London's Newgate Prison[13]—feelings not exactly calculated to create or sustain support for the death penalty. The Texas Board of Corrections seemed less worried about brutalizing the public through exposure to mind-numbing scenes of legal execution than it was worried about arousing opposition to them.

As the events surrounding Autry's attempt to get his execution on television showed, the rights of a free press are not the only important issue raised; there are at least two others. First, there is the issue of privacy. Does the condemned prisoner surrender his privacy to the public, so that whether or not he consents to the broadcast of his last moments, the public and the media have the right to make an audiovisual taping of the scene and then use it however they see fit? Second, there is the issue of paternalism—of protecting the prisoner and the public from indulgence in activities that will cause both parties more harm than good, even though all the parties are adult and give their free and informed consent.

The controversy over paternalism, in particular, was prominently revived in a major national debate that erupted in the spring of 1990, occasioned by a then-impending execution in California, the state's first since 1967. San Francisco television station KQED revived the arguments first heard in Dallas thirteen years earlier. *New York Times* columnist Anthony Lewis, one of the nation's staunchest defenders of free speech and equally known for his opposition to the death penalty, objected that executions, "whose broadcast would further coarsen our society and increase its already dangerous level of insensitivity," deserved no protection under the First Amendment.[14] I agree in part with Lewis; at the time of the impending execution of Autry, I told a journalist that "television manages to make us relatively insensitive . . . to human horror and violence. It arouses interest, gratifies curiosity, and utterly destroys our judgment."[15] But I also believe we must keep distinct (as it seems Lewis did not) whether a television station has a *right* to film and broadcast an execution, and whether a station *ought* to exercise such a right. I cannot see any reason for governmental paternalism nullifying the right, but neither can I see any good reason for the media to exercise that right.

Paternalism in a different direction has been urged by Robert Johnson, the author of *Death Work: A Study of the Modern Execution Process* (1990), who argued that even consenting prisoners should not get their wishes to have their execution filmed, because doing so would only add to "the poverty of their lives and the degradation that has been visited upon them by the death penalty."[16] Whether Johnson thought this argument showed that prisoners had no *right* to have their execution filmed, or only that no prisoner *ought* to seek to exercise such a right, was left obscure. One of the nation's most ardent civil libertarians, Nat Hentoff, finished his discussion of these issues with an ill-concealed sneer: "As Anthony Lewis stereotypes 'the masses,' Professor Johnson dismisses all victims of execution as 'brutalized' if they want their final exit to bear public witness against the death penalty. It's awful enough to be on death row without having to endure all these friendly experts further diminishing you as your time runs out."[17]

In opposing the claim of the television station to film the execution, the state of California alleged that such a broadcast would jeopardize prison security. The state's attorney argued that "By revealing identities, cameras would endanger witnesses and prison staff participating in an execution. . . . [T]he 300 inmates on death row—who have television in their cells—will be incited to revolt if they actually see guards putting one of their own to death."[18] The attorney for station KQED was unimpressed by this argument, as am I. "The public has seen Ceaucescu's execution in Romania," he aptly observed, "beheadings in Saudi Arabia and executions in Iraq, Iran and Vietnam. . . . The state cannot seriously contend that only the executions performed by our

government are inappropriate for television."[19] The court took a different view and ruled, much as the federal circuit court in Dallas had
done, that television stations had no right to film executions if prison
regulations did not permit it. The station decided not to appeal, and
there the matter stands.

By far the most sensitive remarks on the whole controversy came
from Michael Kroll, then director of the Death Penalty Information
Center in Washington, D.C. Kroll ignored the free press issue as well
as the paternalism and privacy issues. Instead, he focused on the issue of
public education, pointing out how misleading and uninformative it
would be to televise an execution—and nothing more, which is precisely what KQED had planned to do. Kroll argued: "What will not be
shown—but what is essential to the understanding what a real execution means—is the systematic and conscious process of dehumanizing
that takes place over time before this final act can occur." This process
involves, among other things, the "repeated drilling of the execution
team" so that it can perform its duties with robotlike precision. To leave
this phase out is to falsify the human reality of executions today. More
than that, a camera in the death house will never present the story of
how the prisoner got into the execution chamber—the typical child
abuse, the family or neighborhood culture of brutality and neglect in
which the offender took his first steps toward violent crime that culmi-
nated in his walk to the gas chamber or electric chair. "It is as if KQED
wanted to show us the reality of AIDS," Kroll observed, "by having its
cameras at the ready to record the moment of death."[20] But no television station so far has shown any interest in, say, an hour-long show
that would present to the viewer something of the full truth about the
crime, the trial, the appeal process, the defendant's family history, his
wait on death row, and then his death in the execution chamber.

III

Since 1976 a criminal court in the United States may impose a death
sentence only if the court has conducted a separate hearing that follows
the trial at which the defendant was judged guilty. As originally under-

stood by the Supreme Court's decisions in *Gregg v. Georgia* (428 US 153 [1976]) and *Woodson v. North Carolina* (428 US 280 [1976]), all capital trials would be bifurcated; in the second or sentencing phase, defense counsel and the prosecution would put before the jury whatever evidence each could assemble pertinent to the various factors specified by statute that would either mitigate or aggravate the offender's guilt and thus determine, or at least guide, the sentencing decision. Accordingly, defense counsel might argue that since the statute specified the youth of the offender as a mitigating factor, the jury ought to keep in mind the fact that the defendant was under eighteen at the time of the crime. Similarly, the prosecution might argue that since the statute specified a prior felony record as an aggravating factor, and since the defendant had such a record, the jury must weigh that factor, too. (How a jury was to weigh a plurality of such factors, some mitigating and others aggravating, is a nice question that cannot be answered with any coherence.) Thus, as of 1976, statutory provisions governed what was admissible at the sentencing phase of a capital trial. Only two years later this practice was radically changed.

In *Lockett v. Ohio*, the Supreme Court ruled that the trial court in the sentencing phase must "not be precluded from considering *as a mitigating factor,* any aspect of a defendant's character or record and any of the circumstances of the offense that the defendant proffers as a basis for a sentence less than death."[21] As a result, statutory mitigating factors no longer defined the range of admissible evidence in the sentencing phase of a capital trial. Instead, it was up to the initiative and imagination of each defense attorney to decide what to bring forward on behalf of his client at the sentencing phase. In the two and a half decades since that decision, many commentators have decried the holding in *Lockett*, on the ground that it opened the gates to the consideration by the jury of arbitrary and irrelevant factors the result of which is precisely the sort of inequitable sentencing that the Supreme Court had ruled unconstitutional in its pioneering decision some thirty years ago in *Furman v. Georgia* (408 US 238 [1972]). Other commentators have drawn attention to the frequent failure of defense counsel to present any evidence of a mitigating sort at the sentencing phase of the trial, thereby all but ensuring that the defendant will receive a death sentence.

The question might naturally arise, however, why the capital sentencing system should allow the apparent asymmetry crafted by the Court in *Lockett*. Why should defense counsel have the opportunity to sway the sentencing court by introducing as mitigating evidence whatever counsel deems of possible influence, whereas the prosecution remains limited to introducing only what the statute defines as an aggravating circumstance? In particular, why shouldn't the jury be entitled to hear from the surviving members of the victim's family just how acute and prolonged their pain and suffering has been, how deeply they mourn their murdered loved one, how much society has lost through the untimely death of their son or daughter, mother or father? How can the court fairly decide what punishment the convicted offender deserves if it cannot hear firsthand from the bereaved about the quality and magnitude of their loss?

Argument in this vein to introduce victim-impact evidence was first submitted to the Supreme Court in 1987 *(Booth v. Maryland)* and reconsidered two years later in 1989 *(South Carolina v. Gathers)*, and by the narrowest of margins the Court turned it down. In the words of Justice Powell, the guiding principle of capital sentencing ought to be "the defendant's 'personal responsibility and moral guilt,' " and that the typical victim-impact testimony not already admissible at trial on the issue of guilt was strictly irrelevant to the defendant's culpability and therefore to his sentence.[22] But in *Payne v. Tennessee* (decided June 27, 1991), the Court made a complete about-face.

During the sentencing phase of the murder trial of Pervis Payne, the mother of one of Payne's victims, who was also the grandmother of one of his other victims, explained to the jury how her surviving grandson "cries for his mom. He doesn't seem to understand why she doesn't come home. And he cries for his sister Lacie. . . . He says, I'm worried about my Lacie."[23] The jury sentenced Payne to death. The Tennessee state supreme court denied that the trial judge had erred in allowing the jury to hear such testimony. Indeed, the Tennessee court went further and openly approved it on the ground that it offends "the civilized members of the human race to say that at a sentencing in a capital case, a parade of witnesses may praise . . . [the] Defendant . . . but nothing may be said that bears upon the character of, or the harm imposed upon, the victims."[24] By a vote of six to three, the Supreme Court over-ruled itself and upheld the Tennessee court.

Writing for the majority, Chief Justice Rehnquist argued that the Court's prior rulings "created an unfairly imbalanced process" to the advantage of the defendant.[25] Justice Scalia, in language more suitable to a politician seeking elective office than to a member of the nation's highest judicial tribunal, added a concurring opinion that the ruling in *Payne* would help restore a "public sense of justice," championed by "a nationwide 'victim rights' movement," by adequately channeling the outrage and righteous indignation felt by murder victims' families.[26] Justice Stevens thought otherwise. The decision in *Payne*, he said, enables the prosecutor to "introduce evidence that sheds no light on the defendant's guilt or moral culpability, and thus serves no purpose other than to encourage jurors to decide in favor of death rather than life on the basis of their emotions rather than their reason."[27] Justice Marshall, in his final dissenting opinion prior to his retirement, sharply criticized the Court majority, arguing that the reasoning behind its earlier decisions in *Booth* and *Gathers* remained unrebutted and unchanged; what had changed, he lamented, was nothing but "the personnel of this court."[28] He was right.

At least three features of the Court's ruling in *Payne* deserve criticism. First, the concern for balance between prosecution and defense at the sentencing phase is completely misplaced. Under the Constitution, the entire criminal justice system is tilted toward the defense (for example, the burden of proof of guilt is on the prosecution, and the prosecution may not appeal an acquittal but the defense may appeal a conviction). It is a remarkable step in the opposite direction to start tipping the scales in favor of the government by permitting zealous prosecutors to parade angry and grieving witnesses before the jury for the sole purpose of getting a death sentence.

Second, the proportion of non-white offenders sentenced to death for the murder of white victims will very likely increase. Indeed, perhaps the most troubling feature of the holding in *Payne* is that it will play into the hands of white juries judging the fate of so-called black-on-white murders. As a wide variety of evidence has amply demonstrated, the likelihood that a black offender charged with killing a white victim will be indicted for a capital murder, convicted, and sentenced to death in the United States today is far greater than can be explained by any identifiable factors other than the race of the victim. The Supreme Court has put into the hands of the trial jury in many, if not all, capital cases a new weapon with which to disguise its racist leanings. Vivian Berger, attorney on appeal for defendant Payne, put it well when she observed: "At the very least, *Payne* will tend to reinforce the widespread view among black citizens that the predominantly white system of criminal justice has dealt them an unequal hand."[29] Even if these disparities connected to race fail to materialize, it is virtually certain that the sentencing phase will become an opportunity for the trial jury to practise social class eugenics—unethical "cleansing," in the jargon of headlines from Bosnia.

Finally, the sentencing phase of capital trials will now become nastier and meaner. Defense counsel will of necessity be forced to dig into the background of the murder victim in an effort to discredit the testimony of witnesses who extol the virtues of the deceased. To fail to do so would be to allow the defendant to suffer at the hands of a jury that believes the murder victim was a saint rather than just another sinner, like most of the rest of us.

Quite apart from these outcomes, the Supreme Court has permitted capital trial juries to weigh a factor having no relevance whatever to the culpability of the offender—namely, the social and personal status of the victim—in order to determine the proper punishment of the offender. To be sure, according to what has been called "the new retributivism," criminal desert is supposed to be measured by the offender's culpability and the harm caused by the crime. However, while in theory the harm caused in crimes such as arson or robbery will vary with the value of the property destroyed or money stolen, the harm caused in criminal homicide is deemed uniform in all cases, on the tacit ground that all human lives are of equal worth. American criminal law has typically recognized only the distinctions in *mens rea* that yield three different kinds of unjustifiable and inexcusable criminal homicide: first-degree murder, second-degree murder, and voluntary manslaughter. It has not recognized as relevant the status and other defining circumstances of the victim in any given unlawful homicide—murder of a father of two versus murder of a homeless vagrant versus murder of a teenage girl. There have, of course, been exceptions to this rule, as when assassination of the President, for example, or the killing of a police officer in line of duty, is singled out as a specific statutory offence, thereby putting the public on notice that such a crime is in a special category relative to other murders. Now, however, it will be up to each capital trial jury to decide for itself whether the murder of which the defendant has been found guilty is deserving of a death penalty because of some special features about the victim, features not defined by any statute, possibly not evident to the defendant at the time of the crime, and not specifiable by the trial court or in any uniform manner from case to case.

IV

The terrifying thing about the politics of democracy is that the people get the officials and policies they deserve, no worse, perhaps, but rarely any better. Whatever may be true in other countries, in the United States today the death penalty receives significant public support and increasing public involvement. Witnessing executions in person, agitation to show executions live on television, and public testimony during the trial itself by friends and family members of the murder victim designed with but one purpose in mind, a death sentence for the defendant—these are but three of the ways in which the death penalty is increasingly not only a popular but a populist practice in America. No wonder politicians run scared before the electorate on this issue, rarely commuting a death sentence, rarely vetoing new death penalty legislation, rarely introducing bills to reduce or abolish the death penalty.

Thirty years ago, shortly after *Furman* was decided, it would have been possible—or so Franklin Zimring and Gordon Hawkins have argued—for the Supreme Court to abolish the death penalty by declaring it to be unconstitutional per se, as a violation of the Eighth and

Fourteenth amendments to the constitution, which bar the states and the federal government from imposing any "cruel and unusual punishments" and require the "equal protection of the law."[30] Zimring and Hawkins may be right; perhaps if the Court had so ruled popular agitation for the death penalty would by now have abated and the nation as a whole would have settled, even if somewhat uneasily, into fighting crime and protecting the public without further use of capital punishment, as Canada, Great Britain, and all European nations have. Instead, in 1976, in its *Gregg* decision, the Court held that the death penalty was not per se unconstitutional. Throughout the 1980s, voices from the White House, Congress, and the Supreme Court all endorsed preserving— even expanding—the death penalty. In 1987, facing the last major opportunity to overthrow capital punishment on constitutional grounds, the Court declared in *McCleskey v. Kemp* (481 US 279 [1987]) that even though the death penalty was administered in a fashion with undeniably racist results, the Constitution was not offended.

With that decision, two decades of effort to obtain a nationwide repeal of the death penalty by means of a constitutional ruling came to an end. Meanwhile, the practice of the death penalty and the illusions it fosters of deserved retribution for terrible crimes, superior deterrence, and inexpensive incapacitation continue to flourish. The American public will not soon be talked out of its embrace of the death penalty, especially when there is no national vocal and visible leadership endeavoring to teach this message and no longer any prospect (at least in the short run) of the insulated federal appellate judiciary saving the people from themselves. Probably Winston Churchill was right when he said that democracy was the worst form of government, except for all the others. In any case, the American people have the death penalty in their midst because they want it.

Whether there is much ground for optimism among those of us who wish it were otherwise is not clear. In the mid-1930s, public opinion polls showed national support for the death penalty rather like that reported today. Yet by the mid-1960s, the same polls showed that public opinion for the death penalty was evenly split between those who favored and those who opposed it. Who knows, it is possible that in another twenty or thirty years—not all that long even in the life of a nation as young as the United States—we may see a comparable reversal in public attitudes. We will certainly see a new Supreme Court, several presidents, many Congresses. And as for the American people, it can still be hoped that as they learn more about the actual practice of capital punishment in their society, they will become steadily disenchanted with it.

CONVICTING AND EXECUTING THE INNOCENT

I

In February 1997, the (usually conservative) House of Delegates of the American Bar Association (ABA) overwhelmingly adopted a report from its section on Individual Rights and Responsibilities and went on record as being formally opposed to America's current system of capital jurisprudence, calling for an immediate moratorium on executions.[1] The motion was supported by twenty former presidents of the ABA (some who counted themselves as supporters of the death penalty), and passed in the House of Delegates by a two-thirds margin. Among the issues of concern to the ABA were the lack of competent counsel in death penalty cases, restricted access to appellate courts even when new evidence of innocence is present, and racial disparities in the administration of capital punishment.[2] In this article, I focus on one of the problems that gave rise to the ABA resolution: the continuing and regular incidence of American trial courts sentencing innocent defendants to death.

Elsewhere, my colleagues and I have published accounts of more than four hundred cases where persons were wrongfully convicted in capital (or potentially capital) cases and described several dozen of these cases in detail.[3] The discussion falls into three parts. First, the conceptualization of the term "innocence" needs to be explained. (Without a precise concept, there is no suitable criterion for deciding who should and should not be considered innocent despite a criminal homicide conviction.) Second, I review the kinds of evidence we have relied on to support our conclusion that some defendants sentenced to death and executed were actually innocent. Finally, I consider how government officials and the general public are currently reacting to the issue of possible executions of the innocent and what role this issue plays in contemporary death penalty debates.[4]

II

If we are to study how often innocent people are convicted of murder, sentenced to death, and/or executed, special care must be taken in determining when a given convicted defendant can and cannot be judged to be innocent. Previous work on this problem[5] touches what is probably only the tip of an iceberg. Undoubtedly, there are many more cases in which innocent persons have been convicted of homicide that have yet to be thoroughly documented and acknowledged by government officials, much less publicized in a way that will allow those who care to learn lessons from them.

In our initial research on this problem, we included in our inventory of exonerated defendants only those who were totally uninvolved in the capital offense of which they were convicted, or who were convicted of a capital crime that never occurred (for example, consensual sexual relations tried in court as capital rape),[6] or a criminal homicide in which the victim was later discovered alive, which happened, most recently, to our knowledge, in 1974 in California.[7] Such narrow inclusion criteria yield an extremely conservative set of cases. Almost any other plausible conceptualization of innocence would yield a much larger set.

Of course, including only cases where government officials admitted error would result in an even more conservative estimate. To be sure, in some ninety percent of the cases described in our previous publications, there is some acknowledgement by public officials in one or more branches of government that the trial court's judgment of guilt was incorrect. But our investigations failed to disclose a single case in the twentieth century where a government official in this country admitted that an execution carried out under his authority, or to his knowledge in his jurisdiction, took the life of an innocent defendant.[8] By itself, however, that is hardly reason to believe that innocent defendants have not been executed.

Although the conceptualization of innocence could be broadened in several different ways from the conservative definition we have used in our research, we have made no attempt to do so or to investigate the new types of cases that would, as a result, need to be included in our inventory. The task is simply overwhelming. However, we can cite examples of cases that illustrate these alternative ways to broaden the conceptualizations of innocence.

Acquittal after Appellate Reversal   One way to broaden the definition is to include all those cases in which the indictment of the defendant was ultimately dismissed or the defendant was acquitted at retrial. To be sure, in our research, we treat a dismissal of charges after reversal of a defendant's conviction, or a verdict of acquittal at retrial, as evidence of innocence, but we do not regard it as either a necessary or sufficient condition of innocence.[9] Prosecutors sometimes fail to retry the defendant after a reversal not because of doubt about the accused's guilt, much less because of belief that the defendant is innocent or that the defendant is not guilty "beyond a reasonable doubt," but for reasons wholly unrelated to guilt or innocence (for example, the prosecution's chief witnesses may have died or disappeared). Such cases could be included among those we count as miscarriages of justice, on the rationale that, if a trial court conviction is to be treated as conclusive evidence of (legal) guilt, then by parity of reasoning *nolle prosequi* after a reversal could reasonably be treated as evidence of (legal) innocence. Other reasonable observers have used such a criterion, notably the authors of a 1993 House Subcommittee Staff Report on innocence and the death penalty. They collapse the distinction between being acquitted of charges and being innocent, arguing that "[u]nder the law, there is no distinction between the definitely innocent and those found innocent [that is, acquitted] after a trial but about whom there may remain a lingering doubt."[10]

Other ways to expand the concept of innocence would permit us to include cases where a capital crime was indeed committed but by accident, in self-defense,[11] or by an offender who is certifiably mentally ill. Yet another class of cases consists of defendants who are guilty of criminal homicide, but not of first-degree murder, and who—for any of several reasons—are erroneously convicted of capital murder nevertheless.

Accidental Killings   There are many cases in which a defendant, after being convicted of homicide and even sentenced to death, wins a retrial and is acquitted after persuading the jury that the homicide was accidental. Legally, such a defendant is innocent of murder and always was; the original conviction of criminal homicide was a miscarriage of justice.

In this context, consider the Florida case of Clifford Hallman, sentenced to death for killing a waitress in a barroom brawl in Tampa in 1973. Hallman's death sentence was eventually commuted to life imprisonment after it was shown that with proper medical care, the victim would not have died (indeed, the victim's family successfully sued Tampa General Hospital for malpractice). Hallman unquestionably cut the victim during the brawl, but almost certainly did not intend for her to die. Despite being guilty only of accidentally causing death, he remains imprisoned for murder a quarter of a century later.[12]

Homicides in Self-Defense   Depending on what theory of legal excuse and legal justification one accepts, homicide in self-defense is either excusable or justifiable and thus not criminal. Yet, persons have been sentenced to death for killing others in self-defense. In 1979 in California, Patrick "Hooty" Croy was sentenced to death for killing a police officer, but at retrial in 1990 he was acquitted when he was able to show his jury that the killing had been done in self-defense.[13] In South Carolina in 1979, Michael Linder was sentenced to death for killing a highway patrol officer, but he was acquitted two years later at retrial when ballistics evidence supported Linder's self-defense claims.[14]

Homicide by the Mentally Ill   In another class of cases, the defendant does cause the death of another person but lacks the requisite *mens rea* to be held responsible for the crime. Nevertheless, the trial court convicts the defendant and sentences him to death. Why? Because of the incompetence of his attorney, or the absence or incompetence of expert psychiatric witnesses, or the jury's refusal to believe defense experts, or for other reasons.[15] The result in any case is the same: Innocent defendants (that is, defendants not properly held responsible for their acts) are convicted and sometimes sentenced to death.

A classic example of this type of error involves Erwin Charles Simants, sentenced to death in 1976 for killing six members of a Nebraska family.[16] At retrial in 1979, he was found not guilty by reason of insanity.[17] Not so lucky was Varnall Weeks. On May 13, 1995, readers of the *New York Times* learned that "Varnall Weeks, a convicted killer described by psychiatric experts as a paranoid schizophrenic who believed he would come back to life as a giant flying tortoise that would rule the world, was put to death . . . in Alabama's electric chair."[18] At trial, Weeks's inexperienced court-appointed attorney never raised the issue of the defendant's insanity. As the *Times* editorialized a few days before the execution, "if Alabama is allowed to take this sorry life, it will . . . expose just how barbaric and bloodthirsty this nation has become in its attempt to see justice done."[19] No one knows how many mentally ill convicts there are on America's death rows who do not deserve to be punished, but the number is unquestionably significant.[20]

These three categories of cases are familiar and have been discussed before by others, notably Charles Black; all illustrate what he rightly called the "caprice and mistake" in the criminal justice system where the death penalty is used.[21] But three other categories of innocence that have received less recognition also deserve attention.

Noncapital Murderers   Not all convicted murderers are candidates for the executioner. Death penalty abolitionists and retentionists alike agree that capital punishment is not supposed to apply to all murderers; it is to be applied only to the worst among the bad. David Baldus and his colleagues have estimated that "death-eligible" murder cases number at present around 2,000–5,000, or 10 to 25 percent of all murders and nonnegligent manslaughters in the nation.[22] Data on death sentencing practices in Florida suggest the number of death-eligible defendants may be even smaller; in any case, the system transforms only a few of these defendants into death row prisoners. In Florida, there are about a thousand homicides per year. Yet, despite the popularity of the death penalty, only about three dozen defendants, 3.6 percent, are actually convicted of first-degree murder and sentenced to death.[23] If we arrange Florida's thousand murders per year on a scale from the most aggravated (perhaps a multiple rape-murder) to the least aggravated (perhaps a mercy killing), we can define "capital murder" (based on the verdicts and sentences of the trial courts themselves) as the crimes committed by the worst 3 or 4 percent.

However, some of those three to four percent are not sentenced to death, while some of the others are. Ted Bundy, for example, qualifies in the judgment of most people as one of the nation's worst murderers. Yet he was offered a plea bargain in both of his Florida murder trials.[24] Had he wished to do so, he could have escaped a death sentence by pleading guilty to noncapital murder. His case is not unique. It is common for defendants accused of some of the worst murders to escape the death penalty through plea bargaining. Often the prosecution has little choice: either accept a plea bargain or risk not getting a conviction because of lack of convincing evidence. As the O. J. Simpson case showed, prosecutors may quickly decide not to seek the death penalty—even for those they believe are multiple murderers—when they learn the defendant is able to employ top-notch attorneys.[25]

Other defendants are not so lucky. If measured by statutory "aggravating" circumstances, their crimes do not place them among Florida's worst three to four percent, yet they end up on death row nonetheless. Many examples could be cited here, but consider only the case of Ernest Dobbert, executed in Florida on September 7, 1984. He had been convicted of killing his nine-year-old daughter. His Jacksonville jury, obviously troubled, recommended life imprisonment by a vote of ten to two; Florida's unusual death sentencing law allows the trial judge to reject the jury's recommendation, and the judge sentenced Dobbert to death. The key witness at trial was Dobbert's thirteen-year-old son, who testified that he saw his father kick his daughter.[26] In a dissent from the Supreme Court's denial of *certiorari* written just hours before Dobbert's execution, Justice Thurgood Marshall argued that while there was no question that Dobbert abused his children, there was substantial doubt about his premeditation, necessary to sustain his conviction of first-degree murder. "That may well make Dobbert guilty of second-degree murder in Florida, but it cannot make him guilty of first-degree murder there. Nor can it subject him to the death penalty in that state."[27] If Justice Marshall's assessment was correct, then Dobbert was not guilty of a capital offense, and—in this qualified sense— Florida executed an innocent man.

Although defendants like Dobbert may be unquestionably guilty of some form of criminal homicide, they are arguably not guilty of capital murder. They do not belong among the death-eligible defendants. We rarely think about this category when discussing innocence and the death penalty, but it is relevant and extremely important. The problem has been with us for at least two centuries, ever since the invention of the distinction between first-degree (capital) murder and second-degree (noncapital) murder and the inclusion of felony murder (any homicide committed in the course of committing a felony, such as rape or robbery) within first-degree murder. Proper administration of the death penalty requires us to draw careful lines in several different dimensions simultaneously, but a substantial amount of evidence shows we are doing a poor job distinguishing between those who do and those who do not deserve—in a strict legal sense—to be found guilty of capital murder and sentenced to death.[28]

Some of those who are guilty of criminal homicide but factually innocent of capital murder end up on death row because of a politically ambitious prosecutor, a lazy or angry jury, incompetent or over-worked defense counsel, or just bad luck.[29] Others are on death row not out of arbitrariness, but because of systematic bias and discrimination. In Florida[30] and in several other states,[31] taking into account all the relevant facts, those who kill whites are between three and four times more likely to end up on death row as are those who kill blacks.[32] In short, the race of the victim is a strong predictor of which defendants end up on death row, and explains why some who are innocent of capital murder are nonetheless sentenced to death.

Sentencing defendants to death who are innocent of capital murder—or innocent of any homicide—is especially risky in states where the trial judge has the authority to disregard the jury's sentence recommendation, as in Alabama, Delaware, Florida, and Indiana. After interviewing fifty-four jurors from a dozen Florida capital juries (including the jury that judged Ernest Dobbert), William Geimer and Jonathan Amsterdam concluded, "The existence of some degree of doubt about the guilt of the accused was the most often recurring explanatory factor in the life [imprisonment] recommendation cases studied."[33] Clearly, even when jurors believe that certain defendants are "guilty beyond a reasonable doubt," lingering doubts often remain about whether the defendant is guilty of a capital crime, and those doubts understandably make the jurors reluctant to recommend the extreme penalty.

Innocent Victims in the Death Row Inmate's Family   No discussion of innocence and the death penalty can be complete without considering how the death penalty affects the inmate's family.

Consider for a moment why some Americans want the death penalty rather than life imprisonment. They argue that the inmate does not suffer enough if punished only by life imprisonment. What is it about the death penalty that makes the inmate suffer more than if he had been sentenced instead to a long term of imprisonment? In many cases, the primary pain felt by men facing execution is seeing what their plight and their anticipated execution does to their families. Life in prison is a miserable life; the inmate knows that even if he were to leave death row via commutation of his sentence, he would be resentenced to life without possibility of parole and would die in prison. Given the widespread availability of life-without-parole sentences, almost all of those sentenced to death, absent the death penalty, will still die in prison. Being executed would end the pain of imprisonment sooner rather than later.

But the pain felt by the inmate anticipating execution is often overshadowed by the pain that innocent family members experience in anticipating the death of their loved one. Their pain arises out of their helplessness, the scorn directed at them, and what they endure immediately prior to, during, and after the execution itself.[34] Families of death row inmates are often indigent and almost always powerless to resist public and political outcries aimed at their incarcerated loved one. While the inmate's suffering is terminated at the instant of death, that of the family members goes on, from the moment they learn the death sentence has been carried out through the years of living with the memories and second guesses. Arguably, the only thing worse than being executed is to see a member of your family executed.

Sentimental though this may seem to some, I make this point in the context of discussing the execution of the innocent for the following reason. Today, the main rationale generally given for retaining the death penalty is retribution.[35] Retribution gives us the simplest and most direct argument for the death penalty: Execute murderers because they deserve it. However, the death penalty inflicts its harm not with a laser but with a shotgun, injuring the guilty and the innocent alike. In ways very unlike prison sentences, the death penalty creates an ever-widening circle of victims. And many of those caught in the circle as it widens do not deserve it. Obviously, families of homicide victims do not deserve their pain either, but the discussion about the death penalty is foremost a discussion of how much misery society should deliberately inflict in the future, not about the misery that has already been inflicted wrongfully in the past (and is therefore unretractable) by the offender.

III

In 1985, when we released the first draft of our research on erroneous convictions in capital cases,[36] the reaction by the Reagan Administration took us by surprise. Then–Attorney General Edwin Meese III, who in California in 1967 (with then-Governor Ronald Reagan) presided over the next to last pre-*Furman*[37] execution in America,[38] ordered the Justice Department to prepare an immediate response.[39] We had evidently hit a sore spot in the Administration's support of the death penalty; neither before nor since has the Attorney General's office taken such an interest in academic research on the death penalty. The government's response was not, as one might naïvely have hoped, to confirm or disconfirm our findings by throwing its resources behind a more comprehensive study of the problem. We carried out our initial research over four years on a budget of $9,000; it is anyone's guess what could have been discovered if the vast resources of the Justice Department had been available for more extensive research into the 350 cases we studied, much less into any of the thousands of cases still waiting to be reexamined. Instead, the Attorney General's Office designed its response solely to discredit our work and by implication to insulate the death penalty from the charge that even in our society, with all the legal protections afforded the accused or convicted or sentenced capital defendant, there is still an undeniable risk of executing the innocent.[40] As events would prove, the government's hostile reaction to our work was far different from that of other informed observers.[41]

The Justice Department's response focused on ten of the twenty-three cases about which we declared our belief that the executed defendant was innocent. Our critics did little more than rehash the case for the prosecution, because they thought, or wanted their readers to believe, that we had denied or forgotten that these defendants had been found guilty in court "beyond a reasonable doubt." Our judgment to the contrary was explained as the result of our careless methodology and excessive anti–death penalty zeal. In 1994, the conservative magazine *National Review* recycled the views of our critics.[42]

Some of the nation's leading judges have given our work more positive attention. For example, Supreme Court Justice Harry Blackmun used our research to support (in part) his decision to abandon any further tinkering with "the machinery of death," as he called it, in the futile hope to make the administration of the death penalty in our society fair and efficient.[43] And, in 1998, the Chief Justice of the Florida Supreme Court, Gerald Kogan, pointed to our work as one reason why he had decided to urge Florida lawmakers to abandon the death penalty.[44]

We should mention in passing that despite not having demonstrated any lack of integrity or reliability in our research, the Justice Department's critique of that work has been very effective. The critique is frequently cited by those who support executions, though they give no evidence of having actually read the critique, much less of having read our law review article, our reply to our critics, or our book. Perhaps this is another example of the complacency that has for so long surrounded the public's attitude toward the death penalty and issues of fact on which that attitude ought to depend.

Again and again, our critics point out that no responsible official in any of the nation's capital jurisdictions has ever admitted to executing an innocent person in this century, a point we were the first to make on the basis of our extensive research into the question.[45] Obviously, the government's failure or refusal to acknowledge that an innocent defendant has been executed is hardly evidence that none has been executed.

Getting the state to concede that it has convicted (let alone executed) an innocent defendant is clearly no easy matter. Once an innocent person is convicted, it is almost impossible to get that conviction reversed on grounds of the accused's innocence.[46] Even when prisoners do get released, usually the prosecutor or some other state official will continue to insist publicly that they really are guilty. The Jacobs-Tafero case powerfully and painfully illustrates this point.

In May 1990, Jesse Tafero was executed in Florida. His case gained notoriety because the electric chair malfunctioned and his head caught on fire before he died.[47] Two years later, Jesse's co-defendant, Sonia Jacobs, who had been convicted and sentenced to death on exactly the same evidence that sent Tafero to his death, was released after a U.S. Court of Appeals concluded that her conviction was based on prosecutorial suppression of exculpatory evidence and perjury by a prosecution witness (who was the real killer).[48] Jacobs now lives in Los Angeles, and in early 1996, a television movie of her case was aired.[49] But Tafero is dead. Had he been alive, the evidence that led to Jacobs's release would have led to his release, too.

Did Jacobs's vindication and release cause any Florida official to admit the error in convicting Tafero, much less to apologize on behalf of the state, or even to express second thoughts about Tafero's execution? No. To be sure, a few newspaper articles pointed out the error,[50] but no politician, prosecutor, judge, or ex-juror involved in the case has so far made any public comment on Tafero's fate in light of Jacobs's vindication. Tafero's mother, living impoverished in Pennsylvania, does not have the resources to mount a campaign to clear her son's name. His attorneys have long since moved on to other cases.

So, given that we cannot point to admission of erroneous executions by government officials involved in the cases we have studied, on what grounds can we confidently infer that innocent defendants have been executed? Apart from rare cases like Tafero-Jacobs (where one codefendant is executed before the other codefendant is exonerated), there are at least three kinds of evidence that we believe ought to convince any reasonable person that innocent defendants have been executed: close calls, calculation of the odds, and the role of "Lady Luck."[51]

Close Calls   Between 1972 and early 2003, 103 death row inmates in the nation were released because of doubts about their guilt.[52] These releases do not prove that the system works, as some defenders of the death penalty would argue. Representative Bill McCollum, for example, one of the executioners' best friends in Congress, was "encouraged" by the findings, claiming that sixty-eight such errors between 1972 and 1996 "shows that the system is working quite well."[53] Contrary to such political spin, however, our research indicates that if "the system worked," the defendants would be dead. In virtually all of these cases, the defendants were released only after an expensive and exhausting uphill struggle, unsupported by public funds or public officials, and almost always fiercely resisted by the prosecution and ignored by those with the power to commute a death sentence.

Some of these prisoners, now free, came within a few days of being executed. Randall Adams, sentenced to death in Texas in 1977 and exonerated in 1989, came to within one week of his execution.[54] Andrew Mitchell, sentenced to death in Texas in 1981, came within five days of death by lethal injection before being vindicated in 1993.[55] Two half-brothers in Florida, William Jent and Ernest Miller, came within sixteen hours of being executed before they were released from prison in 1988.[56] More such cases have been cited elsewhere.[57]

Today, there are nearly four thousand prisoners on America's death rows.[58] As things stand, it would be preposterous to believe that all the innocent death row defendants have been identified and exonerated. If the history of the last thirty years is any guide to the future, an average of three death row inmates per year will continue to be vindicated and released. How many equally innocent death row inmates will be unsuccessful in obtaining relief is impossible to know, but the number most certainly is not zero.

Calculation of the Odds   Assume we execute two death row inmates, each of whom we believe is guilty "beyond a reasonable doubt" on the evidence. Let belief in guilt "beyond a reasonable doubt" mean that we are ninety percent confident of guilt, and that our belief in both these cases is correct. Nevertheless we are not (and rarely could be) 100 percent certain, and so, on these assumptions, we are implicitly accepting a 10 percent error rate even when we are 90 percent confident. However, because the odds of error are multiplicative, the probability that any two death row prisoners chosen at random are guilty is not 90 percent (0.9), but only 81 percent (0.9 $\times$ 0.9). Thus, the probability that all 3,700 death row inmates today are guilty, even if we are 90 percent confident of guilt in each case, is minuscule.

To put this another way, if we executed 100 inmates and we were 95 percent certain of guilt in each case, we would be implicitly accepting a 5 percent error rate; in being willing to execute all 100, we are in effect willing to execute five out of the hundred who might be innocent (even though, of course, we do not know which five are innocent, or whether more or any are). If our perceptions on the odds of error are accurate reflections of the real occurrences of error, the number of innocent persons legally executed is quite high—and much higher than our admittedly selective and incomplete research into identifiable cases suggests.

The Role of "Lady Luck"   In the heat of its attack on our claim that some two dozen of the several hundred cases we studied involved the execution of the innocent, the Justice Department simply ignored the vast majority of cases where we claim an innocent person was convicted of a capital offense but was not executed.[59] In effect, their silence tacitly concedes that our judgment is correct in more than 90 percent of all the cases and wrong in fewer than 10 percent. Why these critics think that small percentage matters they have yet to explain. What they conveniently overlook are scores of cases in which they do not—and could not reasonably—dispute our claims, namely, that innocent persons have been convicted and sentenced to death, and that innocent prisoners who were not executed would have been, or might have been, executed except for extraordinary good fortune.

Consider some of the ways good fortune has smiled on innocent death row prisoners. Some of the cases involve a defendant whose release was owing to the timely discovery of a hitherto unknown eyewitness (for example, the case of Jerry Banks).[60] What if that witness had not stepped forward? In other cases, the true culprit confessed in time to save the innocent prisoner (for example, the case of James Foster).[61] What if the true culprit had kept silent about his involvement? In still other cases, vindication depended on a dedicated journalist who took up the cause and established that the convicted defendant is really innocent (for example, the case of Freddie Pitts and Wilbert Lee).[62] What if no journalist had developed a timely interest in the case? In 1993, Kirk Bloodsworth was freed from death row in Maryland when technology not widely available at the time of his trial (DNA testing) proved his innocence.[63] What if this technology had not been developed for another decade, or semen on the body of the victim had not been preserved, or the victim had not been raped as well as murdered? Under any of these conditions, Bloodsworth would not have been exonerated.

In one way or another, virtually every case in which death row inmates are able to prove their innocence is a story of exceptional luck. Only when we realize how lucky the exonerated death row defendants have been can we realize how easy it is for fatal mistakes to go undetected. The more such cases are discovered the greater the likelihood there are other cases as yet undetected—and that some of these cases involve the execution of the innocent. Just because boats filled with illegal drugs are regularly intercepted by the police near our shores, it does not follow that all boats carrying such drugs have been intercepted.

IV

The fact that innocent persons (in one or another sense of "innocence") are executed seems to have had a very mixed impact on opinion toward the death penalty. Four deaf audiences can be identified: the appellate courts, clemency boards, legislatures, and the general public.

Appellate Courts   The Supreme Court has in effect said that appellate courts need not listen to postconviction evidence of a defendant's innocence, unless the circumstances are truly exceptional, as when the inmate has a videotape supporting his alibi that he was not at the scene of the murder. The Court issued a ruling of this very sort in 1995 in the case of Lloyd Schlup.[64] While incarcerated at the Missouri State Penitentiary, Schlup was accused of, and eventually sentenced to death for, the murder of a fellow inmate. Scheduled to be executed in 1993, he came to within nine hours of his death before Governor Mel Carnahan granted a stay and appointed a panel to reinvestigate the case.[65] In addition to the videotape, Schlup had affidavits from twenty other prisoners and a former guard stating that he was not the killer.[66] Schlup's demand for a full hearing on his innocence prevailed in the Supreme Court by the narrowest of margins—one vote.[67] In this case, the Court continued its unremitting effort to reduce access to appellate review via federal habeas corpus by raising the threshold for relief. It ruled that before an inmate could present evidence of his innocence in federal courts in search of a hearing to reopen the case, he must show that "a constitutional violation has probably resulted in the conviction of one who is actually innocent."[68] By "probably," the Court seems to have meant "more likely than not." Prior to *Schlup*, the defendant seeking habeas corpus relief in federal courts had to show by "clear and convincing evidence" that "no reasonable juror would have found him guilty except for a constitutional error at his trial." Although this was a victory for Schlup (a victory that, thanks to Congress, other inmates will not be able to secure; see the discussion below), it demonstrates how reluctant the appellate courts are to hear evidence of innocence. Had there been no videotapes to present to the courts, Schlup would have been executed.

Clemency Boards   Government officials with the power to commute death sentences to terms of imprisonment have not been receptive to arguments of the condemned defendant's innocence.[69] In the period from 1988 to 2000, only twenty-five death sentences were commuted to prison terms for humanitarian reasons by executive clemency;[70] doubt about the defendant's guilt was a factor in nine of these cases.[71] Few of these commutations came from Texas or California, states with the largest death row populations; in Florida, the only other state with more than three hundred prisoners on death row, there has not been a commutation of a death sentence in more than a dozen years.[72] A defendant's possible innocence has begun to seem almost like an argument against clemency: No one, least of all members of clemency boards, wants to embarrass the state officials who worked to get the prisoner convicted, sentenced, and executed. The solitary exception, as of this writing, to these generalizations is the mass clemency issued by then-Governor George Ryan to all 171 death row prisoners in Illinois early in 2003. This included pardons of four prisoners and commutation to life imprisonment for the rest. Ryan's actions were motivated in large part by his belief that at least four prisoners were innocent and his concern that some (many?) of the rest were also in fact innocent.

Legislatures   Worry that the innocent might be executed has not persuaded state legislatures to create higher standards for death sentencing, much less to repeal the death penalty. In 1994, Kansas reenacted the death penalty;[73] New York's legislature did so in 1995,[74] and Massachusetts came within one vote of following suit in 1997,[75] despite evidence of wrongful capital convictions in each of these states,[76] evidence virtually placed in the hands of every member of these state legislatures prior to their votes. In New York, extensive protections demanded by concerned legislators were built into the new death penalty law,[77] with what effect remains to be seen. But the history of wrongful convictions in capital cases did not in the end persuade the majority to vote against reenacting the death penalty. Nor is there any reason to believe that if Governor George Pataki in New York (elected in part for his vigorous pro–death penalty stance)[78] were confronted with a plea for clemency from a death row prisoner, he would follow the lead of his predecessors, Alfred E. Smith (1923–28) and Herbert H. Lehman

(1933–42). When Smith and Lehman served as New York's governors, death sentences were routinely commuted every time one or more Court of Appeals judges dissented from a ruling that affirmed a conviction.[79]

In recent years, Congress, like the courts, has made it easier to execute the innocent. In 1995, federal funding for attorneys serving indigent death row inmates was severely cut, resulting in the closure of "Resource Centers" in twenty states that provided legal services for condemned inmates.[80] Congress has also restricted the ability of federal courts to hear claims of innocence. Several new barriers to obtaining habeas corpus relief are in the Anti-Terrorism and Effective Death Penalty Act signed into law on April 24, 1996.[81] For example, the act includes a provision that requires "clear and convincing" evidence of innocence rather than simply evidence of "probable" innocence.[82] This supersedes the broader standard articulated by the Supreme Court in the *Schlup* case discussed above. Under the provisions of this legislation, even with his videotapes, Schlup would have been executed.

General Public   The risk of executing the innocent appeared to be a rather weak anti–death penalty card in the public debates over the death penalty. In a 1985 Gallup Poll, 15 percent of those who opposed the death penalty justified their position by saying "persons may be wrongly convicted."[83] By 1991, this figure had fallen to 11 percent.[84] Since 1998, in the aftermath of the conference on wrongful convictions in capital cases held in Chicago in November of that year, the documented cases of such convictions has sensitized the public to their magnitude and frequency. There are dozens of cases in which it can be said the defendant might be innocent,[85] and death penalty opponents are absolutely right to point that out and stress the risk involved. Whether journalists and their audiences will tire of the issue with an attitude that amounts to a "Ho hum, another 'innocent' death row inmate" remains to be seen.

In the end, arguing that the death penalty should be abolished because it will eventually kill the innocent is not the best kind of argument to make, just as it is not the best argument against torture to point out that some false confessions will result. Protesting the execution of the innocent does not make one a death penalty abolitionist; the true test is whether one opposes it for the guilty. The innocence argument is important because it undermines the justification of capital punishment on the ground of retributive justice.

As things stand now, we have precise knowledge about the effect of information about wrongful convictions of capital defendants on the public's support for the death penalty. Here as elsewhere, the Marshall hypothesis (that the public is ignorant of the basic facts about the death penalty but that if it were informed, there would be a tendency to oppose the death penalty)[86] remains untested in recent years.[87] In the years since our research on miscarriages of justice in capital cases was first published, we have some vivid anecdotal evidence from various conversations and courtroom testimony showing that jurors in capital trials who learn about our work find themselves rethinking their support for the death penalty.[88] However, more systematic research is needed before we can gauge the effect of such knowledge on various constituencies.

It is here that the ABA's call in 1997 for a nationwide moratorium on executions might have its strongest impact.[89] The ABA's call has been joined (as of the end of 2001) by twenty state and local bar associations across the nation, as well as about fifty state, county, and municipal governments.[90] In the past several years, the religious community has joined forces, creating a grass-roots organization, Moratorium 2000, chaired by Sister Helen Prejean, and renamed in 2001 the Moratorium Campaign. It claims more than a thousand member organizations and nearly 400,000 individual members.[91] While the campaign so far may not have turned many of those who strongly support the death penalty into abolitionists, the call for a moratorium may have increased the public's ambivalence on the topic.[92] This, in turn, promises to lower the volume on calls for vengeance and to make opposition to the death penalty in general (by the public) or in a specific case (by a troubled juror) more tolerable, leading to fewer death sentences.

Nonetheless, for the immediate future it appears that most Americans will either ignore the risk of executing the innocent or simply accept its inevitability. A letter to the *Houston Post* by Rex L. Carter is all too typical.[93] In November 1994, we wrote to the newspaper, pointing out the inevitability of executing the innocent and mentioning the case

of Gary Graham.[94] Graham had admitted to a string of armed rob-
beries but denied he was guilty of the murder that sent him to Texas's
death row. And, indeed, much of the evidence of his guilt of that crime
was suspect.[95] Here is Mr. Carter's response:

> Hugo Bedau had best come in out of the heat. As a defender of
> the death penalty, I have no problem in admitting innocent
> people can be executed and couldn't care less what happens
> to Gary Graham. He should have been executed for what he
> confessed to. There is a war going on in our own country—
> against crime and thugs like Graham. It is sad that innocent
> people get killed in war, but that is the way it is. Ask any war-
> time veteran. Try 'em, give 'em 90 days for appeal and then
> hang 'em slowly at noon on the courthouse lawn. Just maybe
> killers-to-be will get the message, just as Japan did when we
> dropped the A-bomb.[96]

Mr. Carter's rhetorical flourishes get in the way of his logic, but we have
no doubt his sentiments coincide with the feelings of many citizens.

Dale Volker, the state senator from New York whose ten-year quest
to reinstate the death penalty in the Empire State finally succeeded in
1995, had this to say about executing the innocent: "I would never
think it's impossible. You would hope that it would never happen, but
the mere fact that you might fail does not argue that you shouldn't
do it."[97]

Or consider the comments of Paul D. Kamenar, executive director
of the Washington Legal Foundation, who early in 1995 was quoted in
the *New York Times* saying, "I would gladly give them a couple of ques-
tionable cases that they are harping about in return for their agreeing
to recognize that in the vast majority of cases, there is no question of
the guilt of those being executed."[98] This trade we would happily accept; few abolitionists would deny that most of those now on death row
are guilty. We doubt, however, that most retentionists would be willing
to agree that the vast majority of murderers on death row are not geno-
cidal maniacs, psychopathic serial or multiple murderers, recidivist

killers, and thus that they are not the worst among the bad and so do not belong there.

Finally, consider the comments of Florida State University criminologist Larry Wollan. Although a supporter of the death penalty, Wollan realizes that the risk of executing the innocent is undeniable, and he phrases the argument in a responsible way: "Innocent people have been executed," he concedes, but "[t]he value of the death penalty is its rightness *vis-à-vis* the wrongness of the crime, and that is so valuable that the possibility of the conviction of the innocent, though rare, has to be accepted."[99] Elsewhere, Ernest van den Haag made the same point when he said that our documentation of twenty-three erroneous executions in this century in America "[does] not tell us anything unexpected,"[100] and this liability to grave error does not outweigh the deterrent and moral benefits of the death penalty. Since, in our judgment, those benefits are entirely illusory[101]—we gain nothing in public safety or moral rectitude by the practice of the death penalty—the constant and unavoidable risk of executing the innocent cannot be so complacently tolerated.

V

One of the amazing things that has happened in the decades since our research was first released to the public is that those who defend the death penalty now concede the inevitability of executing the innocent, even though they challenge individual cases that we and others have identified as probably involving the execution of an innocent person. It is a major concession. We know of no defender of the death penalty who, prior to 1985, was willing to make such a public concession. Moreover, this concession has the effect of forcing responsible defenders of capital punishment to rethink their argument in two important respects. First, as retributivists, they must acknowledge that convicting and executing the innocent—those who do not deserve to die—is a terrible wrong, and avoiding it is no less important on retributive grounds than convicting and punishing the guilty. Second, they must explain in convincing detail how a cost/benefit argument, on which they rely, shows that the benefits from the death penalty outweigh the admitted cost of executing the innocent. Elsewhere, we have shown why we believe these arguments must fail.[102]

We are left to ponder how future generations, when they look back, will evaluate America's current love for the executioner.

4 EXECUTIVE CLEMENCY IN CAPITAL CASES

I

Of all the times in the year at which one might consider the issue of executive clemency, it is uniquely appropriate to have done so in the season of Passover, when the lecture on which this essay is based was first delivered. The first phase of one of the most distinctive events in the history of Christianity arose at Passover from the refusal of a certain governor, with the power of executive clemency, to exercise that power in a capital case. There are four versions of the story;[1] here is how it is told by the Apostle Mark:

> Now at the feast he used to release for them one prisoner for whom they asked. And among the rebels in prison, who had committed murder in the insurrection, there was a man called Barabbas. And the crowd came up and began to ask Pilate to do as he was wont to do for them. And he answered them, "Do you want me to release for you the King of the Jews?" For he perceived that it was out of envy that the chief priests had delivered him up. But the chief priests stirred up the crowd to have him release for them Barabbas

instead. And Pilate again said to them, "Then what shall I do with the man whom you call the King of the Jews?" And they cried out again, "Crucify him." And Pilate said to them, "Why, what evil has he done?" But they shouted all the more, "Crucify him." So Pilate, wishing to satisfy the crowd, released for them Barabbas; and having scourged Jesus, he delivered him to be crucified.[2]

Over the past two thousand years, the release of Barabbas has given much pause for reflection. It has also been the occasion for one impressive novel and one awful joke. The novel is *Barabbas*—disturbing and fascinating—by the Swedish Nobel Prize–winner Par Lagerkvist, a book much read in the 1950s but largely ignored today.[3] The joke is more recent, and is credited to New York's former state Senator James Donovan. During a speech in which he defended the death penalty, Senator Donovan is reported to have asked, with rhetorical disdain and finality, where Christianity would be today if "Jesus had got eight to fifteen years with time off for good behavior."[4]

The subject of executive clemency in capital cases is triangulated on one side by its history, on another by the current state of the law, and on the third by its rationale. The long history of executive clemency in capital cases begins even prior to the confrontation between Jesus and Pilate. It commences in another biblical episode, the judgment of Jehovah on the murderer Cain. For killing his brother Abel, Cain was banished, and all others were prohibited from assaulting him in revenge.[5] In spite of the biblical contributions, the history of the subject has rarely been examined.[6] On the current state of the law, however, reasonably complete, up-to-date information on executive clemency does exist owing to a survey published as a government document.[7] This document obviates any need to review the matter here.

What is needed is more focus on two aspects of executive clemency: its declining use in capital cases nationally, and the problem of adequately explaining this decline. It will prove useful to look at these two topics against the rationale of executive clemency in general and as exercised in particular capital cases.

II

At present, there are more than 3,700 persons under death sentence in over three dozen states.[8] In each of these states, the governor, acting alone or in concert with a board of pardons or some other administrative body, has the authority to commute these death sentences to lengthy prison terms.[9] Each of these death row prisoners has the privilege or the right to some form of clemency review by the chief executive or other official body. Normally, the most relevant and important form of clemency in a capital case is not pardon (because it entails release from custody) or reprieve (because it constitutes only a delay in carrying out sentence) but commutation of the sentence to a less severe punishment.

The laws governing the exercise of clemency are diverse among the jurisdictions, but they share these basic features: Clemency decisions—even in death penalty cases—are standardless in procedure, discretionary in exercise, and unreviewable in result.[10] Short of a constitutional amendment to remove or regulate this power, political and moral factors usually dominate the outcome of a clemency hearing.[11] As a result, the clemency hearing in capital cases constitutes a terminal stage of lawlessness in criminal justice decision making that is symmetrical with the lawlessness of the initial stage, controlled as it is by the prosecutor's similarly unregulated and discretionary decision-making authority.[12]

Shifting attention from the laws to their underlying rationale, one finds considerable uncertainty, as Kathleen Dean Moore has convincingly demonstrated.[13] There are at least three different accounts of the rationale for clemency. First, there is the traditional version that clemency generally and a fortiori commutation of a death sentence is a free "gift" of the executive,[14] an "act of grace,"[15] or an act of arbitrary "mercy."[16] Chief Justice John Marshall, in a passage often cited from the Court's opinion in *United States v. Wilson*,[17] observed: "A pardon is an act of grace. . . . It is the private, though official, act of the executive magistrate. . . ."[18]

A second version of the rationale, favored by governors who take seriously their power to grant clemency, is that it is a quasi-judicial power providing the opportunity for a final review, one in which considerations not admissible in ordinary appellate review become relevant. Here is how Governor Winthrop Rockefeller put it in 1971, explaining his decision to commute the death sentences of Arkansas's entire death row population: "In a civilized society such as ours, executive clemency provides the state with a final deliberative opportunity to reassess the moral and legal propriety of the awful penalty which it intends to inflict."[19]

The third version might be said to stem from a passage in *Ex parte Grossman*, in which the Supreme Court, a century after Marshall's opinion in *Wilson*, wrote:

> Executive clemency exists to afford relief from undue harshness or evident mistake in the operation of the criminal law. The administration of justice by the courts is not necessarily always wise or certainly considerate of circumstances which may properly mitigate guilt. To afford a remedy, it has always been thought essential ... to vest in some other authority than the courts' power to ameliorate or avoid particular criminal judgments. It is a check entrusted to the executive for special cases.[20]

The not altogether unambiguous view expressed in this passage has been transformed by Moore in her recent study of pardons[21] into a full-blown, single-minded retributive account of the rationale of pardon. Inspired by the extraordinary rise to dominance in recent years of retributive justifications for punishment generally,[22] she proposes that pardons, too, be justified solely on retributive grounds. Accordingly, she declares that pardons "are duties of justice, not supererogatory acts [like mercy]";[23] they "should be granted only when deserved";[24] unsurprisingly, she claims that the pardoning power "is abused when a pardon is granted for any reason *other than* that punishment is undeserved."[25]

It is tempting but not feasible at this point to argue about the merits of these different conceptions of the nature of clemency power. Nevertheless, two observations can be made. First, it may seem a matter of little moment to the issue of frequency with which clemency is granted in capital cases which of these three rationales dominates the thinking of governors and their advisers. Whereas such records as have been made public on the exercise (or denial) of clemency in capital cases readily show that each of these three alternative conceptions has played a role,[26] there is no evidence to show that the frequency of commutations in capital cases dramatically increases or decreases as a function of which rationale for its exercise prevails in gubernatorial thinking. Second, however, were the retributive theory of clemency to become dominant, it would have one of two effects: Either it would guarantee that few if any murderers on death row would receive executive clemency, or governors and their advisers would have to be convinced that retributive justice does not require (or even permit) the carrying out of the death sentence in many cases.[27] Neither alternative is very attractive to opponents of the death penalty. The retributive attack on the death penalty is not without its articulate and persuasive advocates,[28] and it may be that the governors of death penalty jurisdictions can be persuaded by this reasoning. One cannot be confident, however, that this can be done. The three most recent mass commutations of death row prisoners—in 1971 by Governor Winthrop Rockefeller, in 1986 by Governor Tony Anaya of New Mexico, and in 2003 by Governor George Ryan of Illinois—were not based on the judgment that the death penalty is retributively unjust. To that extent, at least, those who find attractive the retributive rationale of executive clemency must conclude that mass commutations such as these probably are an abuse of power and therefore wrong.

If one turns from the rationale for executive clemency to some practical considerations, especially where the death penalty is concerned, it is easy enough to see good reasons for preserving the clemency power and expecting it to be exercised with some frequency. First, the appellate courts can be counted on to define narrowly what will count as legally reversible error and what suffices to secure relief on this ground. The result is that not every error will be remedied by the courts, and these errors will go unremedied unless the executive steps in. Second, the legislature knows or should know that its criminal statutes are not self-enforcing any more than they are self-interpreting. As in the past, there will be inequities and inconsistencies in application of the laws. These can be remedied, if at all, only after they have occurred, and not all such remedies will be forthcoming from the appellate courts. Third, society should want some branch of government to have the power to reduce sentences where the punishment is inappropriately severe or excessive in a particular case. This concern should be especially strong where the failure to reduce a sentence entails the death of a prisoner by lawful execution. The natural place to lodge such power is with the executive, whose responsibility it is in any case to carry out legislatively authorized and judicially imposed sentences.

III

Against this background, let us take a closer look at the reasons that governors have offered in explanation and justification of their exercise of the power to commute a death sentence to a prison sentence. The reasons are many[29] but the following ten suffice to indicate their range:

1. *The offender's innocence has been established.* In 1975, Florida Governor Reuben Askew granted a full pardon to two death row prisoners, Wilbert Lee and Freddie Pitts, despite reaffirmance of their conviction on appeal. Governor Askew said: "I am sufficiently convinced that they are innocent."[30]

2. *The offender's guilt is in doubt.* In 1963, Maryland Governor J. Millard Tawes commuted the death sentences of John G. Giles, James V. Giles, and Joseph E. Johnson, Jr. Newly discovered evidence supported the claim of innocence by the defendants, and Governor Tawes declared: "From what I know now, I would now have to vote for a verdict of not guilty."[31]

3. *Equity in punishment among equally guilty co-defendants requires reduction of a death sentence to life imprisonment.* In 1960, New Jersey Governor Robert Meyner commuted the death sentence of Willie Butler, stating that since three of his co-defendants had been permitted to plead *non vult* to second-degree murder, "it

would be manifestly unfair for this one defendant to suffer death when his co-defendants, all of whom may be of equal guilt, have received comparatively light punishment."[32]

4. *The public has shown conclusively albeit indirectly that it does not want any death sentences carried out.* The 1964 campaign in Oregon to abolish the death penalty by constitutional referendum was in part a campaign over the fate of two men and one woman then under sentence of death. When the electorate gave its verdict at the polls to repeal the death penalty, Governor Mark Hatfield immediately commuted the three death sentences.[33]

5. *A nonunanimous vote by the appellate court upholding a death sentence conviction leaves disturbing doubt about the lawfulness of the death sentence.* Two New York governors, Herbert Lehmann and Alfred E. Smith, refused to affirm any death sentence in which the appellate courts were nonunanimous in upholding the underlying conviction.[34]

6. *The statutes under which the defendant was sentenced to death are unconstitutional.* In 1976, Virginia Governor Mills E. Godwin, Jr., commuted the death sentences of all five prisoners on death row, arguing: "Until Virginia has a death sentence statute over which there is no legal question, I do not feel anyone should be executed."[35] Governor Godwin also was quoted to the effect that he would urge the next General Assembly to enact a death penalty law that could pass constitutional muster.[36]

7. *Mitigating circumstances affecting the death row prisoner's status warrant commutation to a lesser sentence.* In 1971, South Carolina Governor John C. West commuted the death sentence of Edward Williams on the ground that nine years on death row for a man then eighty-one years old "might well constitute cruel and unusual punishment."[37]

8. *Rehabilitation of the offender while on death row undermines the rationale for carrying out the death sentence.* In 1962, Illinois Governor Otto Kerner commuted the death sentence of Paul Crump. The Governor argued that after seven years awaiting execution, "the embittered, distorted [Crump] who committed a vicious

murder no longer exists," and said that he was commuting the sentence because "[u]nder these circumstances, it would serve no useful purpose to take this man's life."[38]

9. *The death penalty is morally unjustified.* The mass commutations of death row prisoners in Arkansas by Governor Rockefeller and in New Mexico by Governor Anaya, as well as commutations in earlier years by such governors as Oregon's Robert Holmes and Massachusetts' Endicott Peabody, were rooted in their strong convictions that capital punishment was morally wrong.[39]

10. *Executions must cease until it can be shown that the process is free from arbitrariness and unfairness; meanwhile, any death row prisoners must be resentenced to prison.* This was essentially the rationale used by Governor Ryan in 2003[40] when he emptied Illinois's death row after reviewing the report of a special commission he appointed to evaluate whether death sentences in Illinois were "fair, just, and accurate."[41]

Today, all these reasons, except for the rationale that the public has shown that it does not want the death penalty to be imposed, remain plausible grounds for the exercise of clemency in capital cases. They also show that there are good reasons—even retributive reasons, in many cases—for granting clemency to a death row prisoner. Nor is it necessary for a chief executive or pardon board to base a commutation on personal moral opposition to the death penalty. As these cases show, neither extraordinary political courage nor a suicidal desire to end one's political career is always a necessary condition of exercising the power of executive clemency in a capital case.

IV

Let us now turn from the rationale for executive clemency to the role that it has played in capital cases during the past century in the United States, and the role that it currently plays and is likely to play in the immediate future.

What is known about the frequency, jurisdictional distribution, and the demographic characteristics of those who sought and received, and those who were denied, commutation of a death sentence? Readily accessible published information leaves much to be desired. The statistical data are of two kinds; statistics compiled by the federal government that purport to present a national picture and statistics compiled by states to present a local picture.

Concentrating on the national picture, in 1952 one observer reported that for the seven-year period 1940 through 1946, 771 persons were sentenced to death throughout the nation but only 587 executed.[42] Of the remaining 184, it was conjectured (though without any evidence or explanation) that "[m]ost of [these prisoners] undoubtedly received commutations."[43] If so, then between a fifth and a quarter of all death sentences during the early and mid-1940s were disposed of by commutation. This may be the only information about the nation as a whole that is currently available for the period in question; in any case, the official source being relied upon by the author, the annual publication of commutation statistics by the Department of Justice's Bureau of Justice Statistics (as it is now called), did not commence until 1960.[44] The series of national data provided by the Department of Justice on death sentences presents a very incomplete picture; it is nonetheless the best available. Only further research in the archives of clemency proceedings, state by state, is likely to improve upon it. Meanwhile, Table 1 presents what the available published records from this federal source show:[45]

Table 1   U.S. Death Sentences and Commutations, 1961–2000

Year	Death Sentences[46]	Commutations[47]
1961	140	17
1962	103	27
1963	93	15
1964	106	9
1965	86	19
1966	118	17
1967	85	13
1968	138	16
1969	153	20
1970	133	29
1971	113	**

Year	Death Sentences[46]	Commutations[47]
1972	83	**
1973	42	9
1974	149	22
1975	298	21
1976	233	15
1977	137	7
1978	185	8
1979	152	5
1980	173	7
1981	224	5
1982	266	7
1983	252	7
1984	295	6
1985	267	4
1986	300	6
1987	289	2
1988	296	3
1989	259	4
1990	253	2
1991	266	3
1992	288	5
1993	289	5
1994	318	2
1995	320	1
1996	318	1
1997	278	0
1998	303	0
1999	280	0
2000	214	0
Total	8,295	339

SOURCE: United States Department of Justice, Bureau of Justice Statistics.

As Table 1 shows, there is a two-year informational hiatus for commutations, from 1971 through 1972, which falls in the years of the moratorium on executions brought about by constitutional litigation that began in 1967 and ended in 1976.[48] This is probably the very period when annual commutations began their precipitous drop, starting in 1977, that is so conspicuously documented in Table 1. The year 1976 was the last in which commutations reached double digits (prior to 2003). In the decade 1961 through 1970, death sentences totalled 1,155 and commutations 182. This yields a ratio of one commutation for approximately every 6.3 death sentences. In the decade 1991 through 2000, death sentences totalled 2,874 but there were only 17 commutations. This yields a ratio of one commutation for approximately every 170 death sentences. Thus, in the 1990s, death row prisoners had about one-twenty-seventh as many commutations as did their counterparts of the 1960s.

A certain caution, however, is advisable in the interpretation of these data, which apparently document a radical decline in the commutations of death sentences.[49] Table 1 gives a measure of frequency of commutation relative to the number of death sentences. It does not give a measure of commutations relative to the number of applications, or to the number of death row prisoners applying, for clemency. Filing an application is a necessary condition of receiving clemency; it is not known how many death row prisoners since *Gregg v. Georgia*[50] have filed such an application and been turned down. It is known that not every death row prisoner executed since *Gregg* has filed for clemency; some post-*Gregg* death sentences have been carried out on "volunteers"— prisoners who by definition refused to seek full appellate review or clemency.[51]

A somewhat different picture emerges, one that partially overlaps with the national data reported in Table 1, when information from various states is examined. The data reported in Table 2 come from a non-random sample of a dozen state jurisdictions scattered across the nation and spanning different years (with the sole exception of Georgia, the periods covered antedate the death penalty moratorium of the 1960s and 1970s). Unfortunately, there is no uniform reporting scheme or locus of publication for state data on commutations of death sentences.[52]

Table 2 Death Sentences and Commutations in Selected States for Selected Years, 1900 to 1985

State	Span	Total Years	Death Sentences	Commutations
California[53]	1943–66	24	192	35
Florida[54]	1925–65	41	**	57
Georgia[55]	1976–85	10	**	0
Maryland[56]	1936–61	46	122	34

State	Span	Total Years	Death Sentences	Commutations
Massachusetts[57]	1900–58	59	101	30
New Jersey[58]	1907–60	54	232	34
New York[59]	1920–36	17	252	83
North Carolina[60]	1909–54	46	660	229
Ohio[61]	1950–59	10	60	23
Oregon[62]	1903–64	62	92	26
Pennsylvania[63]	1914–58	45	439	71
Texas[64]	1924–68	45	483	85
Total			2,633	707

These data show that in the years prior to *Furman v. Georgia*,[65] the ratio of commutations to death sentences was approximately three to eight. (Even if one excludes North Carolina, which accounts for 25 percent of all death sentences and nearly a third of all commutations, on grounds that it is an anomaly, the ratio drops only to two in eight.) Of these dozen states, the one whose pattern of clemency in capital cases has been studied most closely over the course of the century is Florida. Between 1935 and 1979, Florida governors extended clemency to death row prisoners in about one-third of all cases.[66] In the decade following *Gregg v. Georgia*,[67] from 1976 to 1986, Florida governors gave clemency review in 202 capital cases.[68] In Governor Robert Graham's first six years in office, his forty-four reviews resulted in clemency in six cases.[69] Since 1982, neither he nor Governor Robert Martinez, his successor, has granted clemency in even one case,[70] despite efforts to obtain it in more than one case where substantial doubts lingered over the guilt of the condemned man.[71] Governor Graham, to be sure, did not sign some twenty death warrants, thereby creating a kind of halfway house on death row for these inmates, suspending them indefinitely between execution (for which no date was set) and a life term in prison.[72]

V

Some years ago, observers reported that about one out of every four or five death row prisoners had had his sentence commuted to life in prison.[73] As was shown in Table 1, the frequency has dwindled to barely one in sixty, a reduction by at least a factor of four. Commentators have noticed this decline, leading some to conclude that clemency for death row prisoners has become unavailable in practice.[74] What explains this precipitous decline in commutations (assuming, without evidence, that the rate of clemency applications per death row prisoner has been relatively constant)? There are several hypotheses to consider; they are not mutually exclusive.

Beginning in 1967, with the national litigation campaign to abolish the death penalty on federal constitutional grounds, the courts stayed all executions for roughly a decade.[75] This judicially imposed moratorium on executions had several interrelated consequences. First, no death sentence could receive final appellate review during the pendency of a federal judicial decision on the very constitutionality of the death penalty itself.[76] As a result, few death row prisoners were in a position to file a clemency application, and governors could indefinitely defer clemency hearings on the ground that no death case was ripe for such a final review. Governors, for the first time in history, thus found themselves positioned safely outside the network of decision making in particular capital cases. To some extent they could also stand aside from the growing controversy over abolishing or restoring the death penalty. The typical governor was loath not only to intervene in individual death cases but also to play any conspicuous role in the legislative arena on this issue, since intervention on either side could only result in lost votes. What governors first learned a generation ago and enjoyed for a decade, their successors practice today.

Attractive though this hypothesis may be, it is largely conjectural and is, at least in part, apparently contradicted by the facts. Table 1 shows that during the first five years of the decade 1967 through 1976 for which data are available, commutations proceeded at a fairly steady annual rate and constituted a significant percentage (about 13 percent) of the final disposition in all death sentences. So governors during at least the first half of this period did not entirely stand aside; they did intervene to grant commutations, just as their predecessors had intervened prior to the litigation campaign that began in 1967.

A second hypothesis concerns commutations granted by Governor Rockefeller of Arkansas and most other governors during the decade from *Maxwell v. Bishop*[77] to *Gregg*. They were done in the belief (or, as in Rockefeller's case, the hope) that capital punishment would soon be declared unconstitutional and abolished by the federal courts once and for all. Commutations made under this belief were quite unlike those made in earlier years, and not surprisingly they dried up after 1976, when it was clear that the campaign to abolish the death penalty nationally on constitutional grounds probably would not succeed.

Like its predecessor, this hypothesis suffers from a lack of empirical evidence to support it; at present, it is entirely conjectural. At best, like the first hypothesis, it warrants further investigation. At the moment, all one can do is put it to one side and move on to other considerations.

There is a third hypothesis, also to some extent conjectural, but worthy of consideration and not without support from a fairly steady observation of the domestic political scene over the past generation. Some agreement with, and perhaps even support for, the following arguments can also be found in a report by Amnesty International on the death penalty in the United States,[78] as well as in some other sources.[79] For reasons that will become clearer, it is tempting to call the central feature of the hypothesis the Pilate Syndrome. On reflection, however, this name has one conclusive objection against it. After all, though Pilate refused to spare the innocent Jesus, he did spare the (presumably) guilty Barabbas.

The hypothesis now to be considered is based principally on three perceptions widely held by those in public life, especially over the past two decades or so. First, there is the perception that a governor who commutes a death sentence verges on committing political suicide. This perception appears to be the inevitable consequence of two factors in electoral politics: the high level of apparent public support for capital punishment[80] and the proven willingness of gubernatorial candidates to use a rival's opposition to the death penalty in whatever form it might take (commutation of a death sentence, veto of a death penalty bill, or the intention to so act) as evidence of being a "bleeding heart liberal" and "soft on crime."[81] In 1966, what may have been the first of the modern "law and order" political campaigns was run with great success in California; its triumph was the election of Ronald Reagan, then a second-rate Hollywood actor, as governor.[82] Two years later, on the national scene, the same strategy succeeded in putting Richard Nixon in the White House and Democrat liberals in the outhouse.[83] Examples of governors in the past twenty years in death penalty states who have achieved election or reelection despite a publicized record of commuted death sentences, or of an advertised willingness to commute death sentences, are hard to find.

Second, there is the perception—at least, in the states in which executions have once again become frequent—that death sentences are now meted out by trial courts with all the fairness that is humanly possible, even if in the dark pre-*Furman* past they were not. The constitutional collapse of that old standby, mandatory death sentences,[84] the introduction of the bifurcated capital trial that divides the deliberation over guilt from the deliberation over sentencing,[85] and the constitutional authority for the defense to introduce just about anything in mitigation during the sentencing phase, on the ground that it might persuade the jury to favor a prison sentence[86]—these are three important features of the post-*Furman* system of capital punishment at the trial level that make any death sentence (except in states like Florida, with a judicial override provision)[87] appear more than ever before to be the product of democratic process. Any chief executive who commutes a death sentence thus appears to flout the popular will—and to do so on unprincipled or perplexing grounds.

Third, there is also the perception that if a death sentence is unfairly imposed in a particular case by the trial court, then the appellate courts—and especially the federal courts—can be counted on to rectify the injustice and order a new trial. Appeal at the state level is now virtually mandatory, automatic, and universal,[88] and some form of appeal in the federal courts (although neither mandatory nor automatic) is virtually guaranteed.[89] Significantly, half or more of all death sentences are reversed in state or federal appellate courts;[90] this is hardly surprising given the mediocre quality of defense counsel in many capital trials and the superior quality of defense counsel on appeal—indeed, the very best that pro bono services can provide.[91]

As a result, the perceived performance of trial and appellate courts in capital cases is a powerful factor in rationalizing gubernatorial refusal to commute death sentences.[92] Of course, in the judgment of critics with considerable experience litigating capital cases, there is no basis whatever for complacency about any aspect of the way the criminal justice system currently handles capital cases. In the view of these critics, what is really happening is the "deregulation of death"[93] and the "death of fairness"[94] in the administration of capital punishment in this country. The conspicuous fight over the future of habeas corpus litigation[95] is but one of many such indications. There is much evidence that in recent years the federal courts, especially the Supreme Court, increasingly refuse to act in accordance with the belief that "death is different."[96] The nadir was reached when the Supreme Court ruled in *Herrera v. Collins* (1993) that a condemned prisoner could always seek clemency, and so the refusal of the courts to provide habeas corpus review in successor petitions did not close every door to relief.

Given the prevailing perceptions, however contrary to the facts they may be, to commute a death sentence requires an unusual combination of personal attributes in a governor. These attributes are rarely manifested except when combined with the loss of further political ambition. This last factor played a considerable role in the commutation decisions of Governor Rockefeller in 1971 and Governor Anaya in 1986. Each made commutation of his state's death row prisoners his political swan song. Few governors with death row populations want to sing that tune.[97]

VI

If the foregoing hypothesis, with its stress on both the perceived fairness of capital sentences and the risks of intervention, does indeed explain the decline of clemency in today's capital cases, what can be done to keep clemency hearings from becoming an empty formality, as some observers have complained has already happened?[98] What, if anything, can be done to get governors and pardon boards to exercise their authority to review meaningfully:

whether an execution should take place . . . , whether a death sentence is imposed because of the race or social status of the victim, or because the jury wanted to keep the defendant in jail longer, and whether a death sentence is unfair in view of such mitigating factors as the defendant's mental retardation?[99]

One possibility is to elect more courageous governors, or governors with no ambitions beyond one term in office. This is not a promising tactic; one can pretty well dismiss it out of hand. Another possibility is to change public opinion so that it no longer supports capital punishment and instead tolerates commutation of death sentences, at least in certain cases. A cynical observer might sneer that this is impossible, arguing that it is evident that efforts by abolitionists in this country over the past three decades have left death penalty opponents worse off today than ever before (not a judgment with which I concur).[100] Another possibility is to sentence to death offenders that evoke more sympathy than the present lot. Yet another is to return to the old pre-*Furman* system of death penalties that cried out for executive intervention to remedy flagrant injustices. Many will consider all of these to be frivolous suggestions.

Here, then, are a few suggestions that are more serious. First, opponents of the death penalty have to give sober consideration to advocating the severe alternative to the death penalty of life without possibility of parole (LWOP).[101] In this way, and perhaps only in this way, given the present climate of public opinion, something can be done to alleviate public anxiety over parole or other releases of convicted murderers deemed either unrehabilitated or undeserving of leniency. Coupled with persuasive argument showing that the overwhelming public support for the death penalty is really only skin deep and to some extent an artifact of inadequate survey research,[102] it might well be possible to make room for the serious consideration of commutations. Second, opponents of the death penalty have to consider whether it might not be more effective to concede that clemency should be viewed, like punishment itself, from a retributive point of view. This would free them to launch an attack on at least some death sentences as retributively unfair or unjustified, as indeed many are. Third, opponents of the death penalty need to explore whether it may be possible to persuade a governor or two to consider clemency earlier in the post-sentencing phase, before, rather than after, hundreds of thousands of tax dollars have been spent in the appeal process.[103] Perhaps governors could be persuaded that real savings in public expenditure could be made if the current system of protracted appeals was smothered in the crib. Not by speeding up federal appeals (favored in some quarters),[104] but by preemptive commutation of the death sentence itself. One should not be optimistic that any of these suggestions, separately or together, will come to pass, until such time as the public is less tolerant of the practice of capital punishment.

America enters the twenty-first century surrounded by a disheartening climate of public opinion that envelops many issues on the nation's domestic social agenda. The lingering presence of opinion tolerant of the death penalty is only one of them. Executive leadership at the state and federal level shaping this agenda is increasingly rare, as negative sound-bite electoral politics confirms anew the inescapability of Gresham's Law. Nor is it likely that the experience of signing death warrants, followed by actual executions, will provoke governors to reconsider their current all-too-enthusiastic support for the death penalty. What governors in southern states have proved capable of doing when appellate litigation fails and death row prisoners finally confront the executioner probably can be learned by their northern, eastern, and western counterparts.

The prospect is not cheering, at least not for those who oppose the death penalty, and only small consolation can be offered. Government by executive decree is in principle not one that constitutional democrats should favor. The criminal justice system in its normal operation should not be expected to allot a large role to executive clemency. The exercise of clemency is and must remain a rare exception in the final disposition of an offender's sentence. Those who oppose the death penalty cannot realistically hope to have state governors save them from popular folly. At a time when trial courts in this nation are willing to send two to three hundred prisoners to their deaths each year,[105] popularly elected chief executives cannot be expected to block the execution of those sentences except rarely. Opponents of the death penalty can only make renewed efforts to secure commutations wherever possible and to expose unrelentingly the moral and other harms that our system of capital punishment inflicts.[106]

5

THE CHOICE BETWEEN IMPRISONMENT AND DEATH

I

Perhaps the oldest of all the issues raised by the struggle in western civilization to end the death penalty is this: If we abolish the death penalty, what alternative mode of punishment shall we mete out to convicts who otherwise would have been executed? Some who are opposed to hanging, electrocution, and all the other methods of execution are in favor of no punishment whatever, not even for the worst criminals. What they offer is an alternative to punishment, not an alternative punishment. Exactly what their alternative to punishment is they will have to explain, not I. I accept the principle that wrongdoers deserve to be punished, as well as the principle that those who have committed the gravest wrong, namely murder of another person, deserve the severest punishment short of execution.[1] Precisely what this severe, but not intolerably cruel, alternative punishment should be has been a topic for much disagreement and debate. It is my purpose in this discussion to identify this alternative punishment and explain why it is preferable to death.

It is appropriate to begin by noticing a well-known but under-appreciated principle governing the advancement of science. The principle in question—self-evident upon inspection—is that no field of inquiry counts as fully developed until it is replete with concepts, theorems, lemmas, axioms, equations, and phenomena named after their discoverers. Philosophy, of course, led the way. It began with Zeno's Paradoxes, added Occam's Razor, and later, Mill's Methods.[2] Mathematics has its Cartesian Coordinates, just as quantum physics has its Planck's Constant. Where would thermodynamics be without Maxwell's Equations, economics without Say's Law, or medicine without Hodgkin's Disease? However, the overlapping fields of criminology and penology, in which our subject is located, suffer from a complete dearth of proper names designating the concepts crucial to the field. A skeptic might infer from this that there are no concepts crucial to this field, but that would be needlessly uncharitable. The best way to banish doubt on the point is to begin to reformulate our field in the requisite manner. Here I hope to make a modest contribution to that goal and to inspire others to more imaginative contributions in due course.

Sheleff's Dilemma is the fundamental deduction from the argument advanced by Leon Sheleff in his excellent book, *Ultimate Penalties*.[3] Sheleff argues that torture, a life sentence in prison, and the death penalty are all "ultimate penalties"—ultimate in their severity and ultimate in that each is morally objectionable. For our purposes, we can safely ignore Sheleff's critique of torture[4] since no serious opponent of the death penalty has ever, to my knowledge, proposed torture as an acceptable alternative to outright execution. The dilemma that concerns us arises solely between the death penalty and the third of Sheleff's "ultimate penalties"—life imprisonment. As Sheleff knows, the alternative to the death penalty advocated by most opponents of execution is some form of life sentence to prison.[5] Currently, the most popular version of this alternative is a mandatory prison term for the duration of the prisoner's natural life without possibility of parole or commutation of sentence, known by the acronym LWOP (pronounced "ellwop").[6] Sheleff is one of those who finds this alternative completely unacceptable. In his view, repealing the death penalty and substituting LWOP is going from the frying pan into the fire.[7] Unlike the late Oxford philosopher J. L. Austin, Sheleff does not believe in the principle of "any frying pan in a fire."[8] But if society refuses to consider torturing its worst criminals, and may neither execute nor forever imprison them, then what is society to do with them? This is the dilemma to which Sheleff directs our attention.

For the other half of my theme I am indebted to the late Henry Schwarzschild. On many public occasions (but not, so far as I know, in print) he observed that although there are many methods of inflicting the death penalty, some of which are clearly worse than others (electrocution is clearly worse than lethal gas, and lethal gas is probably worse than lethal injection), paradoxically no method of inflicting this penalty is better than any of the others. The point of Schwarzschild's Paradox, of course, is to remind us that all methods of carrying out the death penalty are irredeemably tarred with the same brush: All are administered with the same lethal goal, namely to kill the prisoner, even if some are administered with a further intention, laudable or deplorable as the case may be, to make the death as painless or as painful as possible. As the discoverer of this paradox, Schwarzschild deserves to have his name forever associated with it.

The solution to Schwarzschild's Paradox, as he is quick to point out, is to abolish the death penalty. Indeed, the whole point of his paradox is to turn us in this direction. But surely this lands us squarely in Sheleff's Dilemma. How are we to escape it? Can we avoid Schwarzschild's Paradox only by being impaled on the horns of Sheleff's Dilemma?

II

At the threshold, it is desirable to inform our inquiry with some historical reminders because they show how remote recent thinking among liberals and reformers really is from the views of their predecessors in the abolition movement. All students of the subject know that the abolition movement, or at least its literate advocacy, begins with the short treatise *On Crimes and Punishments*, published in 1764 by the young Italian nobleman and jurist Cesare Beccaria.[9] What did Beccaria propose as the alternative to the death penalty and why did he favor this alternative?

Beccaria favored perpetual imprisonment at hard labor—"penal slavery," as Thorsten Sellin described it[10]—rather than the death penalty, for several reasons.[11] The first he mentions is thin and formalistic, the sort of reason only a philosopher (and not a very good one, at that) could formulate. Beccaria believed (much as Hobbes had argued a century earlier) that it is conceptually impossible for any individual social contractor to alienate his right to life because it is so contrary to self-interest to do so—no one could willingly transfer to another the right over his very own life.[12] Since the rights of legitimate government are derived entirely by tacit transfer of the natural rights of persons, the government as the agent of society has no right to take in punishment the life of any member of society.[13]

Notice that Beccaria makes no moralistic appeal; it is not respect for the value of human life, much less any religious appeal to the sanctity of human life, nor even the desire to reduce the pain suffered by the convict on which Beccaria rests his argument. It is rather an alleged inference from within the theory of the social contract, an inference that most other social contract theorists (such as Locke, Rousseau, and Kant) rejected. They rejected it for a simple reason: Even if one grants that it is psychologically or conceptually impossible for a person to *alienate* his right to life, that does not make it impossible for a person to *forfeit* that right. The major social contract theorists who favored the death penalty (except Hobbes) relied on this argument. Beccaria simply ignored it.[14]

Beccaria's second reason is more familiar to us. He stated, "It appears absurd to me that the laws, which are the expression of the public will and which detest and punish homicide, commit murder themselves, and, in order to dissuade citizens from assassination, command public assassination."[15] What is this but the familiar rhetorical question of the current abolition movement: Why do we kill people to show that killing people is wrong? This is not, I am afraid, a very telling objection. By parity of reasoning, one might ask why do we deprive persons of their liberty and property in order to show that kidnapping and theft are crimes? Punishments necessarily involve deprivations, so Beccaria's rhetorical objection to the death penalty would, if consistently applied, effectively tie our hands against using any alternative punishment as well.

Beccaria's third reason is simpler and more convincing. He believed the death penalty to be a "cruel" punishment; its infliction "gives to men," he said, "the example of cruelty."[16] Well put, indeed. Ever since Beccaria wrote these words, abolitionists have echoed them and have never tired of explaining why the death penalty is a cruel punishment and why it therefore ought to be abolished.[17]

The death penalty, however, is not the only form that cruelty in punishment may take. Imagine a person whose legs are rigidly shackled together at the ankles, but who is otherwise free to move about. Or imagine someone condemned to spend his days and nights confined to a tiny space the size of a telephone booth. Would anyone seriously deny that such punishments are cruel, even if not as cruel as drawing and quartering or burning at the stake? We are here at the edge of Sheleff's Dilemma, and so it is important to see whether Beccaria escaped it.

He did not; he was fatally impaled on its horns, as we see when we look at his final reason for favoring abolition. Beccaria believed that the spectacle of endless drudgery in prison—"the constant example,"[18] in his words, of a convict undergoing punishment—would serve far better as a deterrent (would make a "much stronger impression")[19] than the brief spectacle of death on the scaffold. To this extent he believed that imprisonment of the sort he favored was worse—harsher, more painful, more severe—or at least was perceived by the average citizen as worse, than the death penalty. Soft-headed liberalism, soft-hearted concern for the welfare of the wretched criminal, the desire to achieve reform of sociopathic behavior rather than retribution—none appears to play any role in Beccaria's opposition to capital punishment. As a result, Beccaria in effect gave a much needed rationalization to brutal forms of imprisonment already well known in his day, such as hauling barges by roped teams of prisoners and annual public floggings coupled with "severe" incarceration for thirty years—in short (and again I borrow the words of Thorsten Sellin) to "forced labor of excruciating kinds or frightful imprisonment" that amounted to "a prolonged death penalty."[20] A cynic might well argue that Beccaria completely deceived himself as to his own "enlightened" opposition to executions. His insistence on resting the choice of punishments entirely on their alleged deterrent effect caused him and his supporters to embrace savage, ruthless, inhumane, and cruel alternatives with a clear conscience—the very worst result of self-deception caused by thralldom to an abstract ideology.

III

At some point, the argument is bound to be raised that it is impossible to decide whether death or LWOP is the worse punishment. The argument goes like this: No one can tell which of the two experiences is worse without experiencing each and comparing the two in the relevant respects. (One might think here of John Stuart Mill's argument that no one can rationally choose which of two pleasures is the greater unless he or she has had "experience of both.")[21] The argument proceeds by pointing out that no one ever has experienced both of these alternatives; at most a person experiences one of the alternatives—perhaps some fragmentary portion of life imprisonment (say, thirty or forty years in prison out of a lifetime of seventy years) or the first stages of death by execution (as in the famous case of Willie Francis, who survived the first attempt to electrocute him).[22] The conclusion then follows that no one knows or can ever hope to know which of these two punishments is worse.

There are many objections to this argument but I want to consider only one. Even if the argument that no one can ever know which punishment is worse were sound, this would not rule out the possibility that a person might still have a preference for one punishment over the other. For example, it will be recalled that in 1977 Gary Gilmore expressed a preference for death by firing squad rather than spending the rest of his life in prison—and the State of Utah happily obliged him.[23] Gilmore knew something about imprisonment from prior experience, but he knew no more about death and dying than you or I. Yet the force of the previous argument is to raise a doubt about whether it is possible for a preference such as Gilmore's to be rational since the sole, allegedly relevant evidence on which to base a rational preference is unavailable.

Even if we can evade this conclusion, we stare another problem in the face: the complete subjectivity of any judgment concerning which of the two punishments is worse. Even if it were possible for a Gilmore to have a rational preference for death over imprisonment, this in no way would require any other convicted offender to have the same rational preference. Rational preference may be intersubjective, but it need not be; it might even be radically subjective and individual.

How might the rational legislator (if there is such a creature outside the pages of Jeremy Bentham) respond to such a conclusion? One response would be to enact the subjective rational preference of the legislature or of the general public. But there is another and better possibility. The rational legislator might argue that the statutory punishment for murder (and other capital crimes, if any) ought to include the provision that the choice between the alternatives of death and LWOP is to be made by each convicted capital offender on a case by case basis.

But are we really content with the conclusion that the judgment regarding whether prison or death is the worse punishment must be an irreducibly subjective one? Surely, the rational legislator prefers to believe otherwise. He or she prefers to believe that there is an objective basis on which to argue that of two different statutory punishments, A and B, either A is worse than B, or B is worse than A, or both are equally mild or severe, humane or cruel.

Leon Sheleff, for example, seems to believe something like this: He points out that "the life sentence [has] not been subjected to the kind of scrutiny that has been given the death penalty,"[24] and he urges that "there may well be a need for a probing investigation aimed at ascertaining the relative severities of these two punishments."[25] But the point of such scrutiny presupposes the possibility of arriving at some kind of objective or at least intersubjective judgment on the issue of relative severity. Sheleff's Dilemma is so acute for its author partly because he neither indicates how such "scrutiny" might proceed nor identifies the factors on which a nonsubjective judgment of relative severity might rest.

IV

I want to argue that there is a purely objective basis on which to make the choice between these two punishments, a basis that is indifferent to and that should prevail over any subjective preference, however rational that preference may be.

As a first step, it is useful to return to the history of the problem. Unquestionably, the first thinker to lavish serious attention on the question of the relative severity of the death penalty versus life imprisonment was Jeremy Bentham. Within little more than a decade after Beccaria's pioneering book, Bentham wrote his *Rationale of Punishment*, in which he devoted two chapters to the death penalty.[26] Although in this book, written around 1775, he did not oppose capital punishment categorically, by the end of his life, in 1832, he did,[27] and his arguments then were essentially the same as his early objections. They deserve careful consideration even today. (I have discussed his views in greater detail elsewhere.)[28]

Bentham was a utilitarian and he believed that the choice between alternative punishments must rest on which best serves the public welfare at the least cost. The task of the rational legislator was to carry out what today we would refer to as a cost/benefit analysis of the alternatives and enact into law the mode of punishment best calculated to maximize net benefits. Bentham believed that, on balance, penal servitude had the edge over the death penalty.[29]

Today, we can most conveniently model the way Bentham set up the problem by means of a decision matrix for pairwise comparison.[30] The two rows of the matrix represent the two alternative punishments; the several columns of the matrix are the independent variables by means of which any punishment can be analyzed and any set of punishments compared.[31] We then simply assess the value numerically of each punishment under each variable, plug in these several numerical values one by one, do a bit of arithmetic, and inspect the result. (Actually, Bentham's own analysis of the matter cannot be directly presented in such a decision matrix because a crucial step—evaluating the weight of each independent variable and ranking the variables accordingly—is missing from his discussion. This omission fatally weakens the modeling of his actual reasoning by this method. Nevertheless, a modern Benthamite would readily enough adjust to the demands of the model.)

Let us focus on the eight independent variables that Bentham identifies as sufficient and necessary to capture every relevant feature through which punishments vary, and see what they tell us about the relative merits of the death penalty and LWOP for the crime of murder.[32] Arrayed in favor of the death penalty, according to Bentham, are four factors: (1) death bears a closer "analogy" to the crime than does imprisonment; (2) death is the more "popular" punishment of the two; (3) death is the more "exemplary" punishment, because its real cost to the offender more closely approximates its apparent cost; and (4) death has greater "efficacy" than imprisonment because it incapacitates better.[33]

Arrayed on the other side are four quite different factors: (5) prison is far more "profitable" to society and to the offender than is death because the imprisoned offender can labor productively; (6) prison is more "frugal" than death because the deprivation death imposes on the offender is way out of proportion to the sheer delight it affords the rest of society; (7) prison is more "equable" than death because it admits of infinite variation in degree and quality, whereas death admits of no degrees (one might think of Schwarzschild's Paradox as a natural product of what Bentham would have called the inequability of death as a punishment); (8) finally, and above all, death is "irremissible" whereas imprisonment is not.[34]

Although the number of factors favoring death is the same as the number of factors favoring the alternative, Bentham clearly thinks the latter four factors are weightier than the former four.[35] If he is right, the rational legislator must favor prison over death in all cases (except possibly those few where factor [4] decisively and by a wide margin favors death).

Let us grant that Bentham has found as objective a way of evaluating alternative penalties as one could want. Unfortunately, it sheds little light on our problem. Bentham has shown us, at least in principle (and if we are utilitarians), how to choose rationally between two punishments from the point of view of society as a whole. But he has not therewith shown us which of the two punishments is the more severe or the less cruel, as these factors might figure in the judgment of someone who had to choose between the two alternatives for himself. Of the eight Benthamite variables that bear on rational choice between punishments, at most three—exemplarity, frugality, and remissibility—clearly bear on that choice from the perspective of a person about to be punished the one way or the other. To put this point another way, the set of eight factors that enable a rational legislator to choose one and reject another mode of punishment on behalf of society is not identical with the set of three factors that make the one mode of punishment better—less severe, less cruel, less of a deprivation—than the other.

What, then, can we learn from this exercise about resolving Sheleff's Dilemma? Rather less than we might have hoped because the true character of Bentham's alternative punishment as actually lived by someone sentenced to endure it plays almost no role whatever in his pairwise comparison of the two punishments, not even in the three variables from among his eight that I singled out above. Accordingly, if there is to be any intersubjective (much less objective) measure of the relative merits of death versus LWOP, it is not provided by Bentham's analysis.

V

Two decades ago I laid out a set of reasons why I believed that imprisonment, even long-term imprisonment, perhaps even LWOP, is a less severe, less cruel, and in short, a better punishment than death.[36] I still believe that these reasons are as powerful and conclusive as they seemed to me then, and so I want to reexamine them here. I also believe that they are objectively valid and exhaustively relevant.

Crucial to my analysis is the following principle of evaluative comparison. Roughly, of two punishments, one is more severe than the other, depending on its duration and on its interference with other pursuits a person undergoing the punishment might undertake. There are at least four dimensions in which to make the pairwise comparison of death and LWOP as punishments, and in each death emerges as the more severe.

- Death is interminable, whereas it is always possible to terminate by revocation a life prison sentence.
- Death makes compensation for error impossible, whereas it is always possible to compensate (at least in part) any wrongly convicted life term prisoner.
- Death permits no concurrent experiences or activities, whereas life imprisonment permits many.
- Death eliminates the presupposition of all experience and activity—life itself—whereas life imprisonment only restricts the scope, range, variety, and duration of the experiences and activities that the punishee undergoes.[37]

As a fifth consideration, I would also add that if being alive is not only a necessary condition of good things but is a good in and of itself, as we might suppose to be true of autonomy, liberty, and privacy, then life is the greatest of these goods and so a greater good than any of the other intrinsic goods it makes possible.

I am aware that my fifth point is disturbingly metaphysical and that some evidence for each of my prior four points may need to be brought forward to convince the skeptical. Nonetheless, I infer from these pronounced differences between the punishments of death and long-term imprisonment that, of course and in general, death is the more severe punishment, no matter what any given prisoner in a fit of despondency may say. As advertised above, this argument purports to be both intersubjective and objective; it is not vulnerable to counterclaims based upon nothing more than the subjective experience or preference, by anyone, of either type of punishment, much less on a comparison of the experiences involved in undergoing each punishment. The argument, rather, depends entirely on objectively ascertainable facts about the two kinds of punishments.

Yet, there is a line of possible rebuttal to the argument above, to the effect that other considerations enter beyond those identified so far, and they tip the balance. These considerations point out that under LWOP, the quality of life can so deteriorate that it undermines the value of the life itself. The same kind of considerations that make suicide or euthanasia preferable to continued life under certain adverse conditions can also make death by execution preferable to year after year in prison when there is no hope of release. The accommodations the young and robust prisoner must make with his hopes and desires, this objection maintains, simply are not worth it—or might reasonably be judged not worth it, at least by some such prisoners.

How conclusive is this objection? I am inclined to say not very, and I would appeal to three kinds of empirical facts. First, very few capital convicts awaiting sentencing seek a death sentence rather than a sentence to life in prison. (Of the 7,000 persons sentenced to death since the 1970s, as of January 2000, 784 had been executed, 93 of whom were "volunteers," in the sense that at some point after sentencing, they refused any further attempts to block their execution.)[38] Second, very few life term prisoners try to commit suicide—or try until they succeed. (Statistics on the point are difficult to obtain, but consider the suicide rate for prisoners on death row. In the five year period 1985–89, 14 death row prisoners died by suicide out of approximately 1,500–2,500 persons on death row for those same years.)[39] Third, very few life term prisoners indicate, after twenty or thirty years in prison, that if they had known in advance what these decades behind bars would be like, they would have preferred death to such a life. In short, those in the best position to judge overwhelmingly prefer imprisonment. If I had to give an explanation for such facts as a reflection of rational judgment by the prisoners, I would appeal to the factors (at least the first four, if not all five) mentioned earlier in this section.

One might try to undermine the force of this argument in any of three ways. First, objections may be made that my empirical data are inconclusive because the imprisonment that convicts prefer to death is not LWOP—and if the only alternative to a death penalty were LWOP, the empirical data might be very different. All quite true. Thanks to the growing popularity of LWOP, we may have the opportunity to find out whether this objection really is sound. Meanwhile, I remain unpersuaded.

Second, one might press the point that imprisonment can be made a living hell, so much so that death would be a welcome relief from its horrors. This objection had weight in Beccaria's day but not in ours, or at least it has less weight today than it once did. The kind of aggravations to incarceration that gave penal servitude its deservedly bad reputation are not today permissible under law anywhere in the civilized world (even if they are occasionally practiced in spite of the law).[40]

As a third objection, one might argue that it is the interminable and irrevocable character of LWOP that makes it so awful. This is the feature, above all, that Sheleff's Dilemma rests upon. In effect, echoing Sellin's observation about the penal servitude of Beccaria's day, Sheleff insists that "if a person has no prospect whatsoever of being released, no scintilla of hope to sustain and encourage him that one day he may be free, then his punishment is tantamount to a delayed death penalty."[41] This makes it "qualitatively different" from any other form of punishment except, of course, outright execution.

I beg to disagree. One might as well argue that being alive itself is, after all, nothing but delayed dying, a kind of natural death sentence, since eventually everyone is dead. But this simply points to the exaggeration, not to say the absurdity, of Sheleff's claim. Of course, it is a platitude to observe that whichever side of the prison bars one is on, being alive results eventually in being dead. But then, surely, it is simply unconvincing to assert that a "delayed death penalty" in the form of perpetual imprisonment in and of itself is to be regarded as a cruel or unnecessarily severe or otherwise objectionable punishment, when the alternative punishment is a wholly unnecessary death brought about in an untimely manner by lawful execution.

I argue as I have without wishing to disagree with Sheleff that LWOP is probably completely unnecessary as an alternative to the death penalty. Its current popularity is owing not to rational judgment of its necessity to protect the public or to mete out deserved retribution, but to public anxiety over premature or irrational release of still-dangerous felons and by those opponents of the death penalty who are willing to clutch at any straw, any frying pan in a fire.

VI

Elsewhere I have argued that the preferred alternative to capital punishment is not LWOP but a much less severe punishment.[42] Inspired by the alternative to the death penalty proposed nearly a century ago by

New York's Lewis E. Lawes,[43] warden of Sing Sing Prison and one of the founders of the American League to Abolish Capital Punishment, my proposal amounts to a bold and humane way through the horns of Sheleff's Dilemma.

The proposal has seven features: (1) every person convicted of first degree murder would be sentenced to life imprisonment; (2) no consideration for release, commutation, or reduction in sentence would be made until ten years of the sentence had been served; (3) during the period of imprisonment, the prisoner would be expected to work in prison industries and would receive appropriate compensation for his labor, from which half of the earnings would be contributed to a fund for indemnification of dependents of murder victims; (4) after the tenth year of imprisonment, the offender would be considered annually for release; (5) release from prison for a convicted first-degree murderer would be contingent upon convincing evidence of rehabilitation while in prison, a feasible job opportunity in the community into which the prisoner is to be released, support from community agencies, residency in a halfway house or comparable supervised setting for one year, and parole supervision for an additional four years (except where old age or illness of the prisoner warranted a waiver of some or all of these conditions); (6) judgment of a prisoner's suitability for release under the above conditions would be made either by a duly constituted parole and release board or, in the absence of such a body, by a special ad hoc committee appointed by the legislature and chief executive; and (7) repeated failure of a prisoner to secure release under the foregoing conditions would result in the prisoner serving a natural life sentence.[44]

Essential to the proposal is the distinction between life without possibility of parole and life without the probability of parole. The proposal repudiates the former and thus is not a strict version of LWOP. But the proposal does not rule out the latter in some cases; how large a fraction of life term prisoners this proposal would require to remain in prison for the duration of their natural lives is impossible to say. Other conditions and variations would need to be considered, but the seven listed above are the central ones. None is novel; many are familiar and found in the law. Nowhere, however, to my knowledge, is any statute with all these provisions currently in force.[45]

This is explained by the two major objections to the proposal. First, as penal statutes currently stand, such a punishment for first-degree murder would be less severe than the punishments currently applicable for offenses of lesser gravity.[46] Second, even if this were not true, the alternative proposed here to the death penalty and to LWOP is probably politically unfeasible at this time in most, and probably all, jurisdictions in this country.

My response to these objections can be stated quite briefly. As to the first, I conclude that other crimes are punished too severely if the punishment proposed here for first-degree murder is not the severest of them all. The way to meet the first objection, then, is not to ignore the alternative I propose but to reassess current sentencing practices for other felonies. As to the second, I suggest that it is not the task of penal reform—or of the movement against the death penalty—to present to the public whatever it will accept. The task, rather, is to argue for a punitive policy that is humane, feasible, and effective, whatever the crime and whoever the offender, and regardless of the current climate of public opinion. Temporary compromises are no doubt necessary and advisable in order to make some practical progress. But the goal must be kept firmly in mind. The death penalty is not the only outrageous form of punishment practiced in our society, even if it is the worst. Only an alternative to the death penalty and to LWOP, such as I have proposed, recognizes the truth in Schwarzschild's Paradox without embracing or ignoring Sheleff's Dilemma.

A MORAL READING OF THE EIGHTH AMENDMENT

I

In his recent book *Freedom's Law*,[1] Ronald Dworkin argues for what he calls "the *moral* reading" of the American Constitution.[2] He explains that such a reading—an interpretation of the written text of the Constitution—requires lawyers, judges, legislators, and the general public "to find the best conception of constitutional moral principles . . . that fits the broad story of America's historical record."[3] As an example, consider the Equal Protection Clause of the Fourteenth Amendment. Dworkin contrasts a narrow versus an expansive reading of that clause and argues that only the latter can do justice to what "equal protection" really means. On a narrow reading, for example, the Court's decision in *Brown v. Board of Education*,[4] based on the Equal Protection Clause, is unintelligible and unwarranted. That decision, however, is fully justified if we realize that the Equal Protection Clause tacitly invokes a *principle* to the effect that "[our] government must treat everyone as of equal status and with equal concern."[5] Schools racially segregated by law cannot do this if (as was true in the United States fifty years ago) the segregation was imposed by a majority on a minority in part as a badge of the latter's inferiority. Only a broad, tacit principle can do justice to the American idea of equal protection.

Arrayed against this theory of constitutional interpretation is mainly the *originalist* theory, perhaps best known in the version advanced by the unsuccessful Supreme Court nominee Robert Bork,[6] and applied to the death penalty two decades ago by Raoul Berger in his book *Death Penalties: The Supreme Court's Obstacle Course*.[7] According to the originalist view, "the great clauses of the Bill of Rights should be interpreted not as laying down the abstract moral principles they actually describe, but instead as referring, in a kind of code or disguise, to the [F]ramers' own assumptions and expectations about the correct application of those principles."[8]

Such a theory rests on a fundamental confusion, however: the error of mistaking what the Framers *thought* their language in the Bill of Rights referred to (or what they *intended* the political and legal results of their constitutional language to be) with what that language really *does* mean. As Dworkin realizes,[9] originalists such as Bork and Berger cannot attach any significance to this distinction between intention and meaning, because they are moral skeptics or moral subjectivists. Skeptics and subjectivists cannot make sense of a contrast between what someone *thinks* is a correct and relevant moral principle and what *is* a correct and relevant moral principle; only objectivists in moral theory can make that distinction. The generic distinction we all make between our attitudes or feelings and the reality to which they are directed ought to make us cautious in rejecting that distinction where morality is concerned. Why, for example, should we collapse the *fact* that torturing babies is cruel into someone's *belief* that such torture is cruel?[10] But undermining moral skepticism and subjectivism is a task for another day.

What is the chief objection to the moral reading of the Constitution (subjectivism and skepticism to one side)? According to Dworkin, it is the mistaken belief that such a reading "offends democracy."[11] It supposedly does that by violating what he calls "the majoritarian premise,"[12] namely, "that political procedures [including the interpretation of the Constitution by the Supreme Court] should be designed so that, at least on important matters, the decision that is reached is the decision . . . a majority or plurality of citizens favors, or would favor if it had adequate information and enough time for reflection."[13] If you accept the majoritarian premise, then you must believe "that it is *always* unfair when a political majority is not allowed to have its way."[14]

Dworkin proceeds to argue against the majoritarian premise in favor of what he calls "the constitutional conception of democracy."[15] On that view, "the defining aim of democracy" is to develop institutions and practices of government designed to show "equal concern and respect" for all persons—and if this requires nonmajoritarian procedures on occasion, that is not unfair or otherwise morally or constitutionally objectionable.[16]

A careful study of Dworkin's argument repays the investment of time and energy, but it will not advance my purpose here to sketch his argument in further detail. For although one might have thought Dworkin could not have done better than to illustrate the moral reading of the Constitution by undertaking to show the effect of such a reading on the constitutional status of the death penalty under the Eighth Amendment prohibition against "cruel and unusual punishments"[17] and the Fourteenth Amendment requirements of "equal protection of the laws" and "due process of law,"[18] his book, alas, presents no such undertaking. Apart from a few scattered allusions to the death penalty, he is silent on the subject, reserving extended application of his "moral reading" of the Constitution to other issues. I propose to remedy this neglect and to show how an appropriate moral reading of the Eighth Amendment yields the conclusion that the death penalty is, indeed, unconstitutional. The fragment of that large task to be addressed here concerns the quarrel between the moral reading and an alternative majoritarian or populist reading of the Eighth Amendment.

II

As one reads through the more than two hundred pages that constitute the *per curiam* decision and the nine opinions by the Supreme Court in *Furman v. Georgia*,[19] one cannot fail to notice the paucity of structured argument by any of the five Justices in the majority[20] or the four in the minority.[21] Political and legal history in varying degrees of detail, evidence provided by social science investigations, sketchy conjectures, and ripostes and rebuttals of diverse scope and persuasiveness are most of what one finds. The striking exception to this pattern is the fifty-page opinion by Justice William J. Brennan, Jr.[22]

Justice Brennan's opinion is suggestive of how to give a moral reading to the Eighth Amendment's prohibition of cruel and unusual punishment. His strategy was to propose four "principles" to elucidate that brief and cryptic constitutional text, principles he claimed were "recognized in our cases and inherent in the Clause," and that when taken in conjunction with the relevant empirical facts would provide a sound basis for "a judicial determination whether a challenged punishment" is or is not unconstitutional.[23] Justice Brennan's identification and application of these principles was a bold and original contribution to constitutional interpretation. Here are his four principles (in the order in which he presented them, perhaps also what he believed to be the order of their importance):

1. "The primary principle is that a punishment must not be so severe as to be degrading to the dignity of human beings."[24] The sheer painfulness of the punishment, however, is not the only factor determining its severity. "[A severe] punishment may be degrading [to human dignity] simply by reason of its enormity."[25]

2. "[T]he State must not arbitrarily inflict a severe punishment. . . . [It] does not respect human dignity when, without reason, it inflicts upon some people a severe punishment that it does not inflict upon others."[26]

3. "[A] severe punishment must not be unacceptable to contemporary society. . . . Rejection by society . . . is a strong indication that a severe punishment does not comport with human dignity."[27]

4. "[A] severe punishment must not be excessive. A punishment is excessive under this principle if it is unnecessary: . . . The infliction of a severe punishment . . . cannot comport with human dignity when it is nothing more than the pointless infliction of suffering."[28]

It too frequently goes unnoticed that no other Justice in the *Furman* majority, and none of the four dissenting members of the Court, took up explicitly the challenge in their opinions implicitly presented by Brennan's four principles—the principles that constituted the major premise of his constitutional argument against the death penalty. To do so would have required a Justice to decide, first, whether to endorse all and only those principles. If the Justice decided to endorse them, his next task would be to assess their application to the death penalty; this would amount to addressing the minor or factual premise of Brennan's overall argument. However, if the Justice decided to reject these principles, then he would have to offer alternative interpretive principles or else explain why no such principles were available or needed. One instructive way to read the other eight opinions in *Furman*—as well as the Court's opinions in subsequent major death penalty cases, notably *Gregg v. Georgia*[29] and *Woodson v. Carolina*[30]—is to see how each Justice implicitly responded to the challenge of Brennan's principles. In *Furman*, for example, Justice Marshall endorsed virtually all four of Brennan's principles, but without expressly acknowledging that he was doing so.[31] Justices Stewart[32] and White,[33] on the other hand, in their very brief concurring opinions, endorsed at best only one or two of those principles (and they did that only implicitly). The same is true of Justice Douglas in his *Furman* opinion.[34]

Because of the neglect and nonjoinder of issues visited on Justice Brennan's four principles, the major death penalty decisions by the Supreme Court in the 1970s have left unsettled the status of the only explicit attempt ever made by anyone on the Court to articulate the interpretive principles implicit in the Eighth Amendment prohibition of cruel and unusual punishment. It remains true today, as it was a generation ago, that the best way to develop an intelligible Eighth Amendment jurisprudence is by grappling with Justice Brennan's four principles.

Helpful as these principles are, however, they are not beyond criticism; I suggest they are both under- and overinclusive. They are underinclusive because they omit one obvious relevant principle to any moral reading of the Eighth Amendment—a principle, not surprisingly, recognized by the Supreme Court at least as far back as the non-capital case of *Weems v. United States*.[35] I refer to the principle of proportionality, in both its versions: A punishment may be cruel and unusual if in its severity it is not proportional to the gravity of the offense; and the greater the gravity of the offense the greater is the deserved severity of punishment. These principles are virtually unanimously endorsed by modern theorists of punishment.[36] Confronted by the realization that these principles are omitted from Justice Brennan's analysis of the Eighth Amendment, a supporter of the death penalty will be sorely tempted to explain their absence by pointing out that if they are included, then it will prove difficult, perhaps impossible, to obtain the result that Justice Brennan wants, namely, a set of principles under which it is possible for the Court to conclude that the death penalty violates all of them, no matter what the crime, including murder. For, as a dissenter in *Furman*[37] and the majority in *Gregg*[38] pointed out (though not in express criticism of Justice Brennan for his failure to address the proportionality principles),[39] it is difficult to argue that the death penalty is disproportionate for the crime of murder. I think there are ways to make such an argument, but doing so is not part of my present purpose.

Second, for anyone interested in a moral reading of the Eighth Amendment, the third of Justice Brennan's four principles is especially important. That principle declared "that a severe punishment must not be unacceptable to contemporary society."[40] Here, installed in the very center of his interpretation of the Eighth Amendment, is a populist, majoritarian consideration indicative of an interpretative strategy Justice Brennan otherwise seems to reject. So this principle and the facts relevant to it need our careful scrutiny. Let us look first at the facts that shed light on whether the death penalty was, or is today, "unacceptable to contemporary society." We can then consider whether Justice Brennan's populist principle of constitutional interpretation is a valid principle.

III

Justice Brennan expressly pointed out that "[t]he acceptability of a severe punishment is measured, not by its availability, for it might become so offensive to society as never to be inflicted, but by its *use*."[41] Accordingly, he went on to point out that in the 1960s, "society will inflict death upon only a small sample of the eligible criminals,"[42] "a mere 100 or so cases among the thousands tried each year where the punishment is available."[43] Justice Brennan in effect defends what I will call the Irregular Infrequency Hypothesis as the best interpretation of the administration of the death penalty in the 1960s.

In much the same vein, Justice Thurgood Marshall in *Furman* offered as a general principle relevant to interpreting the Eighth Amendment that even if "a punishment is not excessive and serves a valid legislative purpose, it still may be invalid if popular sentiment abhors it."[44] Justice Marshall went on to declare that the death penalty "is morally unacceptable to the people of the United States at this time in their history."[45] His evidence? He cited, but without much enthusiasm, a public opinion poll showing that in 1966, 47 percent of the public opposed the death penalty and 42 percent favored it;[46] he also mentioned the "few people . . . executed in the past decade"[47]—even though he knew that beginning in mid-1967, the moratorium on executions was judicially imposed and not a consequence of any general public discontent with the death penalty.[48] What he mainly relied on was the claim that a public fully informed about the death penalty would oppose it. This came to be called the "Marshall Hypothesis," and I will return to it below.[49]

The Brennan-Marshall line of argument paraphrased above did not go uncriticized by other members of the Court. The criticism developed in two stages, and it focused exclusively on the empirical (or minor) premise of the Brennan-Marshall argument. Chief Justice Warren Burger, in his *Furman* dissent, and Justice Stewart, in his plurality opinion in *Gregg*, completely ignored whether Justice Brennan's major normative premise could be relied on as a sound principle of constitutional interpretation. Justices Burger and Stewart were content, it appears, to concede *arguendo* that it did. But as to the facts of public attitudes and behavior regarding the death penalty, their dissent was quite explicit. The Chief Justice insisted that it was "unwarranted hyperbole" to describe "the rate of imposition" of the death penalty in the 1960s as "freakishly rare,"[50] quoting language used in the opinion of Justice Stewart,[51] but implied in the opinions of Justices Douglas,[52] Brennan,[53] and White[54] as well.

The Chief Justice also insisted that "[t]he selectivity of juries in imposing the [death penalty] is properly viewed as a refinement on, rather than a repudiation of, the statutory authorization for that penalty. . . . [J]uries have been increasingly meticulous in their imposition of the penalty."[55] Thus, in contrast to Justice Brennan, the Chief Justice defended what I will call the Meticulous Scrutiny Hypothesis as the best interpretation of how the death penalty was being administered. The reader will look in vain, however, for any supporting evidence in the opinion. The Chief Justice also claimed that the petitioners themselves, who presumably bore the burden of the argument, offered "no empirical basis" to support their claim of arbitrary and infrequent irregularity of jury imposition of the death sentence.[56] This was not correct, as inspection of the amicus brief filed by the NAACP Legal Defense and Educational Fund shows.[57] One could argue, of course, that the evidence presented there was far from conclusive. So far as the empirical evidence was concerned, then, it is arguable that each side failed adequately to support its claims.

Four years later a more extensive challenge to the Brennan-Marshall minor premise was advanced by Justice Potter Stewart in his plurality opinion for the Court in *Gregg*.[58] He cited four populist facts: (1) "the legislative response to *Furman*," involving the swift reenactment of the death penalty by three dozen states;[59] (2) "the only statewide referendum occurring since *Furman*," in which California voters amended the state constitution to permit the death penalty;[60] (3) "jury verdicts," in which more than two hundred convicted murderers "had been sentenced to death since *Furman*,"[61] and (4) current support for the death penalty by a large proportion of American society, according to the most recent survey research.[62] Justice Stewart had argued, in effect: If public opinion and behavior are relevant to interpreting the Eighth Amendment, and opponents of the death penalty in *Furman* not only concede but insist they are, then there is no reason to think that this consideration in interpreting the Eighth Amendment requires abolition of the death penalty—at least, not in 1976. The Brennan-Marshall claim of diminished, if not zero, public support for the death penalty simply flies in the face of the facts.

As for Justices Brennan and Marshall themselves, the fifteen pages of their dissenting opinions in *Gregg* run closely parallel to the argument of petitioner's brief: They contain no direct or even indirect reply to the attack on this part of their own minor premise.[63] What else is this but a tacit concession that if the majoritarian principle of Justice Brennan's major premise is valid, then the constitutional opponents of the death penalty have failed to make out their claim? So much, then, for where things stood in 1976.

IV

Where do they stand today? An evaluation of the current status of the minor premise in the Brennan-Marshall argument involves two steps. First, we need to look at the relevant survey research on the death penalty. Second, we need to fix our minds on the basic facts regarding use of the death penalty. Using both these kinds of information, we can evaluate which of the two hypotheses before us—Irregular Infrequency or Meticulous Scrutiny—is the more plausible.

For some years now, the American public apparently has given substantial, even overwhelming, support to the death penalty. The evidence is various and considerable:[64]

- In 1979, three years after the Court's decisions in *Gregg* and related cases, *The Playboy Report on American Men* reported that 68 percent of American men favored the death penalty, ranging from a high of 74 percent (men between the ages of thirty and thirty-nine), to a low of 60 percent (men between the ages of eighteen and twenty-two).[65]
- *The Figgie Report Part II*,[66] published in 1980, reported that 92 percent "of senior executives with *Fortune* 1,000 corporations favor" the death penalty for murder.[67]
- In New York City, nearly half of the 1,329 city residents polled in 1985 reported that the death penalty would "help reduce crime a lot."[68]
- In South Carolina, a 1985 newspaper survey reported that among

those asked in the local population, the death penalty was supported by more than three to two (68 percent versus 21 percent); only 11 percent were undecided.[69]

- A Media General/Associated Press survey in early 1985 reported that of the 1,476 adults asked nationwide, "[a]n unprecedented 84 percent of Americans approve of the death penalty. . . . [Of these,] 57 percent said the death penalty was appropriate in certain circumstances and only 27 percent said it should be used in all murder cases."[70] (One wonders whether these respondents knew or cared that, nine years earlier, the Supreme Court had ruled that a mandatory death penalty for murder was unconstitutional.)[71] According to the same poll, half of those who support the death penalty also believe that the death penalty is not imposed fairly from case to case.[72]

- *Parade* magazine reported in 1987 that of the "nearly 40,000" persons from all over the country who volunteered their views on the death penalty, "[n]early 80% believe there should be capital punishment in general," and "[a]lmost 55% think there should be no minimum age for the death penalty."[73]

- In Texas, a sample of 1,008 persons polled by telephone in 1988 reported overwhelmingly (86 percent) that they thought "Texas should have capital punishment."[74] This was an increase over 1985, when 75 percent of Texans favored the death penalty.[75]

- The annual survey of the attitudes of students entering college, *The American Freshman*, reports a steady decline in support for abolition: In 1971, almost 58 percent of entering college freshmen favored abolition of the death penalty.[76] That figure dropped to 26.6 percent in 1985,[77] to 21.2 percent in 1991,[78] and in 1994 plummeted to the all-time low of 20 percent.[79]

These reports are typical. Public support for the death penalty appears to have steadily increased from around 65 percent in the early 1970s to an all-time high of 80 percent, according to a Gallup Poll in September 1994.[80] This poll also showed that a majority of the public favored the death penalty for juveniles (an attitude perhaps fueled in part by an overestimate of the volume and rate of juvenile crime;

though statistics do show that the volume of teenage murder more than doubled in the period from 1985 through 1991[81] and the arrest rate for young teenagers more than tripled).[82]

In their thoughtful survey of public opinion on the death penalty in the United States, psychologist Phoebe Ellsworth and law professor Samuel Gross summarized the situation succinctly: "Support for the death penalty is at an all time high, both in the proportion of Americans who favor capital punishment and in the intensity of their feelings."[83] As I noted in Chapter 1, however, survey research during 2001 showed a measurable drop in public support to 63 percent, a drop of 10 to 15 percent.[84] How much farther that support will fall cannot be predicted; it may not even stay at this lower rate for long, given the pressure to support the most violent measures at the government's disposal, fueled by our foreign policies in the Middle East.

V

Three different kinds of arguments have been advanced to discredit the apparent nationwide popular support for the death penalty reported in the sources cited above.

The Marshall Hypothesis   As noted earlier, this argument emerged in 1972 in Justice Marshall's concurring opinion in *Furman*.[85] He argued that public opinion polls cannot settle whether a punishment is cruel and unusual in the constitutional sense of those terms:

> [W]hether or not a punishment is cruel and unusual depends, not on whether its mere mention "shocks the conscience and sense of justice of the people," but on whether people who were fully informed as to the purposes of the penalty and its liabilities would find the penalty shocking, unjust, and unacceptable.[86]

This counter-factual conditional has two parts. First, it assumes that the public is uninformed or misinformed about the death penalty as it is actually employed; second, it assumes that if the public were "fully informed," then "a substantial proportion of American citizens would . . . [find the death penalty to be] barbarously cruel . . . in the light of all information presently available."[87]

Justice Marshall himself cited no empirical support for either part of his hypothesis, thus leaving it as little more than conjecture; an unfriendly critic might even go so far as to regard his hypothesis as little more than whistling past the graveyard. However, within two years of the decision in *Furman*, social scientists did put the issue to test. Austin Sarat and Neil Vidmar tested the Marshall Hypothesis with undergraduate students, and confirmed both that their respondents "were generally uninformed about the death penalty and that receiving information about it caused a substantial diminution of support for it. . . ."[88]

Whether a test of the Marshall Hypothesis today would show that factual information about the death penalty can change attitudes from support to rejection of the death penalty is unknown, but there is reason for doubt. In the early 1980s, Phoebe Ellsworth and psychologist Lee Ross discovered that of their respondents, "two-thirds (66 percent) claimed that they would still favor capital punishment even if it were proven to be no better than life imprisonment as a deterrent."[89] Ellsworth and Ross also discovered "that fairness and equal protection were not important considerations in [the respondents'] judgments of the acceptability of capital punishment."[90] Ellsworth's and Ross's research did, however, confirm Justice Marshall's belief that the public "know[s] very little about capital punishment"[91]—though they offered no support for his belief that further information would undermine approval of the death penalty and strengthen the desire to see it abolished.

I would conjecture that, in the years since the Ellsworth and Ross research, support for the death penalty has been based increasingly on (or has increasingly found expression in professed) belief in the *retributive* features of capital punishment. Support for the death penalty based on retribution is difficult to change. Considerations of the usual sort—deterrence, unfair application, racial bias, cost and delay, effective available alternative penalties—play little or no role in a retributive rationale for punishment.

What does, or ought to, play a role is the guilt of those punished and the fairness of the procedures used to determine their guilt, because—

taken abstractly—the retributivist is interested only in the accused getting what he deserves,[92] and that entails being at least as interested in the innocent being fairly acquitted as in the guilty being fairly convicted. Now, there is considerable evidence that the innocent have been wrongly convicted and sentenced to death;[93] there is also evidence that worry over the risk of executing the innocent often is a very significant factor in opposition to the death penalty. For instance, the Death Penalty Information Center has reported that "[f]ifty-eight percent of those polled said the question of innocence raised doubts in them about the death penalty,"[94] a far higher percentage than were influenced by any other factor.

Nevertheless, as the retributive basis for death penalty support has increased and the importance of crime-preventive effects of the death penalty has decreased, trying to undermine popular support for the death penalty by the strategy proposed in the Marshall Hypothesis is less plausible today than it once seemed to be.

Broad versus Shallow Support   The second important argument undercutting apparently strong public support for the death penalty is the belief that although this support is undeniably a mile wide, it is only an inch deep. The *New York Times* reported in 1989 "that support for the death penalty falls sharply if there is a stern, certain alternative. . . ."[95] In that same year, research by criminologists James Fox, Michael L. Radelet, and Julie Bonsteel confirmed this point. They showed that several surveys commissioned (but not conducted) by Amnesty International reveal that "death penalty support diminished considerably when respondents were given adequate alternatives to death"[96]—on average, the support for the death penalty was cut in half.[97] A year later criminologist William J. Bowers reported that "when people are asked about the death penalty relative to a sentence of life without parole [so-called LWOP] and a requirement that the offenders pay a part of what they earn in prison industries to the victims' families [so-called LWOP + R]," support for the death penalty plummets.[98]

In California, for example, the Field Institute reported in 1992—only a few days before the first execution in the Golden State in thirty years—that "82 percent favor[ed] the death penalty in principle. But . . .

only 26 percent favored execution over a true life sentence with restitution to the families of victims."[99] Similar results were reported in 1993 by the Death Penalty Information Center and reported in the *Wall Street Journal:* The percentage of those who "strongly favor" the death penalty drops from a majority (57 percent) to a minority (44 percent) when the alternative sentence of LWOP + R is available.[100] Bowers and his collaborators summed up the matter by pointing out a distinction not adequately recognized: Public opinion survey research data show that there is public "acceptance" of the death penalty, but the same data indicate public "preference" for a severe alternative to the death penalty.[101]

There are, however, at least three problems with using this interesting information as a basis for arguing that there is latent majoritarian support for abolishing the death penalty. The first is the problem of transforming abstract preference for LWOP into actual sentencing policy. Legislatures (state and federal) so far have shown very little interest in enacting LWOP, much less LWOP + R—except to enact it alongside the death penalty, rather than as a substitute for it. In the foreseeable future, most jurisdictions are likely to have *both* the death penalty and LWOP; few, if any, will abolish the death penalty in favor of LWOP (with or without R). Thus, it will fall to capital trial juries to decide whether to punish the convicted with death or to extend "mercy" in the form of LWOP. How many death sentences will be (or already have been) averted by juries who favor a sentence of LWOP is anybody's guess; I am unaware of any empirical research on the point.

A second problem is that, even if legislatures were to enact LWOP + R as a substitute for the death penalty, restitution by life-term prisoners would be no more than a token, a symbolic gesture, at best. Defenders of the death penalty are unlikely to greet LWOP + R as an acceptable alternative to the death penalty, once they realize that even a lifetime of labor behind bars can produce only a pittance by way of restitution. I see no real prospect of prisoner-contributed restitution weaning away support for the death penalty.

Finally, LWOP itself (with or without R) is hardly a humane form of punishment; except for a few cases, it is not necessary for incapacitation or deterrence. Thus, it comes perilously close to a leap in desperation from the frying pan into the fire.[102] Not so in the past, however. As I discussed in Chapter 5, the original impetus more than two hundred years ago to abolish the death penalty in Europe was fueled by Cesare Beccaria's little book, *On Crimes and Punishments*,[103] and by Jeremy Bentham in England.[104] Both of these pioneering abolitionists believed that life imprisonment at hard labor was (or ought to be) a better deterrent than hanging because it was a more severe (but less cruel) punishment, and that this was one reason why they preferred it to hanging.[105] Today's advocates of LWOP do not make this argument. Nevertheless, if the only way to abolish the death penalty in this country is to substitute LWOP (with or without R), we should be cautious before we embrace such a development as a significant moral improvement.[106]

Sentencing   The third kind of reason casting doubt on the popular support for the death penalty is the actual sentencing practices of our capital trial juries. Some years ago Phoebe Ellsworth discovered that in Connecticut, although "55 percent" of her respondents said they "favored the death penalty in the abstract," when presented with a real-life murder case "only 15 percent said they would consider the death penalty for that case."[107] What she found in her research is substantially what in fact happens in the courtrooms where capital cases are tried. Out of several thousand murder trials each year (the exact number is unknown; experts estimate the number of "death-eligible" defendants in the range of 2,000 to 4,000 per year),[108] on average, fewer than three hundred persons per year have actually been sentenced to death during the three decades since *Furman* was decided.[109] This is around 10 percent of those eligible. For one thing, for whatever reasons—economy of resources, hostility to the death penalty, doubts the jury will bring in a death sentence, plea bargaining with the trigger person in order to convict the co-defendants—prosecutors seek the death penalty only in a fraction of all cases where they could. Again, for a variety of reasons— appropriate mitigating evidence, sympathy for the defendant, lingering doubts about the defendant's guilt—juries bring in a death sentence in only a fraction of all the cases where the prosecutor seeks it. When one considers these facts in conjunction with the fact that each capital trial begins by eliminating on the voir dire every prospective juror who evidences opposition to the death penalty, the number of death sentences is surprisingly small.

The three different arguments discussed above show that public support for the death penalty is far from monolithic and overwhelming, intense and inelastic. But do they also vindicate Justice Brennan's claim in *Furman* that the death penalty today is "rejected by society"? I do not think so. Or, to put the point more cautiously, I do not know how infrequent the death sentences and executions must be before we are entitled to say that the death penalty has been rejected in practice despite its diminished but not diminishing use.[110]

VI

Given that the number of death sentences annually in round numbers averages less than three hundred for each year in the 1980s and 1990s, what light do these numbers shed on whether we should accept the Meticulous Scrutiny Hypothesis or whether we should reject it in favor of its alternative, the Irregular Infrequency Hypothesis? We need to consider as well at least two very different sorts of evidence. One kind comes from the federal government annually in the interpretive sections of the Bureau of Justice Statistics report, *Capital Punishment*. The most recent such report—for calendar year 2000—tells us that among the 3,593 prisoners under death sentence at the end of that year, "64% had prior felony violations, including 8% with at least one previous homicide conviction."[111] In *Gregg*, Justice Stewart had explained the small numbers of death sentences issued during the four years between *Furman* and *Gregg* by the conjecture that "the reluctance of juries in many cases to impose the [death] sentence may well reflect the humane feeling that this most irrevocable of sanctions should be reserved for a small number of extreme cases."[112] Beginning in 1984 under President Ronald Reagan, as though the Department of Justice had the Burger-Stewart Meticulous Scrutiny Hypothesis in mind, the bureau has reported each year the prior felony and homicide convictions of the nation's death row population, thereby giving an indirect and silent endorsement of capital punishment (as currently practiced) as an appropriate incapacitive and retributive punishment.

The bureau has been silent, however, on the point that these same figures also show one-third of all death row prisoners had *no* prior felony convictions, and that nine-tenths had *no* prior homicide convictions. How can one claim the death penalty as currently administered winnows out the worst from among the very bad in the face of these facts? Is there not some reason to think that there is plenty of room for improvement in the death sentencing practice of our trial courts before we accept the Burger and Stewart claim that the worst offenders are being "selectively" sentenced to death, and that a sentence of death is reserved only for "a small number of extreme cases"?

Consider in this light the armchair experiments proposed by law professors Ursula Bentele and Vivian Berger. In 1985, Bentele presented several different murder vignettes involving defendants in Georgia, some of whom were sentenced to death and others sentenced to life in prison; she challenged her readers to identify which defendants received which sentence.[113] The evidence she presented showed there was no discernible rational basis to be found in those cases that ended up with a death sentence and those cases that did not. Three years later, Vivian Berger presented her readers with a version of the same task: After reading five case vignettes from Florida and Georgia that include all the sentencing-relevant factors, readers were asked to decide which defendants (if any) should be sentenced to death and which (if any) should be sentenced to life in prison.[114] Like Bentele, Berger concluded that there is no regularity, no pattern, shared by all the defendants who actually got the more severe sentences. Nor did any of her five cases fit the popular stereotype of the multiple or serial murderer, the depraved torturers who the public believes are to be found by the hundreds on our death rows.[115]

The doubts raised by these informal exercises are considerably strengthened if we look at what goes on in capital trials around the nation. Today, we have ample (anecdotal and—since the research by Professor James S. Liebman—statistical) evidence that the dissenters in *Gregg* lacked. Throughout the 1980s and 1990s observers provided us with a partial record of the deplorable practices present in far too many capital trials: the appointment of incompetent defense counsel;[116] the lack of funds to hire defense investigators and expert witnesses for the defense;[117] the confusion and misbehavior of trial juries during the sentencing phase;[118] the willful overrides of jury-recommended sentences of life imprisonment by judges who decide to sentence the defendant to death instead;[119] the racist practices prominent in, but not confined to, the "buckle of the death belt" in the Deep South;[120] aggressive prosecution of murder cases by politically ambitious district attorneys;[121] and perfunctory clemency hearings in which politically conscious officials show little or no interest in seriously considering a commutation of sentence from death to life[122]—to mention only the most extreme and well-documented shortcomings.[123] Is this what Chief Justice Burger had in mind when he insisted that the infrequency of the death penalty was a mute testimony to the scrupulous conduct of capital trials by prosecutor, defense counsel, trial judge, and jury?[124] Is it what Justice Stewart believed was a system that "reserved [the death penalty] for a small number of extreme cases"?[125]

The foregoing evidence shows, I believe, that "the machinery of death," in Justice Blackmun's phrase,[126] is being and has been administered in what law professor Robert Weisberg has called a deregulated fashion.[127] Exactly as petitioners argued in *Gregg*, the changes introduced by the post-*Furman* capital statutes were largely "cosmetic"[128]— a description even more apt today than when it was first advanced thirty years ago, because it is supported by overwhelming evidence today that was unavailable then.

VII

The discussion so far has proceeded as if Justice Brennan's majoritarian principle of constitutional interpretation were correct. But is it? This question can be reformulated as follows: What should a proper "moral" reading of the Eighth Amendment say about the appropriateness of the way Justice Brennan incorporated majoritarian attitudes and behavior to explain the meaning of the Constitution's prohibition of cruel and unusual punishment? In Chapter 5 I argued, contrary to Justice Brennan, that "it is a grave error to suppose that there is any significant popular dimension to deciding the . . . status of a punishment as cruel and unusual" in the constitutional sense of those words.[129] Rather than repeat that argument here, I will amplify it with two further comments.

First, populist considerations of the sort we have been examining are not to be found in anything that would count as a "moral" reading of other parts of the Constitution and Bill of Rights. We do not attempt to define or explain "due process of law," "equal protection of the law," "an impartial jury," or any other of the fundamental, normative constitutional concepts by making an appeal to what the majority believes or accepts. For example, the Supreme Court in *Griswold v. Connecticut*[130] did not argue that the widespread flouting of the statutory prohibition against physicians giving birth control information and devices to their patients showed, or even tended to show, that the statutes criminalizing such conduct were for that reason an unconstitutional invasion of privacy. Out of considerations of consistency alone, therefore, we should hesitate to incorporate majoritarian considerations into our interpretation of the Eighth Amendment.

Second, since it is universally recognized by all interpreters of the Constitution and the Bill of Rights that these texts consist largely of counter-majoritarian devices and so have as their primary function restraining runaway majorities (and, of course, irresponsible government officials pandering to such majorities), it is difficult to see how this restraining function can be accomplished with optimum effectiveness if a majoritarian principle is incorporated into the very interpretation of these constitutional clauses themselves.

If, however—as I believe—the correct strategy for interpreting the Eighth Amendment prohibition against cruel and unusual punishment not only permits but requires us to set aside irrelevant popular or majoritarian considerations, then we are free to construct a new argument. In doing so, we can rely either on Justice Brennan's remaining three principles or on some of them in conjunction with other more suitable principles appropriate to a "moral" reading of the Amendment.

VIII

Without exception, to the best of my knowledge, commentators who have considered the constitutionality of the death penalty in recent years agree that there is no prospect in the near future of the Supreme Court reopening the question of whether the death penalty is a cruel and unusual punishment. As things stand today, the United States may well be the only nation in the world in which the fundamental law has been officially interpreted by the highest court in the land to shield the death penalty.[131] Instead of providing a moral reading of the Constitution and the Bill of Rights as they bear on the death penalty, the Supreme Court has taken refuge in other principles, using them as fig leaves to cover embarrassing nakedness. I refer to the familiar principles of federalism, judicial self-restraint, and legislative deference— procedural principles by means of which the life appointees of the Supreme Court deny to themselves any authority to play the role of philosopher-kings, even when the application of other principles is no less compelling.

What we need, I suggest, is what constitutional lawyers would call a *substantive due process argument* against the death penalty (see Chapters 8 and 9). A proper "moral" reading of the Eighth and Fourteenth Amendments encourages just such an argument; so does the reasoning of Justice Brennan and Justice Marshall in their separate opinions in *Furman*. One might well begin with Justice Brennan's fourth principle in particular, the principle that declared "a severe punishment must not be excessive"[132] or with Justice Marshall's third principle, to the effect that a punishment must not be "excessive and serve no valid legislative purpose."[133] Here, I will sketch only the main features of such an argument.

In general, substantive due process requires that a fundamental individual right (such as the right to life) may be invaded by government only if it is required by a compelling state interest (such as public security from convicted offenders), the method used is the least restrictive means to that end, and the courts have exercised the strictest scrutiny to establish that these means not only are intended to achieve that end but really do achieve it.[134] This general pattern of substantive due process reasoning is easily applied to the use of the death penalty, as follows: Excessiveness in a state-authorized punishment is to be defined by reference to the least restrictive means sufficient to achieve valid state objectives.[135] Under this test, the death penalty is surely excessive, as the history of long-term imprisonment as an effective alternative to the death penalty in Michigan and in neighboring abolition jurisdictions (Wisconsin, Minnesota) amply proves. Although general deterrence, incapacitation, retribution, denunciation, and vindication of legal and moral order are valid state objectives[136] that appropriate punishment ought to achieve,[137] they may not be achieved at the expense of needlessly infringing on the convicted offender's rights. The death penalty does this because long-term imprisonment is sufficient to achieve these valid objectives. It may not be sufficient to achieve revenge; but revenge—with its unprincipled, personal, emotional qualities[138]—is not a valid state objective, anymore than it is an appropriate private or personal motive.

It seems to me, as it has to others,[139] that whatever the objections to substantive due process arguments may be in other contexts,[140] death as a punishment in our society today is sufficiently different from other punishments or other lawful deprivations to permit—indeed, to invite—reliance on just such an argument. I look forward to the day when our Supreme Court agrees and rules the death penalty unconstitutional, no matter what the crime, no matter who the defendant, no matter how an execution might be carried out, and no matter what a majority of the public thinks.

7 HUMAN DIGNITY AND THE EIGHTH AMENDMENT

> The basic concept underlying the Eighth Amendment is nothing less than the dignity of man.
> —Chief Justice Earl Warren, in *Trop v. Dulles* (1958)

> Even the vilest criminal remains a human being possessed of common human dignity.
> —Associate Justice William J. Brennan, Jr., in *Furman v. Georgia* (1972)

I

Human dignity is perhaps the premier value underlying the last two centuries of moral and political thought. But were we to measure its importance by the prominence accorded it in the writings of moral philosophers or in the texts and documents of constitutional law, we might well reach the opposite conclusion. Explicit reference to and reliance upon the value of human dignity as such plays no more than a minor role (with one conspicuous exception, to be noted below) in the writings of classic modern western moral theory. Similarly, human dignity also plays no explicit role in the federal Constitution and the Bill of Rights. What other conclusions can one reach when the term *human dignity* (as well as equivalent phrases and synonyms) nowhere appear in these constitutional texts and when there are no treatises (or even chapters in them) of any influence explaining the nature of human dignity and stressing its importance?

For several reasons, it is useful to notice a certain parallel between the status of human dignity in our constitutional texts and the role of two other values, autonomy and privacy, which have also become important and familiar in modern moral thinking.

Autonomy and privacy, unlike human dignity, are among the values prominently analyzed and advocated in recent moral and social theory.[1] They are also values whose importance in contemporary constitutional interpretation could hardly be exaggerated.[2] Yet, like *human dignity*, the words *autonomy* and *privacy* nowhere appear in the Constitution or the Bill of Rights. The omission of explicit reference in our constitutional texts to these values has led some commentators to doubt whether any of them are recognized and protected by our fundamental law.

Conceding the absence of these terms, the constitutional interpreter can proceed in one of three main ways: The first is to conclude straightaway that since the terms nowhere appear in the texts, the values to which they refer are not recognized as such in our constitutional law. On this view, the Constitution and Bill of Rights are indifferent to human dignity, neither protecting and advancing it nor thwarting and retarding it. If human dignity is to be protected and advanced, it must be by congressional legislation, or by the sovereign states, or by private persons and their organizations—but not by the federal courts claiming to interpret our constitutional law. The silence of constitutional law leaves no alternative (of course, the Constitution could be amended to introduce explicit recognition of the value of human dignity, but that is another matter).

A second interpretative response is to argue that the values *dignity*, *autonomy*, and *privacy* are recognized by the Constitution, albeit implicitly, because other terms and values expressly incorporated into the Constitution amount to implicit recognition of these particular values. On this view human dignity is inextricably if only tacitly (and perhaps elusively, obscurely) intertwined with values the Constitution plainly recognizes. If this is true, then one of the abiding tasks of the federal judiciary, as well as of the other branches, is to protect and promote human dignity just as though there were language in the Constitution and Bill of Rights expressly commanding such concern.

The third style of interpretation agrees with the first, that the terms in question do not appear in the texts, but argues that their absence creates only a presumption against constitutional protection of the values so named. Moreover, this is a rebuttable presumption, precisely as the second position implies. Whether in regard to the value of human dignity the presumption is overcome is simply a question of what we may infer from the available evidence. In this particular case, according to the third position, we must conclude that the evidence is insufficient to tell one way or the other.

One might object to the foregoing set of alternatives on the ground that it fails to take into account two centuries of congressional legislation, executive and administrative orders, as well as actions by the several states, all of which have been subjected to review and criticism by the federal courts in light of the Constitution and the Bill of Rights; all this history (so the objection goes) sheds considerable light on the role of human dignity (as well as of autonomy and privacy) in our constitutional thinking and practice. But the objection is misplaced. Whatever edification we obtain by taking these developments into account, it cannot create additional basic options. Such historical evidence can only reinforce or undermine one or more of the three basic positions already identified. It cannot by itself create additional basic options to these three.

What is true about the place of human dignity under the Constitution and the Bill of Rights in general is true with particular reference to the Eighth Amendment. The language of the amendment reads in its entirety:

> Excessive bail shall not be required, nor excessive fines imposed, nor cruel and unusual punishments inflicted.

Obviously, in this language there is no explicit reference to human dignity. Either, therefore, the amendment is indifferent to this value, or it tacitly and indirectly supports it (perhaps by expressly and directly supporting other values inextricably related to human dignity). Or we simply cannot tell anything conclusive about the status of human dignity under the Eighth Amendment.

In the ensuing discussion I intend to defend a version of the second alternative, and I propose to argue roughly as follows: Principles invariably defend values and often do so without expressly mentioning the values being defended. What is true of principles in general is true of the Eighth Amendment and the value of human dignity. The laws and practices forbidden as "cruel and unusual punishments" are punishments that violate certain values. Indeed, such punishments are forbidden *because* they are an affront to these values. We cannot make sense of the prohibition without acknowledgment of the underlying values; we cannot accept the prohibition without tacitly embracing the values it protects. The values in question are inseparably connected with human dignity. This can be seen once we analyze the essential concepts—human dignity and cruel and unusual punishment. The connection becomes more plausible once we notice other constitutional provisions in which there is unmistakable evidence of a concern to protect human dignity even though that value is nowhere explicitly mentioned.

Let us suppose a convincing line of reasoning that embodies and advances the foregoing position can be developed. What do we find when we take this argument and confront it with the practice, authorized by state and federal statutes, that a defendant convicted of a certain crime may be punished by being sentenced to death and executed—the death penalty? Elsewhere it has been argued that when one thinks about the death penalty in this nation today and evaluates it in light of all the relevant facts and moral principles, one must conclude that it is an unjustified punishment.[3] The best (if not the only) way to express this conclusion in constitutional language is to affirm the judgment that the death penalty is a cruel and unusual punishment in violation of the Eighth Amendment. Yet the role of the value of human dignity in such a judgment is obscure. One reason for this obscurity is that arguments against the death penalty mounted by philosophers not preoccupied with constitutional interpretation typically fail to allot any explicit role to human dignity, relying instead on other values. Another reason is that arguments against the death penalty mounted by jurists are likely to be focused solely on the explicit language of the Bill of Rights, precedent cases, and related discourse—in which, as we have noted, little or no mention is made of human dignity as such—rather than on abstract values at best tacitly expressed. So at least two questions naturally arise. First, how is explicit connection to be made between the value of human dignity and the Eighth Amendment? Second, does explicit reliance on the constitutional recognition and protection of the value of human dignity really strengthen the argument against the death penalty?

II

Let us begin by noticing that norms, including principles, are designed to guide conduct in order to secure respect for, and discourage indifference to, certain values typically held dear by those who issue, authorize, endorse, or enforce the norms. The point of normative requirements, prohibitions, and permissions is incompatible with viewing them as value-neutral imperatives. Suppose someone were to say, "Don't violate principle *P*—but if you do, that's all right, it doesn't matter." Unless the person who says this rejects (or is indifferent to) principle *P*, the utterance is essentially unintelligible. Its unintelligibility derives from the conflict between the conduct required (or forbidden) by *P* and the indifference expressed toward that conduct's performance by the very person who insists on *P*. Such a conflict presupposes the implicitly value-laden character of *P*.

Very well, then; norms are not value neutral. But must they expressly mention the values that they are intended to defend or protect? Let us look briefly at a few examples.

Take first an example from the Bible, the commandment "Thou shalt not kill." No one would deny that this prohibition arises from a recognition of the value of (innocent) human life; the killing prohibited is the killing of human beings, not other living things; and the kind of killing is usually understood to be confined to murder. Yet no such phrase as *human life is valuable* appears in the commandment. If an argument is needed to persuade that this commandment protects a value that it does not mention, here is one: It makes little sense to prohibit the murder of every person (as the commandment does), to treat murder as a sin against God or as a crime against the person, unless it matters whether people murder other people. Now it cannot matter unless what murder invariably destroys—the life of a person—is *valuable*. (We may ignore here the further question whether only a realist and objectivist account can make sense of such a value.) The universality of the condemnation of murder implicitly but unmistakably recognizes the universality of the value of human life.

Take as a second example language from the Bill of Rights, the portion of the Fifth Amendment that reads: "nor shall [any person] be compelled in any criminal case to be a witness against himself." No competent interpreter of the Bill of Rights would deny that this language establishes a constitutional *right* to be silent under accusation of a crime, even though the term *right* nowhere appears in the text quoted. More than that, this right has constitutional status because of the *value* of the interest it protects—the value of according finality to the accused's own judgment on whether, when testifying under oath, it is in his best interest to be silent or to give testimony against himself. But no such value is expressly mentioned at all in the language of the amendment. Nevertheless, if this value is ignored or repudiated, the purpose of the right itself is undermined; by the same token, refusal to grant the right makes the prohibition pointless.

Take finally an example from social philosophy, the maxim derived from Louis Blanc and made famous in Karl Marx's slogan: "From each according to his abilities, to each according to his needs." This slogan is generally understood to express a principle of distributive *justice*, and to assert it implies acceptance of justice as a *value*, even though the term *justice* is nowhere used in formulating the maxim. Yet it would be wrong to argue from omission of that term that the Blanquist slogan does not express, and is not intended to express, a principle of justice. Again, if argument is needed, here is one. First, the slogan can be reformulated (without loss or addition to its content) in order to make good this omission, so that it reads in revised form: "Justice requires that property and services be provided to persons according to their needs and taken from them according to their abilities." If it is objected that this reformulation begs the question, one can reply by explaining how the slogan in its original form derives whatever force it has by implicitly asserting that fairness requires placing one person's needs and another's abilities in a recriprocal relationship, and that fairness and justice are conceptually or semantically intertwined. If this, too, is unconvincing, then one might argue more elaborately to the effect that the best interpretation of Blanc's intentions in formulating this slogan is to see it as a principle or maxim of justice.[4] These tactics apart, it is clear that the point of the slogan is to advocate practices that secure certain values; in the absence of commitment to those values, asserting the slogan is pointless.

Here, then, are three different norms—different in origin, in content, and in kind—each of which protects a value it does not expressly mention. (For those with a taste for semantics, this is but a special case of the general truth that it is not necessary for a sentence to *use* a given term T in order to *mention* what T refers to.) What has been illustrated with these three examples could be confirmed in countless other cases. There is no general objection, therefore, to the view that the Eighth Amendment, through its language prohibiting "cruel and unusual punishments," aims to protect a value or values it does not mention, and that human dignity is, or is one of, these values. (Notice that I have not tried to provide a general criterion to enable us to tell in any given case what particular value[s] a given norm is intended to protect when the norm makes no explicit mention of the relevant value[s].)

III

We are now in a position to face the question of whether in fact there is good reason to agree with Chief Justice Earl Warren in *Trop v. Dulles* when he claimed (recall the epigraph) that the value of human dignity is centrally relevant to a correct understanding of the constitutional prohibition against cruel and unusual punishments. Is it really true that we must have eventual recourse to this value in order to make sense of the constitutional prohibition? Or is it possible that our Constitution prohibits cruel and unusual punishments as a matter of fundamental rights but without regard to whether doing so protects or respects human dignity? Could one truly declare, for example, "I don't care a fig about human dignity, but of course I respect the constitutional prohibition against cruel and unusual punishments"? Could it be true to say, as some in effect have, "The prohibition of cruel and unusual punishments certainly protects some fundamental albeit implicit values, but human dignity isn't one of them—talk about human dignity, at least in connection with the Eighth Amendment, is empty rhetoric and arrant nonsense"?[5]

The straightforward way to answer these questions requires several steps. First, we need to identify the complex of beliefs, values, and norms that constitute human dignity. Second, we need to understand cruelty and unusualness as they are found in punishments. Third, we need to see what values (presumably, those connected with human dignity) the prohibition against cruel and unusual punishments can be understood to protect. Finally, we need to specify the definitions, empirical generalizations, and "mediating maxims"[6] that connect the language of the amendment with the concepts and values in question. All this is much easier said than done, and easier done with than without any tacit bias (for or against particular kinds of punishments) that tends to prejudge the outcome of the inquiry.

The territory we are about to explore is terra incognita, so far as recent and contemporary philosophy is concerned. For (as noted at the outset) philosophers have shown little or no direct interest in the concept of human dignity, in alternative elaborations of this concept, or in the history and role of this concept in modern moral and political theory. In recent decades moral philosophy has been dominated by reliance on and interest in other values, depending on whether one is a consequentialist (where the values are human feelings, desires, interests, preferences, needs, welfare, or utilities) or a deontologist (where the values are human rights, duties, obligations, or principles). Philosophers have ignored what (if anything) an emphasis on human dignity adds to moral theory and how it is to be integrated with the factors that have captured their attention.

One route, perhaps the safest one to take, in exploring the concept of human dignity is to approach it historically. The concept of human dignity abruptly comes onstage in moral theory two centuries ago in the philosophy of Immanuel Kant.[7] There are, of course, versions of this idea that predate Kant.[8] It may well be that the Kantian idea of human dignity is nothing more than a secular counterpart to the biblical notion of the sanctity of human life, according to which our dignity is established by having been "created in the image" of God.[9] Be that as it may, it is thanks largely to Kant that contemporary moral theory has a concept of human dignity to work with.

Emphasizing a Kantian conception of human dignity is especially appropriate in the present context, since Kant's own retributive defense of the death penalty is based on his belief that respect for human dignity requires the death penalty for murder and other grave crimes.[10] If a Kantian conception of human dignity can nonetheless be shown to be consistent with, and perhaps even support, moral condemnation of the death penalty, it will be implausible to object that the emphasis on this (rather than some other) conception of human dignity has distorted and biased the analysis in favor of the desired outcome.

Although Kant nowhere set out a full-dress account of his conception of human dignity, it is clear from what he did write that there are half a dozen or so important things about human dignity that must be kept in mind if the nature of this value is to be understood.

First, referring to a person's dignity is another way of referring to a person's *worth*. (Our word *dignity* comes from the Latin *dignitas*, and the usual German translation of *dignitas* is *Würde*. *Würde* is usually translated into English as "worth," but English translators of Kant generally render *Würde* as "dignity.") A person's worth must be kept distinct from other attributes of the person, in particular the person's merit or value or usefulness. Above all, a person's dignity, in the sense of that term here, is not to be seen as a result or product of decent conduct, virtuous behavior, moral rectitude, or respect for the moral law. Rather, it is to be seen as a result of the *capacity* for such conduct.

Second, persons vary from one to another and from situation to situation in their merit, value, and usefulness. These variations are owing to variable environment, genetics, luck, effort, skill, and so forth. But persons do not vary in their dignity or worth. Their dignity or worth is a kind of value that all human beings have *equally* and *essentially*. The deepest, least empirical way in which to express the moral egalitarianism of persons is by reference to their inherent dignity. Hence human worth or dignity is invariably described as "intrinsic" or "inherent," to contrast it with values that are instrumental, contingent, extrinsic, or circumstantial.

Third, human dignity is intimately related to human *autonomy*. An autonomous creature is a self-activating, self-directing, self-criticizing, self-correcting, self-understanding creature. Autonomous creatures do not merely have and pursue ends, they create them and thereby confer value on those ends. Autonomy is typically contrasted with heteronomy. (The distinction was popularized a generation ago in a study of the American national character in which the autonomous person was contrasted with those whose heteronomy took the form either of "adjustment" or of "anomie.")[11] At the extreme, a person surrenders his or her autonomy (and dignity) by becoming another's slave. More typically, a person violates the autonomy (dignity) of another when the one exercises patronizing or condescending supervision and control over the other, or (worse yet) manipulates the other by using force or fraud in order to achieve some good or end chosen without regard to the other's welfare or capacity for autonomy. Such patronizing or manipulative behavior is insulting, undignified, an affront to the other person's status as a person.[12]

Fourth, our dignity is inseparably connected to our *self-conscious rationality*, our capacities to evaluate, calculate, organize, predict, explain, conjecture, justify, and so forth, and to prize and appraise things and situations, and thus to choose not only the means to our ends but the ends themselves. Irrational or nonrational creatures do not have or do not exercise these capacities, and so their autonomy is slight to nonexistent. In lacking self-conscious rationality, a creature lacks dignity; only rational creatures can have that.

Finally, human dignity provides the basis for equal human *rights*. All and only creatures with rights (not merely positive legal rights, but the rights that sound moral theory confers) have dignity. We should not be surprised, therefore, to find in the preamble to the Universal Declaration of Human Rights (1948) explicit reference to "the inherent dignity . . . of all members of the human family" and to "the dignity and worth of the human person" as part of the rationale for universal human rights. These rights are the sword and shield that secure our interests and our sense of our own worth in the political arena. Equal human rights is a necessary consequence of equal human worth and dignity. Whatever inequalities (socioeconomic, psychological, physical) may arise owing to the natural lottery or to the contingencies of our social environment, they do not efface, override, or undermine our equal human rights.[13]

Thus, the (Kantian) idea of human dignity involves and consists of a certain cluster of interrelated attributes, which together confer on persons a certain *status*. This status is constituted by the equal worth and capacity for autonomy and rationality of all persons, a status not shared with other things or even other creatures. It is reflected above all in the equal human rights that all persons enjoy. In virtue of this status, persons deserve certain kinds of treatment and not other kinds, whether from each other or from lawful authority. We show that we recognize the worth of persons, whether in ourselves or in others, by the *respect* we accord them. Kant's belief that the value of human dignity requires society to adopt the death penalty for murderers has many sources, one of which turns on what it is to respect another's dignity: I respect another's dignity as a chooser of ends, as a rational agent, only if I treat that person according to the rationale ("maxim") of that person's own actions. Consider the person who chooses to be a murderer; he acts on the rationale that when it suits his purposes, he may kill other persons, disregarding their status as ends in themselves. Therefore, to respect his dignity I must treat him according to the same rationale and authorize or endorse his being murdered in turn (i.e., lawfully put to death).

The major premise of this argument is the chief source of trouble. First, this premise does not follow logically from the idea of human dignity as I have presented it above. Second, even if my dignity is expressed in being a chooser of ends and of rationales for action, and my dignity is equally well expressed no matter what ends or rationales I choose, it does not follow that my respect for the dignity of another is expressed only if I act toward him as he would act toward me (or some third party). Finally, since Kant agrees of course that the rationale of action chosen by the murderer is a paradigm of immorality ("using other persons merely as a means to one's own ends"), it is extremely difficult to see why someone else who wishes to act morally toward and respect the dignity of others *must* authorize or endorse the murder of someone for no better reason than the fact that the latter is himself a (convicted) murderer. Finally, we may say that human dignity is tacitly alluded to whenever at least one of its constitutive concepts—worth, equality, autonomy, rationality—is mentioned or when its expressive concept—equal human rights—is invoked.

Whether the constitutional prohibition against "cruel and unusual punishments" protects human dignity is thus to be decided by the extent to which this prohibition is made more intelligible by being understood as a norm reflecting the equal worth of persons and their equal human rights—despite the fact that the persons in question may also be the duly authorized subjects of deserved punishment.

Although our Bill of Rights omits all use of the language of "autonomy" and "dignity" and "equal worth," it does not omit the use of the language of "rights" and related ideas. It is useful to recall that the Bill of Rights *explicitly* refers to this or that "right" in five of its ten amendments (viz., amendments 1, 2, 4, 6, and 7), as well as to "other . . . rights" not expressly named (Amendment 9). Other amendments unmistakably indicate that considerations of individual or personal rights provide the background of the explicit provisions. For quartering troops, the householder's "consent" is required (Amendment 3); this requirement entails that the householder has a *right* to deny entry. Any punishment or lawful deprivation must be imposed by "due process of law" (Amendment 5); this entails that the person has a *right* to such procedures. To these provisions we may add the later prohibition of slavery and peonage (Amendment 13) and above all the guarantee to all "persons" of "equal protection of the laws" and of "due process of law" (Amendment 14). It is these two later amendments that explicitly establish the equality of all persons before the law, a legal status that makes most sense only if it is presupposed that all persons are of equal worth insofar as the law is concerned, whatever their variable merits and usefulness may be, and whatever their socioeconomic or political status. (As the argument unfolds below, there will be occasion to return to the important provisions of the Fourteenth Amendment mentioned here.)

This explicit language in the Bill of Rights and later constitutional amendments resonates so handsomely with Kant's views that one might almost think the two, concurrent in their historic origins in the last decade of the eighteenth century, had a common source. Indeed, in a sense they did; both are products of the Age of Enlightenment, in which the liberating ideas of the Renaissance and Reformation were consolidated in European moral and political philosophy. If, therefore, we mean by *human dignity* roughly what Kant meant by it—and if this is not what we mean, then it is difficult to give any very exact sense to the term—it is virtually impossible to argue that the Bill of Rights and the Constitution as a whole are indifferent to human dignity. We cannot argue that although our constitutional law certainly acknowledges various equal human rights, it has no interest in the value of human autonomy or the worth of human persons or—in a phrase—in human dignity. And it would be more than surprising if the Eighth Amendment prohibition against cruel and unusual punishments stood apart in this regard from the rest of the Bill of Rights and the Constitution as subsequently amended. After all, as we have seen, the Eighth Amendment must be intended to defend *some* values, or else its prohibitions would be arbitrary and to that extent make no sense. So what values does cruelty in punishment flout, fail to acknowledge, ignore? What rights, if any, would cruelty in punishment violate, repudiate, or nullify? And precisely why does the death penalty amount to an affront to human dignity?

IV

In his thoughtful opinion in *Furman v. Georgia*, Justice William J. Brennan, Jr., proposed four "principles" designed to connect human dignity with the Eighth Amendment prohibition of cruel and unusual punishments (recall the discussion in Chapter 6). On behalf of these principles he advanced two claims. First, they are "recognized in our cases and inherent in the Clause" forbidding cruel and unusual punishments. Second, when taken in conjunction with the relevant empirical facts, these principles suffice to permit a "judicial determination whether a challenged punishment comports with human dignity."[14]

Justice Brennan's elucidation of these principles was a bold and original contribution to constitutional interpretation. Hitherto, in the slender and somewhat scattered string of cases decided by the Supreme Court on Eighth Amendment grounds,[15] no judicial opinion had endeavored to offer any interpretative structure—bridging principles, definitions, sufficient or necessary conditions, empirical generalizations—to supplement and interpret the blunt and abstract language of the amendment.[16] Yet some such structure is necessary if the Court is to evaluate and decide the constitutional status of actual punishments imposed by law. To say this is not to foreclose the question of whether the structure proposed by Justice Brennan is the only or the best one. Nor is it to imply that a close scrutiny of the Court's opinions in the precedent cases would reveal all and only the principles he cited to be tacitly at work. Nor, finally, is this to imply that Justice Brennan was right when he concluded that given his four principles and the relevant facts, one must conclude that the death penalty violates the Eighth Amendment prohibition of cruel and unusual punishments. (It would require a detailed study—inappropriate here—of the reasoning by the majority of the Court in later capital cases, beginning with *Gregg v. Georgia*, to show the subsequent status in the Court's own reasoning of each of Brennan's four principles. In this connection it is worth noting that no member of the Court in dissent in *Furman* or in subsequent capital cases has seen fit to examine and endorse or repudiate any of Brennan's four principles as such.) The worst that can be said about these four principles is that they are only a first approximation to the set of relevant principles pertinent to interpreting the constitutional prohibition against cruel and unusual punishments. Meanwhile, until someone proposes a different set of principles for this purpose, Brennan's deserve the closest scrutiny.

The four principles in question (in the order in which Brennan presented them, perhaps also what he believed to be the order of their descending importance) are repeated here for the reader's convenience:

1. The "primary principle" is that "a punishment must not be so severe as to be degrading to the dignity of human beings."[17] The sheer painfulness of the punishment, however, is not the only factor determining its severity. "[A severe] punishment may be degrading [to human dignity] simply by reason of its enormity."[18]

2. "The State must not arbitrarily inflict a severe punishment. . . . [It] does not respect human dignity when, without reason, it inflicts upon some people a severe punishment that it does not inflict upon others."[19]

3. "A severe punishment must not be unacceptable to contemporary society. . . . Rejection by society . . . is a strong indication that a severe punishment does not comport with human dignity."[20]

4. "A severe punishment must not be excessive. A punishment is excessive under this principle if it is unnecessary. . . . The infliction of a severe punishment . . . cannot comport with human dignity when it is nothing more than the pointless infliction of suffering."[21]

These four principles all concern "severe" punishments; their purpose is to explicate the concept of "cruel and unusual punishments" by laying out the nature of *excessively severe* punishments. It is evidently an implicit tautology in Justice Brennan's reasoning that cruel and unusual punishments are very severe punishments, and that any punishment is unconstitutional when it is excessively severe. (The converse, however, is not a tautology; some punishments very severe by plausible standards—notably, life imprisonment—are not necessarily cruel and unusual, at least not in the relevant constitutional sense of this phrase, because they are not inherently "excessively severe.") It is also assumed that we have an intuitive grasp of what counts as a severe punishment, at least to the extent that everyone will grant that the death penalty is a severe punishment, thereby raising the question of whether it is excessively severe.

How do these principles function in Justice Brennan's argument against the constitutionality of the death penalty? And how successfully do they bridge the gap between the value of human dignity and the prohibition against cruel and unusual punishments? To answer the first question, we need to sketch the structure of his reasoning. His conclusion, we know, is this: The death penalty violates the constitutional prohibition against "cruel and unusual punishments."

His argument for this conclusion relies upon two premises. The major one consists of his four principles, which can be treated as a complex conditional proposition and reformulated in this manner:

> P.1 If a severe punishment is degrading, arbitrarily inflicted, publicly unacceptable, and excessive, then it violates the constitutional prohibition against cruel and unusual punishments.

On this interpretation, the four principles do not quite define the concept of an unconstitutionally cruel and unusual punishment; they leave open whether there might be other, so far unstated conditions needed to perform that task. But the four principles do lay down conditions that are sufficient for judging whether a given punishment is unconstitutionally cruel and unusual.

The correct formulation of principle P.1 is somewhat complicated by the fact that Justice Brennan described the "test" under his four principles as "ordinarily a cumulative one."[22] Assuming that the present instance is not out of the "ordinary," we can give the notion of a "cumulative" role for the four principles two different interpretations. On one interpretation, the four principles form a conjunction in the antecedent of the major premise. This is how they have been treated in the formulation of P.1 above. If so, then *each* of the four principles must be violated for the punishment to be judged cruel and unusual. But there is another interpretation suggested by the term *cumulative*. On this version, it is not necessary that all four principles be violated, because the major premise says in effect: The more of these principles a given punishment violates (or the more extreme the violation of any of these principles by a given punishment), the more cruel and unusual the punishment is.

We need not resolve which is the preferred interpretation, at least not if our only concern is to understand Justice Brennan's argument. It is clear he believes all four of his principles are violated by the death penalty. That is equivalent to asserting as the minor premise of his argument the following:

> The death penalty—indubitably a severe punishment—is degrading, arbitrarily inflicted, publicly unacceptable, and excessive.

There is no doubt the argument from these premises is valid; it remains only to see whether it is sound. Before we can turn directly to that question, however, it is important to consider whether the major premise (the four principles) successfully bridges the concept of human dignity with the Eighth Amendment. It may help to answer this question if we reformulate Brennan's four principles in a more uniform manner that emphasizes their connection to human dignity. Taking them in the order in which he mentions them, this is what we get:

> First, it is an affront to the dignity of a person to be forced to undergo catastrophic harm at the hands of another when, before the harm is imposed, the former is entirely at the mercy of the latter, as is always the case with legal punishment.
>
> Second, it offends the dignity of a person who is punished according to the will of a punisher free to pick and choose arbitrarily among offenders so that only a few are punished very severely when all deserve the same severe punishment if any do.
>
> Third, it offends the dignity of a person to be subjected to a severe punishment when society shows by its actual conduct in sentencing that it no longer regards this severe punishment as appropriate.
>
> Finally, it is an affront to human dignity to impose a very severe punishment on an offender when it is known that a less severe punishment will achieve all the purposes it is appropriate to try to achieve by punishing anyone in any manner whatsoever.

These reformulations link the concept of human dignity explicitly with the concept of "cruel and unusual punishments" via the notion of appropriate limits to the permissible severity of punishments. This is easily seen if we recall several of the constitutive elements of human dignity discussed earlier: Respect for the autonomy of rational creatures forbids its needless curtailment in the course of deserved punishment. Respect for the equal worth of persons forbids inequitable punishments of convicted offenders equally guilty. The fundamental equal rights of persons, including convicted offenders (about whom I shall have more to say below), precludes treating some offenders as if they had ceased to be persons.

V

However, these reformulations do not suffice to show us that the principles are the correct ones to elucidate the concept of "cruel and unusual punishments." Nor do they suffice to show that the argument employing them is sound (that is, that both the major and minor premises of Justice Brennan's argument as reconstructed here are true). Both kinds of criticism deserve our scrutiny.

Some critics have maintained in effect that Brennan's argument is unsound because one or more of his four principles themselves are incorrect. For example, it can be argued that Brennan's final principle, prohibiting excessive punishment, should not be interpreted as a prohibition against unnecessarily severe punishment, but only as a prohibition against disproportionate punishment—and the death penalty is not disproportionate to the crime of murder.[23] The other form of criticism does not dispute the adequacy of Brennan's four principles, but argues that the death penalty as a matter of fact does not violate most, much less all, of them. For example, it can be argued that the death penalty in fact is not "degrading" under the first principle, because there is nothing left for society to degrade in the person who has willfully committed murder; such a murderer has degraded himself by his own criminal acts. His conduct leaves him with no dignity left to stand on, no moral platform from which to demand, or even plead, that society respect his dignity.[24] Let us consider each of these kinds of criticism further, starting with the second.

Consider Justice Brennan's claim that the death penalty is "unacceptable to contemporary society." Criteria for such unacceptability are multiple and complex, and the evidence under them not uncontroversial. Even so, as Chief Justice Warren E. Burger argued in dissent in *Furman*,[25] anticipating the Court majority four years later in *Gregg v. Georgia*,[26] there is considerable evidence that contemporary American society *does* "accept" the death penalty in the most plausible sense of that word.[27] Today, more than three decades after *Furman*, it is difficult to disagree with the Chief Justice: Justice Brennan was almost certainly wrong to argue that American society in the 1970s found the death penalty for murder "unacceptable." If so, then the death penalty at most violates three of Brennan's four principles; and if I have correctly reconstructed the logic of Brennan's argument (and correctly understood the "cumulative" use of his four principles), then he was wrong to think that his argument established that the death penalty really does violate the Eighth Amendment.

It is possible to rescue Brennan's argument against the death penalty from this objection either by abandoning his third principle altogether or by reinterpreting what it means for a punitive practice established in law to be "accepted." Take the second strategy first. This seems to be Brennan's own preferred interpretation, when he wrote that "the objective indicator of society's view of an unusually severe punishment is what society does with it, and today society will inflict death upon only a small sample of the eligible criminals."[28] He argued in effect that society accepts a severe penalty only if it actually carries out that penalty in all or most of the cases where it is legally relevant. But that presupposes that the relevant convicted offenders are actually sentenced accordingly in the first place—and the actual practice of the nation's criminal justice systems violates both of these conditions.

Running against this, however, is evidence of a different sort: the widespread reenactment of death penalty statutes immediately after *Furman*,[29] the willingness of trial juries to convict under these statutes in two or three hundred cases a year,[30] the willingness of Congress to reenact death penalties, and above all public opinion surveys that show a stable and large majority of the public ready to voice at least nominal support of the death penalty.[31] In light of these facts, it is at best arguable whether Justice Brennan's rebuttal succeeds.

Chief Justice Burger insisted that it was "unwarranted hyperbole" to describe "the rate of imposition" of the death penalty in the 1960s as "freakishly rare" (*Furman*, at 387). Instead of trying to decide whether Brennan or Burger had the better of this argument in 1972, when *Furman* was decided, or four years later, when the decision in *Gregg* was announced, let us consider the status of this issue since then.

The *Uniform Crime Reports* tell us that "murders and nonnegligent manslaughters" averaged about 20,000 a year during the 1980s. The National Judicial Reporting Program now informs us that in 1986 nearly 10,000 persons were convicted of "murder." Assuming this to be the annual average for the 1980s, and subtracting the estimated total for all non-first-degree murder convictions as well as all first-degree murder convictions in non-capital jurisdictions, we get a minimum estimated annual total of first-degree murder convictions in capital jurisdictions during the 1980s of 2,500. The Department of Justice's Bureau of Justice Statistics reports an average of 250 persons sentenced to death each year during the 1980s, and an average of 30 executions per year.

Annually, then, during the 1980s we have this: 20,000 criminal homicides, of which perhaps 2,500 result in murder convictions where a death penalty could be handed down, resulting in about 250 death sentences—and 30 actual executions. How much lower would the ratio of executions or death sentences to murder convictions or to murders have to be before they could fairly be described as "freakishly rare" is, of course, unclear. What is clear is that these ratios have never been lower at any time in the past.[32]

So let us turn to the other strategy. Here, I believe, we are on much stronger ground. I believe it is a grave error to suppose that there is any significant popular dimension to deciding the *constitutional* status of a punishment as cruel and unusual. Contemporary acceptability of a mode of punishment, measured in the usual ways, as above, is a plausibly relevant consideration only if unusualness of punishments is taken literally, or if arbitrariness and unequal application of the law are at stake (as they are where due process and equal protection of the law in the Fourteenth Amendment are concerned).[33] It seems quite the wrong kind of partial criterion to use as a measure of excessive severity, which is precisely what is at stake in interpreting the prohibition against cruel and unusual punishment.[34] Popular attitudes and practices under law cannot by themselves *make* a severe punishment hitherto acceptable into one that is not, or preserve a widespread punishment from being judged excessively severe.[35] This is not to deny, as the Court has held, that a "cruel and unusual" punishment is one that is at odds with "the evolving standards of decency that mark the progress of a maturing society."[36] One would like to think that popular disapproval of an extremely severe punishment is to be explained at least in part by public belief that the punishment is cruel and unusual. But the converse argument, which Justice Brennan seems to employ, is inappropriate as well as unsound.

Thus, by removing Brennan's third principle altogether from the set of principles that partially define a cruel and unusual punishment, we can circumvent rejection of his argument on the ground that the relevant empirical evidence undermines his claims.

As for the minor premises of Brennan's argument pertinent to his second and fourth principles. I cannot attempt to review here all the relevant evidence marshaled in the research and writing by others that bears on the arbitrary administration of the death penalty and its excessiveness.[37] I can only declare my belief that this evidence amply supports the requirements of the argument.

That leaves only the objection to Brennan's argument to the effect that it fails because the minor premise needed under his first principle is false. That is, Brennan wrongly believes that imposing the death penalty on a convicted murderer is "degrading" to him—although he is right in believing that the Eighth Amendment implicitly prohibits degrading punishments. One must sympathize with this objection; it seems plausible to accept the idea that human dignity affords anyone (who has it) a platform on which he or she may protest certain kinds of treatment to which they are being subjected. Yet, surely, a guilty and convicted murderer is in the worst possible position to lodge a protest of this sort against his impending punishment, whatever it is.

But is it not obvious that if this objection is given full weight, as some defenders of the death penalty apparently want to do, it will prove too much? It will become impossible to see how there can be *any* upper limit to the severity or brutality of punishments, given the gravity of crimes and the brutality of those who commit them. Or, perplexing though it may be, if there is an upper limit to the severity of punishments even for convicted (mass or serial) murderers, we will have to conclude this limit has nothing to do with (is not derived from) the human dignity of the person being punished, because it arises from some completely independent moral consideration. Surely, morality (quite apart from the Bill of Rights) places a principled upper limit to the severity of permissible punishments; the only issue worth disputing is not whether there is such a limit but what it is and why. The prohibition of cruel and unusual punishments in the Eighth Amendment is intelligible only as a prohibition generated by such a principle. If the principle in question reflects or connects with human dignity, as I believe I have shown that it does, then human dignity *does* provide a platform on which even a convicted murderer may rightfully protest against laws and officials who would punish him in certain ways. Once this is granted, there is no way to prevent arguing that death is among the prohibited punishments.

In order to make this more convincing, a new line of argument needs to be developed that addresses precisely the residue, if we may so speak, of the dignity that even murderers possess, and the cruelty that the death penalty always manifests.

VI

In order to grasp what is at stake in the Eighth Amendment prohibition of cruelty and its tacit recognition and protection of human dignity as a constitutional value, we need to tighten our grip on the idea of cruelty to persons.[38] To do this, we will find it useful to take our cues from reflections not directly or intentionally designed to illuminate cruel punishments under law, and especially not from sources purporting to tell us what the framers and ratifiers of the Eighth Amendment, nor subsequent commentators and interpreters (including the federal courts), have understood by the concept of cruelty as it appears there. Our aim must be in part to test (and not merely repeat or reaffirm) what constitutional authors and interpreters have said and have meant when they condemned cruelty in punishments. To do that without question-begging circularity, we must locate some independent source for the meaning of the term.

In Judith Shklar's account of the nature of cruelty focused on the eighteenth-century French opponents of the more gross cruelties of their day, we find this definition: *cruelty* is "the willful infliction of physical pain on a weaker being in order to cause anguish and fear."[39] When such a definition is used to judge the death penalty as seen from the vantage point of western Europe two centuries ago, it certainly covers the classic paradigms of cruel executions: crucifixion by the Romans, disembowelment by the Tudors, tearing asunder by the Bourbons. It also applies to at least one of the forms in which the death penalty is administered under law in our society (the Supreme Court decisions to the contrary not withstanding),[40] namely, the electric chair. Here is a recent description of death by electrocution: "The body burns bright red as its temperature rises. The flesh swells and the skin stretches to the point of breaking. Sometimes it catches on fire. The force of the electrical current is so powerful that the eyeballs sometimes pop out and rest on the cheeks. Witnesses hear a loud, long sound like bacon frying: the nauseating smell of burning flesh fills the room."[41] Death by electrocution mocks the claims made on its behalf when it was introduced a century ago as a humane advance in carrying out the death penalty.[42]

But what about other ways to carry out the death sentence? What about the death penalty as such? Is it cruel, however it is carried out, under this definition of *cruelty*? It would appear not. Where the death inflicted is not "physically" painful, it cannot be cruel. Where the "intention" of the killing is not to cause anyone—the offender, the witnesses, or other criminals—"anguish and fear" but merely to blot out the criminal once and for all, cruelty apparently evaporates. What emerges from this plausible definition of *cruelty* is exactly what the modern friends of the death penalty (including a majority of the Supreme Court since 1976) insist: Capital punishment is not, per se, an excessively severe or cruel punishment, even if (as all honest observers agree) some of its historic modes of infliction were or its use to punish minor crimes would be.[43]

But *cruelty* as defined so far may not be the best, and is certainly not the only, way to understand the term. Mindful of seminal thinking in the eighteenth century about cruelty as well as sensitive to the widespread horrors of the past century, we can think about cruelty to persons in a more imaginative and thematic fashion. If we do this, we see that "the heart of cruelty"—in the words of Phillip Hallie—is "total activity smashing total passivity."[44] Cruelty, on this view, consists in "subordination, subjection to a superior power whose will becomes the victim's law." Where cruelty reigns—whether in the hands of a Marquis de Sade or in the galvanic charges used by a modern torturer—there is a "power-relationship between two parties," one of whom is "active, comparatively powerful," and the other of whom, the victim, is "passive, comparatively powerless."[45]

These observations reveal the very essence of capital punishment to be cruelty. Whether carried out by impalement or electrocution, crucifixion or the gas chamber, firing squad or hanging, with or without due process and equal protection of the law, for felonies or misdemeanors, there is *always* present that "total activity" of the executioner and the "total passivity" of the condemned. The state, acting through its local representatives in the execution chamber, *smashes* the convicted criminal into oblivion. The government *annihilates* its prisoner; in the strictest sense of that term it reduces him to inert, lifeless flesh. If this is a fair characterization of cruelty, then the death penalty is a *cruel* punishment.

What is most compelling about the concept of cruelty understood as a "power relationship" in the manner sketched above is that it focuses our attention on the salient common factor in all situations where the death penalty is inflicted, however painlessly, for whatever crime the condemned is guilty, and despite whatever punishment the offender may prefer. For western philosophy, the classic example of capital punishment is provided in the case of Socrates, whose death (if we can believe Plato) was painless, a death he accepted in preference to escape or alternative punishment, a death administered by his own hand from the cup of hemlock he drank in compliance with the order of the Athenian tribunal that had convicted and sentenced him. If such a method of execution were revived today, it could not easily be condemned as "undignified" in the ordinary sense of that term, and to that extent could not be judged to be an assault on human dignity. Today, with the unrivaled popularity of lethal injection—and when medical technology in the future may invent an even less burdensome mode of execution—the same difficulty arises. When death is carried out by the state in a manner that does not disfigure the offender's body, apparently causes little or no conscious pain, brings about death within a few minutes, and presents no spectacle of terminal anguish and terror to official witnesses, it is extremely difficult to construct a convincing argument that condemns the practice based on its alleged "cruelty," as that term is often understood. Modern opponents of the death penalty have inadequately acknowledged this difficulty.

But this difficulty is completely outflanked when cruelty is viewed as a power relationship in the manner indicated above. Cruelty seen in this fashion enables us to recognize that the death penalty is and will remain cruel no matter how or on whom or for what reason it is inflicted.

Some will argue that this conception of cruelty is too sweeping, for it condemns *all* punishments—or at least all severe punishments, such as life imprisonment, the usual statutory alternative to death—as cruel. Does not all punishment involve power over the powerless, in precisely the manner essential to the conception proposed and used above to condemn the death penalty?[46] True, punishment requires the punisher to control the punished to whatever extent is necessary to guarantee that the sentence is carried out. But such coercive power usually is not used, and in principle never need be used, to "smash" or "annihilate" the offender, either bodily or spiritually. Its intention is not to destroy life, in body or soul, but only to limit liberty, privacy, and autonomy. Thus the power necessary to carry out severe punishments under law is not "total," even if punitive institutions can be popularly and correctly defined as "total" institutions.[47]

Accordingly, the coercive control needed to incarcerate even dangerous offenders can constitute a morally acceptable alternative mode of punishment not open to attack as excessively severe or inherently brutal or cruel, under the conception of cruelty here being advocated. Imprisonment, including even long-term imprisonment where necessary, also can provide adequate incapacitation, as the long history of its use for dangerous persons convicted of the gravest crimes amply proves.[48] I say this not in complacent dismissal of the miseries of long-term incarceration, but to emphasize the point that incarceration does not *essentially* include annihilative power over any prisoner comparable to what the death penalty manifests over every prisoner.[49] So this alternative to the death penalty cannot be condemned on the ground that it involves merely a subtler form of the very power expressed in, and used here to condemn, the death penalty.

So far, nothing has been said about what makes a punishment "unusual," even though it is only punishments that are "cruel and unusual" that the Eighth Amendment condemns. At face value, cruelty and unusualness are two independent attributes of punishment, each with its own criteria, and capable of various combinations (such as cruel but not unusual punishments, and vice versa). But the Supreme Court has shown little interest in such an interpretation, however plausible the layperson may find it. Instead, unusualness is more typically taken adjectivally, as a feature of the severity in punishments that is a necessary element in their cruelty. This adjectival role has been given mainly two different interpretations. In one, unusualness means *excessive* severity, or *unequal* severity, or perhaps *arbitrary* severity. In the other, it means *unpopular* severity, or *highly atypical* severity.[50] (Justice Brennan's four principles in effect take both these interpretations into account.)

The two interpretations are hardly of equal plausibility; I have already implicitly rejected the latter as inappropriate because it suffers from the same deficiency that led me to argue earlier against the third of Justice Brennan's four principles. Surely, there is no constitutional objection to a punishment that is merely unusual, in the sense of novel, hitherto unauthorized by statute, or otherwise unpopular—so long as it is not also unusual in the sense of excessively harmful or severe and arbitrary. Unusualness in a punishment is a normative, not a purely descriptive, attribute. Accordingly, the constitutional prohibition of a punishment on the ground that it is "unusual" tacitly alludes to some standard or principle by which to judge degrees and qualities of severity in punishment. On the assumption that the standards or principles that relate to unusualness in punishments insignificantly differ from those that govern unacceptable cruelty in punishment, there is no need to dwell further on what constitutes an unusual punishment per se.

We have yet to explain, however, why cruel punishments offend, frustrate, or violate human dignity and thus are prohibited. What is it that cruelty in punishment destroys? And what does the knowing willingness to impose cruel punishments reveal about punishers?

VII

The argument I propose to use to answer these questions starts from the idea that human dignity is most evidently at stake where violation of the most basic human rights are involved. Thus, if the death penalty violates human dignity, there must be a fundamental human right that it violates. What right could that be? Nothing less than "a nonwaivable, nonforfeitable, nonrelinquishable right—the right to one's status as a moral being, a right that is implied in one's being a possessor of any rights at all."[51] Obviously, such a right seems to be violated by officially sanctioned death in the form of punishment. The possession of such a right is a consequence of one's status as a person, a conceptual product of reflection on our common humanity, our human dignity.

The nature of this right can be best seen by contrasting it to the "right to life" as it is found in traditional "natural rights" theories of the seventeenth and eighteenth centuries. According to such theories, the right to life is universal (all and only human beings have it), natural (not conferred by society or law), and inalienable (its possessor cannot use it as a bargaining chip). It is also nonwaivable, since that would open the door to such morally reprehensible acts as suicide and euthanasia. But this set of traits defining the right to life does not entail that someone who possesses this right cannot *forfeit* it. On the contrary, the right to life was traditionally understood to be forfeitable, and it was judged that this right was forfeited by any act of killing another person without justification or excuse.[52] In this way, typical versions of traditional natural rights theories accommodated the lawful (and seemingly necessary) death penalties of their day. The issue before us is whether there is a rational defense of a right connected to human dignity that is invulnerable to demands for its forfeiture.

At the outset, we need to realize how unremarkable such a right is when seen in light of familiar constitutional principles compatible with but having no direct bearing on the Eighth Amendment.

Our Bill of Rights incorporates the principle that even persons accused and convicted of the gravest crimes retain their fundamental rights of due process and equal protection of the law. Whether these rights are absolute in the sense that every countervailing legal consideration must yield before their claims we need not settle here. It is enough to notice that *these rights are not forfeitable* (for present purposes we may ignore whether they can be waived).[53] If government officers violate these rights in the course of their administration of criminal justice, that is normally sufficient to nullify whatever legal burdens were placed on an accused or convicted person arising from such a violation. What this shows is that our Constitution already has in place, and our society to that extent fully acknowledges, a principle of profound importance: The individual *cannot* do anything that utterly nullifies his or her worth and standing as a person, so far as the processes of the criminal law are concerned. Government *must* treat persons in the criminal justice system as having a worth and dignity that prohibits violation of due process and equal protection of the law.

What is at stake in the present argument over the Eighth Amendment and the death penalty is not, therefore, anything very radical or novel. No concept, value, or principle is being advocated without precedent or analogy to what we find elsewhere firmly embedded in our constitutional law. Rather, what is at stake is the extent to which considerations already familiar in criminal procedure under the Constitution can be extended to the evaluation of certain substantive modes of government conduct (viz., lawful punishment) because the same moral factor—human dignity and the equal moral status of all persons—underlies both.

At this point, the overall argument can be advanced by two independent lines of reasoning. The first addresses directly the question of the moral standing of convicted offenders and in particular those guilty of murder and condemned to death, insofar as their standing can be understood as an empirical matter. Convicts on death row typically arrive there with undeniable capacities for action and passion as moral creatures, quite apart from whatever outrageously immoral conduct resulted in their criminal condemnation in the first place. That condemnation and the faulty conduct underlying it does not directly cause these moral capacities to weaken significantly, much less to vanish. The immorality of murder that makes convicted murderers "monsters" in the eyes of the public does not in fact make anyone into a *nonmoral* creature. An act of murder does not cause an offender to lose whatever moral capacities he may have had prior to his crime. Rather, the act of murder is consistent with varying degrees of moral development. (That life, such as it is, on death row sometimes, even if not always, enhances some of these moral capacities in some offenders, and provides surprising opportunity for their manifestation, also cannot be denied.) However dangerous, pathological, and unreformable such convicts may be (excluding, of course, the severely retarded and the certifiably insane), these failings do not overwhelm all capacity in death row convicts for moral action and response—as testimony from friends, relatives, guards, legal counsel, and other visitors overwhelmingly attests.[54] What is true of death row murderers is no less true of the enormously larger number of such offenders who are (dare one say only?) imprisoned for their punishment.

Thus, there is no plausible empirical evidence to support the claim that convicted murderers lose their status as moral agents and patients just because they are guilty of horribly immoral crimes. If it is replied that these offenders nevertheless *do* lack such status, what can this mean and how can it be true? It seems to mean that someone, in effect acting in the name of and on behalf of society, *has taken away* the moral status of the individual, stripped the death row murderer of his worth and dignity. But where does anyone get the authority to make such a devastating judgment? Authority to judge an accused and to punish a convicted offender are troubling enough from the moral point of view. Authority in effect to decree that someone no longer has the status of a moral human being is something else altogether. Indeed, the very idea of such a judgment is bewildering, appalling; it is redolent with the odor of magical, superstitious thinking. It is also disingenuous, because it wraps in deceptive legalistic-moralistic language the fact that it is *we* who have decided the murderer shall die, and that *we* are about to kill him.

Defenders of the death penalty often make the error of supposing that the act of murder destroys the moral dignity of the offender; Walter Berns, for example, claims that the murderer "lost his dignity when he freely chose to commit his vile crimes."[55] Such a view simply ignores the conception of the person as a member of the moral community in the requisite sense. As Gregory Vlastos has noted, "The moral community is not a club from which members may be dropped for delinquency. Our morality does not provide for moral outcasts or half-castes. It does provide for punishment. But this takes place within the moral community and under its rules. It is for this reason that, for example, one has no right to be cruel to a cruel person. His offense against the moral law has not put him outside the law. He is still protected by its prohibition of cruelty—as much as are any kind persons."[56] The abstract and anonymous judgment that the murderer forfeits his very status as a person because of his murder all too smoothly paves the way for the sequence of actual lethal decisions made by identifiable persons involved in administering a death penalty system.

If the authority to render such judgment as this is not entirely specious and unjustified, it must be because the best normative *theory* about the sources and limits of human worth and dignity provides for their forfeiture (cancellation, termination, nullification) under certain circumstances. As was noted above, the judgment that certain persons, who (by virtue of their being persons) are conceded to have had basic human rights prior to their criminal acts, nevertheless forfeit or otherwise relinquish *all* those rights by committing certain crimes—as though they had therewith miraculously ceased completely to be moral creatures—receives no support from experience at all.[57] Everything, then, evidently turns on what the normative theory is that makes this forfeiture the necessary response by society. But there is no adequate theory of the requisite sort at all.

The second line of argument is more abstract and controversial. It

starts with the fact that individual human beings are not merely bio-
logical specimens of *Homo sapiens.* To be sure, the neonate, the hope-
lessly brain-damaged adult, the senile nonagenarian—as well as the
normal and the gifted—are all equally members of the same species.
But not all members of the species are equally *persons;* some never will
be and others never will be again, even if the criteria of personhood are
set generously low.[58] In particular cases, congenital abnormality and
abusive or negligent socialization can prevent the development of the
relevant traits and thus destroy the possibility that a normal person will
ever develop from the human infant that has been given birth. In addition to nature and nurture, what it means to be a person can be understood only as the product of reflective thought about the full range of
our characteristic attitudes, abilities, dispositions, and deeds. The written documents that trace out this story in all its complexity and variety
now span several millennia and dozens of civilizations.

As this record shows, the nature of the person as well as the nature of
human society change subtly over time. These changes are partly a result of changes in our self-perceptions, themselves a product of social
experience and deeper self-knowledge. History, including the history of
morality and moral philosophy, confirms that we are permanently engaged in our own progressive self-understanding, as individuals and
as societies. We are thus, in our very natures, at least to some extent,
what we take ourselves to be. For several centuries, and in particular
since the Age of Enlightenment two centuries ago in Europe, philosophers and other thinkers have been struggling to enunciate a conception of the person as fundamentally social, rational, autonomous, and
relatively immune to change in these respects by the contingencies of
actual particular historical circumstances. Such normal personal traits
and capacities are, of course, no guarantee against the gravest immorality in individual or collective conduct. Nor does possession of these
traits immunize or insulate anyone from mortality.

Short of actual physical destruction, however, these capacities are
not and cannot be sensibly thought of as vulnerable to destruction by
the agent's own acts, or by the immoral or criminal aspects of those
acts. Indeed, there is a paradox at the heart of the idea that a person can

forfeit by his own act his status as a person: Action must be deliberate, intentional, and responsible before it can count as a *person's* action. These are also the very qualities in conduct properly deemed necessary before the person whose conduct is in question can be subjected to the criminal law and properly judged, sentenced, and punished. It is conceptually impossible, therefore, for a person in a given act to deserve condemnation by the law for the criminality of that act *and* for the person to have proved by this act that he is no longer a person at all—but only a creature who now lacks any moral standing in the community of persons. Not even the convicted mass or serial murderer is a mere object, a natural force of flesh and bone, a "monster" to be disposed of by the decision of others, as though that were either the only feasible response to his criminal acts or the best response because it is necessary to the preservation of the human community.

With this in mind, one is bound to require that governments accept severe limits on their use of power and coercive force. In particular, a government can have no authority to create and sustain any institution—a lethal institution—whose nature and purpose is to destroy some of its own members, unless these persons are a permanent threat to the innocent and unless there is no nonlethal alternative method of control available. Capital punishment, which of course is designed to annihilate the offender, does constitute just such a lethal institution. Yet for decades it has operated alongside an effective alternative. To defend the death penalty in the face of these facts requires heroic measures.

Usually, these measures take one of two major forms. One is based, explicitly or implicitly, on the belief that the death penalty is a social defense analogous to individual self-help. The analogy fails, as I have argued elsewhere.[59] The excuse or justification in law and morality that an individual who kills in self-defense may have provides no rationale for the death penalty. (Contrast this weak analogy with another one: The death penalty in peacetime is like shooting disarmed prisoners of war, a classic violation of international law.) The other line of argument claims that morality itself, insofar as it is based on sound moral theory, permits (some would insist that it requires) society to act against persons who show by their own acts their contempt for the moral nature of others, their victims. Such recourse to vindictive and retributive thinking also fails, either because it begs the question or because it is so flagrantly unrealistic.[60]

The conclusion I reach is that the same moral constraints that have long ago produced constitutional requirements of due process and equal protection of the law argue against any punishment that requires the forfeiture of one's very status as a person. This is what the death penalty requires. A society that understands and respects the dignity of persons will not pretend that it can empower other human beings in their official roles as agents of the criminal justice system to exact such a forfeiture.

8 USING MORAL PRINCIPLES TO ARGUE ABOUT THE DEATH PENALTY

I

Argument over the death penalty—especially in the United States during the past generation—has been concentrated in large part on trying to answer various disputed *questions of fact*. Among them two have been salient: Is the death penalty a better deterrent to crime (especially murder) than the alternative of imprisonment? Is the death penalty administered in a discriminatory way—in particular, are black or other nonwhite offenders (or offenders whose victims are white) more likely to be tried, convicted, sentenced to death, and executed than whites (or than offenders whose victims are nonwhite)? Other questions of fact have also been explored, including these two: What is the risk that an innocent person could actually be executed for a crime he did not commit? What is the risk that a person convicted of a capital felony but not executed will commit another capital felony?

Varying degrees of effort have been expended in trying to answer these questions. Although I think the available answers are capable of further refinement, I also think anyone who studies the evidence today must conclude that the best current responses to these four questions are as follows: (1) There is little or no evidence that the death penalty is a better deterrent to murder than is imprisonment; on the contrary, most evidence shows that these two punishments are about equally (in)effective as deterrents to murder. Furthermore, as long as the death penalty continues to be used with relative rarity, there is no prospect of gaining more decisive evidence on the question.[1] (2) There is evidence that the death penalty has been and continues to be administered, whether intentionally or not, in a manner that produces arbitrary and racially discriminatory results in sentencing. At the very least, this is true in those jurisdictions where the question has been investigated in recent years.[2] (3) It is impossible to calculate the risk that an innocent person will be executed—but the risk is not zero, as the record of convicted, sentenced, and executed innocents shows.[3] (4) Recidivism data show that some convicted murderers have killed again, either in prison or after release, so there is a risk that others will do so as well.[4]

Let us assume that my summary of the results of research on these four questions is correct, and that further research will not significantly change these answers. The first thing to notice is that even if everyone accepted these answers, this would not by itself settle the dispute over whether to keep, expand, reduce, or abolish the death penalty. Agreement on these empirical claims about the administration and effects of the death penalty in our society does not entail a decision to support or oppose the death penalty. This would still be true even if we agreed on *all* the answers to the factual questions that can be asked about the death penalty.

There are two reasons for this. The facts as they currently stand and as seen from the abolitionist perspective do not point strongly and overwhelmingly to the futility of the death penalty or to the harm it does—at least, as long as the death penalty continues to be used only in the limited and restricted form of the past three decades (i.e., confined to the crime of murder, with trial courts empowered to exercise "guided discretion" in sentencing, at which defense counsel may introduce anything as mitigating evidence, and with automatic review of both conviction and sentence by state and federal appellate courts).[5] Nor do the facts show that the alternative of life imprisonment is on balance a noticeably superior punishment. The evidence of racial discrimination in the administration of the death penalty, while incontestable, may be no worse than racial discrimination where lesser crimes and punishments are concerned. No one who has studied the data thinks that racial discrimination in the administration of justice for murder reaches the level of discrimination that in the pre-*Furman* era affected the administration of justice in the South for rape.[6] Besides, it is always possible to argue that such discrimination is diminishing, or will diminish over time, and that in any case since the fault lies not in the capital statutes themselves—they are color-blind on their face—the remedy does not lie in repealing them. Nor is it clear that a life sentence in prison without the possibility of release is an enormous improvement over death from the offender's point of view. (Recall the discussion in Chapter 5.)

But the marginal impact of the empirical evidence is not the major factor in explaining why settling disputes over matters of fact does not and cannot settle the larger controversy over the death penalty itself. As a matter of sheer logic, it is not possible to deduce a policy conclusion (such as the desirability of abolishing the death penalty) from any set of factual premises however general and well supported. Any argument intended to recommend continuing or reforming current policy on the death penalty must include among its premises one or more normative propositions. Unless disputants over the death penalty can agree about these normative propositions, their argument on the empirical facts will never suffice to resolve their dispute.

II

Accordingly, the course of wisdom for those interested in arguing about the death penalty is to focus attention on the normative propositions crucial to the dispute, in the hope that some headway may be made in narrowing disagreement over their number, content, and weight.

If this is to be done effectively, the context of these norms in general political ideology needs to be fixed. Suffice it to say here that I proceed from within the context of liberal pluralistic constitutional democracy and the conception of punishment appropriate therein.[7]

Logically prior to the idea of punishment is the idea of a crime. What counts as a criminal harm depends in part on our conception of persons as bearers of rights deserving respect and protection. In this setting, liability to punishment and its actual infliction serve the complex function of reinforcing compliance with a set of laws deemed necessary to protect the fundamental equal rights of all members of society. The normative propositions relevant to the death penalty controversy are interwoven with the basic purposes and principles of liberal society, including the recognition and protection of individual rights to life and liberty, and to security of person and property.

These norms can be divided into two groups: those that express relevant and desirable *social goals* or *purposes*, and those that express relevant and respectable *moral principles*. Punishment is thus a practice or institution defined through various policies—such as the death penalty for murder—intended to be the means or instrument whereby certain social goals are achieved within the constraints imposed by acknowledged moral principles.[8]

Reduction of crime, or at least prevention of increase in crime, is an example of such a goal. This goal influences the choice of punishments because of their impact on the crime rate. No one, except for purists of a retributive stripe, would dissent from the view that this goal is relevant to the death penalty controversy. Because it is assumed to be relevant, there is continuing interest in the outcome of research on the question of the differential deterrent efficacy of death versus imprisonment. The only questions normally in dispute are what that research shows (I have summarized it above) and how important this goal is (for some it is decisive).

Similarly, that no one should be convicted and sentenced to death without a fair trial (i.e., in violation of "due process of law") is a principle of law and morality generally respected. Its general acceptance explains the considerable reformation in the laws governing the death penalty in the United States that have been introduced since 1972 in response to the Supreme Court's decisions in *Furman v. Georgia*.[9] The Court argued in *Furman* that capital trials and death sentencing were in practice unfair (in constitutional jargon, they were in violation of the

Eighth and Fourteenth Amendments, which bar "cruel and unusual punishments" and require "equal protection of the laws," respectively). State legislatures and thoughtful observers agreed. Here again the only questions concern how important it is to comply with this principle (for some it is decisive) and the extent to which the death penalty currently violates it (I have remarked on this point above, too).

The chief use of a moral principle in the present setting is to constrain the methods used in pursuit of policy (as when respect for "due process" rules out curbstone justice as a tactic in crime fighting). However, identifying the relevant goals, acknowledging the force of the relevant principles, and agreeing on the relevant general facts will still not suffice to resolve the dispute. Disagreement over the relative importance of achieving a given goal or disagreement over the relative weight of a given principle is likely to show up in disagreement over the justification of the death penalty itself.

If this is a correct sketch of the structural character of debate and disagreement over the death penalty, then (as I noted earlier) the best hope for progress may lie in looking more carefully at the nonfactual normative ingredients so far isolated in the dispute. Ideally, we would identify and evaluate the policy goals relevant to punishment generally, as well as the moral principles that constrain the structure and content of the penalty schedule. We would also settle the proper relative weights to attach to these goals and constraints, if not in general then at least for their application in the present context. Then, with whatever relevant general facts are at our disposal, we would be in a position to draw the appropriate inferences and resolve the entire dispute, confident that we have examined and duly weighed everything that reason and morality can bring to bear on the problem.

As an abstract matter, therefore, the question is whether the set of relevant policies and principles, taken in conjunction with the relevant facts, favors reduction (even complete abolition) of the death penalty, or whether it favors its retention (or even extension). Lurking in the background, of course, is the troubling possibility, here as elsewhere, that the relevant norms and facts underdetermine the resolution of the dispute. But let us not worry about sharks on dry land, not yet.

III

Where choice of punishments is concerned, the relevant social goals, I suggest, are few. Two in particular generally commend themselves:

G1. Punishment ought to contribute to the reduction of crime: accordingly, the punishment for a crime ought not to be so idle a threat or so slight a deprivation that it has little or no deterrent or incapacitative effects; and it certainly ought not to contribute to the increase of crime.

G2. Punishments ought to be "economical"—they ought not to waste valuable social resources in futile or unnecessarily costly endeavors.

The instrumental character of these purposes and goals is evident. They reflect the fact that society does not institute and maintain the practice of punishment for its own sake, as though it were a good in itself. Rather, punishment is and is seen to be a means to an end or ends. The justification of a society's punitive policies and practices, therefore, must involve two steps: first, it must be assumed or argued that these ends are desirable; second, it must be shown that the practice of punishment is a necessary means to these ends. What is true of the justification of punishment generally is true *a fortiori* of justifying the death penalty.

Endorsement of these two policy goals tends to encourage support for the death penalty. Opponents of capital punishment need not reject these goals, however, and its defenders cannot argue that accepting these goals vindicates their preferred policy. Traditionally, it is true, the death penalty has often been supported on the ground that it provides the best social defense and is extremely cheap to administer. But since the time of Beccaria and Bentham these empirical claims have been challenged,[10] and rightly so. If support for the death penalty today in a country such as the United States were thought to rest on the high priority of achieving these goals, then there is much (some would say compelling) evidence to undermine this support. The most that can be said solely by reference to these goals is that recognition of their importance can always be counted on to kindle interest in capital punishment, and to that extent force its opponents on the defensive.

Whether punishment is intended to serve only the two goals so far identified is disputable. An argument can be made that there are two or three further goals, as follows:

G3. Punishment ought to rectify the harm and injustice caused by crime.

G4. Punishment ought to serve as a recognized channel for the release of public indignation and anger at the offender over crime.

G5. Punishment ought to make convicted offenders into better persons rather than leave them as they are or make them worse.

Obviously, anyone who accepts the fifth goal must reject the death penalty. I shall not try here to argue the merits of this goal, either in itself or relative to the other goals of punishment. Whatever its merits, this goal is less widely sought than the others, and for that reason alone it is less useful in trying to develop rational agreement over the death penalty. Its persuasive power for those not already persuaded against the death penalty on other grounds is likely to be slight to zero. Although I am unwilling to strike it from the list of goals that punishment in general is and ought to be trying to achieve, I am unwilling to stress its preeminence in the present context.

The third proposed goal of punishment is open to the objection that rectification of injustice is not really a goal of punishment, even if it is a desirable goal whenever injustice is discovered. Indeed, it is widely believed that rectification is not a goal of punishment but of noncriminal tort judgments. That point to one side, imprisonment as typically practiced in the United States rectifies nothing. Since mere incarceration by itself does not provide any direct and unique benefit to the victims of crime or to society generally, there is no way it can rectify the unjust harms that crime causes. Nonetheless, this goal is at least indirectly important for the death penalty controversy. To the extent that one believes punishments ought to serve this goal, and that there is no possible way to rectify the crime of murder, one may come to believe the fourth goal is of even greater importance than would otherwise be the case. Indeed, striving to achieve this fourth goal and embracing the death penalty as a consequence is quite parallel to striving to achieve the fifth goal and consequently embracing abolition.

Does this fourth goal have a greater claim on our support than I have allowed is true of the fifth goal, so obviously incompatible with it? Many would say that it does. Some, such as Walter Berns,[11] would even argue that it is this goal, not any of the others, that is the paramount purpose of the practice of punishment under law. Whatever else punishment does, its threat and infliction are to be seen as the expression of legitimate social indignation at deliberate harm to the innocent. Preserving a socially acceptable vehicle for the expression of anger at offenders is absolutely crucial to the health of a just society.

There are in principle three ways to respond to this claim insofar as it is part of an argument for capital punishment. One is to reject it out of hand as a false proposition from start to finish. A second is to concede that the goal of providing a visible and acceptable channel for the emotion of anger is legitimate, but to argue that this goal can justify the death penalty only in a very small number of rare cases (the occasional Adolf Eichmann, for example), or only if its importance is vastly exaggerated. A third is to concede both the legitimacy and relative importance of this goal, but to point out that its pursuit, like that of all other goals, is nonetheless constrained by moral principles (yet to be examined), and that once these principles are properly employed, the death penalty ceases to be a permissible method of achieving this goal. I think both the second and third objections are reasonable, and a few further words here about each are appropriate.

First of all, resentment or indignation is not the same as anger, since the former feeling or emotion can be aroused only through the perceived violation of some moral principle, whereas the latter does not have this constraint. But the question of whether the feeling aroused by awareness of a horrible murder really is indignation rather than only just anger is the question of whether the principles of justice have been severely violated or not. Knowing that the accused offender has no legal excuse or justification for his criminal conduct is not yet knowing enough to warrant the inference that he and his conduct are appropriate objects of our unqualified moral hostility. More about the context of the offense and its causation must be supplied; it may well be that in ordinary criminal cases one rarely or never knows enough to reach such a condemnatory judgment with confidence. Even were this not so, one has no reason to suppose that justified anger at offenders is of overriding importance, and that all countervailing considerations must yield to its claims. For one thing, the righteous anger needed for that role is simply not available in a pluralistic secular society; even if it were, we have been assured from biblical times that it passes all too easily into self-righteous and hypocritical repression by some sinners of others.

Quite apart from such objections, there is a certain anomaly, even irony, in the defense of the death penalty by appeal to this goal. On the one hand, we are told that a publicly recognized ritual for extermination of convicted murderers is a necessary vent for otherwise unchanneled disruptive public emotions. On the other hand, our society scrupulously rejects time-honored methods of execution that truly do express hatred and anger at offenders—beheading, crucifixion, and dismemberment are unheard of today, and hanging and the electric chair are disappearing. Execution by lethal injection, increasingly the popular option, hardly seems appropriate as the outlet of choice for such allegedly volatile energies. And is it not bizarre that this death-dealing technique, invented to facilitate life saving surgery, now turns out to be the preferred channel for the expression of moral indignation?

IV

If the purpose or goals of punishment lend a utilitarian quality to the practice of punishment, the moral principles relevant to the death penalty operate as deontological constraints on the pursuit of these goals. Stating all and only the principles relevant to the death penalty controversy is not easy, and the list that follows is no more than the latest approximation to the task.[12] With some overlap here and there, these principles are seven:

P1. No one's life may be deliberately and intentionally taken by another unless there is no feasible alternative to protect the latter's own life.

P2. The more severe a penalty is, the more important it is that it be imposed only on those who truly deserve it.

P3. The more severe a penalty is, the weightier the justification required to warrant its imposition on anyone.

P4. Whatever the criminal offense, the accused or convicted offender does not forfeit his rights and dignity as a person.

P5. There is an upper limit to the severity—cruelty, destructiveness, finality—of permissible punishments, regardless of the offense.

P6. Fairness requires that punishments be graded in their severity according to the gravity of the offense.

P7. If human lives are to be risked, the risk should fall more heavily on wrongdoers (the guilty) than on others (the innocent).

I cannot argue here for all these principles, but they really need no argument from me. Each is recognized implicitly or explicitly in our practice; each can be seen to constrain our conduct as individuals and as officers in democratic institutions. Outright repudiation or cynical disregard of any of these principles would disqualify one from engaging in serious discourse and debate over punishment in a liberal society. All can be seen as corollaries or theorems of the general principle that life, limb, and security of person—of *all* persons—are of paramount value. Thus, only minimal interference (in the jargon of the law, "the least restrictive means") is warranted with anyone's life, limb, and security in order to protect the rights of others.

How do these principles direct or advise us in regard to the permissibility or desirability of the death penalty? The first thing to note is that evidently none directly rules it out. I know of no moral principle that is both sufficiently precise and sufficiently well established for us to point to it and say, "The practice of capital punishment is flatly contradictory to the requirements of this moral principle." (Of course, we might invent a principle that will have this consequence, but that is hardly to the point.) This should not be surprising; few if any of the critics or the defenders of the death penalty have supposed otherwise. Second, several of these principles do reflect the heavy burden that properly falls on anyone who advocates that certain human beings be deliberately killed by others, even though those to be killed are not at the time a danger to anyone. For example, whereas the first principle may justify lethal force in self-defense and other circumstances, it directly counsels against the death penalty in *all* cases without exception. The second and third principles emphasize the importance of "due process" and "equal protection" as the finality and incompensability of punishments increase. The fourth principle draws attention to the nature and value of persons, even those convicted of terrible crimes. The fifth reminds us that even if crimes have no upper limit in their wantonness, cruelty, destructiveness, and horror, punishments under law in a civilized society may not imitate crimes in this regard. Punishment does operate under limits, and these limits are not arbitrary.

The final two principles, however, seem to be exceptions to the generalization that the principles as a group tend to favor punishments other than death. The sixth principle entails that if murder is the gravest crime, then it must receive the severest punishment. This does not, of course, *require* a society to invoke the death penalty for murder—unless one accepts *lex talionis* ("a life for a life, an eye for an eye") in a singularly literal-minded manner. But *lex talionis* is not a sound principle on which to construct the penalty schedule generally, and so appealing to that interpretation of the sixth principle here simply begs the question. Nevertheless, the principle that punishments should be graded to fit the crime does encourage consideration of the death penalty, especially if it seems there is no other way to punish murder with utmost permissible severity.

Rather of more interest is the seventh principle. Some, primarily the late Ernest van den Haag,[13] make it the cornerstone of their defense of the death penalty. They argue that it is better to execute all convicted murderers, lest on some future occasion some of them murder again, than it is to execute none of them in order to avert the risk of executing the few who may be innocent. For, so the argument goes, a policy of complete abolition would result in thousands of convicted killers (only a few of whom are innocent) being held behind bars. This cohort constitutes a permanent risk to the safety of many millions of innocent citizens. The sole gain to counterbalance this risk is the guarantee that no lives—innocent or guilty—will be lost through legal executions. The practice of executions thus is argued to protect far more innocent citizens than the same practice puts in jeopardy.

This argument is far less conclusive than it may, at first, seem. Even if we grant it full weight, it is simply unreasonable to use it (or any other argument) as a way of dismissing the relevance of principles that counsel a different result, or as a tactic to imply the subordinate importance of all other relevant principles. Used in this objectionable manner, what I have called the seventh principle has been transformed. It has become a disguised version of the first policy goal (viz., Reduce crime!) and in effect elevates that goal to preeminence over every competing and constraining consideration. It has also ceased to be a constraint on policy. Second, the argument fosters the illusion that we can, in fact, reasonably estimate, if not actually calculate, the number of lives risked by a policy of abolition versus a policy of capital punishment. This is false; we do not and cannot reasonably hope to know what the risk is of convicting the innocent,[14] even if we could estimate the risk of recidivist murder. We therefore cannot really compare the two risks with any precision. Finally, the argument gains whatever strength it appears to have by tacitly ignoring the following dilemma: If the argument is to be taken seriously, then death must be understood to be the *mandatory* penalty for everyone convicted of murder (never mind other crimes). But such a policy flies in the face of two centuries of political reality, which unquestionably demonstrates the impossibility of enforcing truly mandatory death penalties for murder or any other crime. The only feasible policy alternative is some version of a discretionary death penalty. But every version of this policy actually tried has proved vulnerable to criticism on grounds of inequality in its administration, as critic after critic has shown.[15]

The upshot is that society today runs both the risk of executing the innocent and the risk of recidivist murder, although it is necessary to run only one of these risks. At the same time, it is politically impossible to avoid running *some* risk of recidivist murder.

V

What has our examination of the relevant goals and principles shown about the possibility of resolving the death penalty controversy on purely rational grounds? First, the death penalty is primarily a means to one or more ends (goals), but it is not the only and probably not the best means to those ends. Second, several principles familiar to us in many areas of punitive policy favor (although they do not demand) abolition of the death penalty. Third, there is no principle that constitutes a conclusive reason favoring either side in the dispute—except, of course, for conclusive reasons (like the fifth goal, or the sixth principle interpreted as *lex talionis*) that either one side or the other simply need not accept. This, too, should not be surprising. If a reason existed that was so conclusive that both sides had to accept it, one must wonder why its discovery continues to elude us. Finally, the several goals and principles of punishment that have been identified have no obvious rank order or relative weighting. As they stand, these goals and principles do indeed underdetermine the policy dispute over capital punishment. Perhaps such a ranking of principles could be provided by one or another general socioethical theory. But the lack of general acceptance for any such theory does not bode well for rational resolution of the controversy along these lines.

Despite the absence of any conclusive reasons or decisive ranking of principles, we may take refuge (as I have done elsewhere)[16] in the thought that a preponderance of reasons does favor one side rather than the other. Such a preponderance emerges, however, only when the relevant goals and principles of punishment are seen in a certain light, or from a particular angle of vision. This perhaps amounts to one rather than another weighting of goals and principles but without reliance upon any manifest theory. One relies instead on other considerations. I shall mention three whose importance may be decisive.

The first and by far the most important is the role and function of *power* in the hands of government. It is preferable, *ceteris paribus*, that such power over individuals should shrink rather than expand. Where such power must be used, it is better to use it for constructive rather than destructive purposes—enhancing the autonomy and liberty of those persons directly affected by it. The death penalty is government power used in a dramatically destructive manner upon individuals in the absence of any compelling social necessity. No wonder it is the ultimate symbol of such power.

A second consideration that shapes my interpretation of the goals and principles of evaluation is an orientation to the *future* rather than to the past. We cannot do anything to benefit the dead victims of crime. (How many of those who oppose the death penalty would continue to do so if, *mirabile dictu*, executing the murderer brought the victim back to life?) But we can—or at least we can try to—do something for the living: We can protect the innocent, console those in despair, and try to prevent future crimes. None of these constructive tasks presupposes or involves the expressive, vindictive, and retributive roles of punishment. The more we stress these roles to the neglect of all else, the more we orient our punitive policies toward the past—toward trying to use government power over the lives of a few as a socially approved instrument of moral bookkeeping.

Finally, the death penalty projects a false and misleading picture of man and society. Its professed message for those who support it is this: justice requires killing the convicted murderer. So we focus on the death that all murderers supposedly deserve, and overlook our inability to give a rational account of why so few actually get what they allegedly deserve. Hence, the lesson taught by the practice of capital punishment is not what its retributivist defenders infer from their theory. Far from being a symbol of justice, it is a symbol of brutality and stupidity. Perhaps if we lived in a world of autonomous Kantian moral agents, where even the criminals freely and rationally express their will in the intention to kill others without their consent or desert, then death for the convicted murderer might be just (as even Karl Marx was inclined to concede).[17] But a closer look at the convicts who actually are on our death rows shows that these killers are a far cry from the rational agents of Kant's metaphysical imagination. We fool ourselves if we think a system of ideal retributive justice designed for such persons is the appropriate model for the penal system in our society.

Have I implicitly conceded that argument over the death penalty is irrational? If I am right, that the death penalty controversy does not really turn on controversial social goals or controversial moral principles, any more than it does on disputed general facts, but instead turns on how all three are to be balanced or weighed, does it follow that reason alone cannot resolve the controversy, because reason alone cannot determine which weighting or balancing is the correct one? Or can reason resolve this problem, perhaps by appeal to further theory, theory that would deepen our appreciation of what truly underlies a commitment to liberal institutions and a belief in the possibilities for autonomy of all persons?[18] I think it can (and elsewhere in this volume I have tried to set out the argument needed)—but this is the right place to end this discussion, because we have reached the launching platform for another one.

9 ABOLISHING THE DEATH PENALTY EVEN FOR THE WORST MURDERERS

I

In the wake of the execution of Timothy McVeigh, convicted in June 1997 for his role in the murderous bombing of the Federal Building in Oklahoma City two years earlier, it is timely to ask this question: Who has the better of the argument, those who believe that some offenders (such as McVeigh) ought to be punished by being put to death, or those who believe that no one ought to be executed (not even McVeigh) and instead should be sentenced to long-term imprisonment?

To focus the question and keep the discussion relevant to the current scene, we can put aside the status of the death penalty for nonhomicidal crimes, for at least two reasons: First, the paradigm crime punishable by death has always been murder ("a life for a life"). It is also now settled constitutional law that nonhomicidal crimes such as rape and armed robbery are no longer subject to the punishment of death, as they had been only a generation ago.[1] Second, we need not discuss whether the death penalty is the appropriate punishment for *all* homicides. A mandatory death penalty for those convicted of killing another person would require abolishing the distinction between murder and manslaughter and between first- and second-degree murder; it would also require abolishing prosecutorial, judicial, and executive discretion in capital cases. Even if those considerations were not persuasive, the Supreme Court has decreed that mandatory death penalties, even for first-degree murder committed by a person under life sentence for murder, are unconstitutional.[2]

For these reasons it is plausible to argue that the only issue worth discussing is whether the majority of the public (some 65 to 70 percent at the present time)[3] is right in approving the death penalty for some murderers; or whether the minority (to which I belong) is right in defending absolute, exceptionless abolition.

We must concede from the start that a pick-and-choose death penalty policy has much to recommend it. It is typical of the contingencies acknowledged by modern morality where issues of life and death are concerned to shun principles that admit of no exceptions. (Thus, most of us do not favor laws prohibiting all abortions, or prohibiting all physician-assisted suicides.) But the absolute abolitionist position by definition allows no exceptions, which has a crucial consequence for the overall argument. It requires that we leave aside issues of great practical importance in the contemporary debate over the death penalty, such as the relatively greater economic costs of our current death penalty systems when compared with a system of long-term imprisonment; the unfairness—arbitrariness and discrimination—with which the death penalty is administered; and the risk of convicting, sentencing to death, and executing the innocent. These issues have been discussed elsewhere,[4] and they provide powerful objections to the death penalty in our society (just as they are the primary factors in the call for a national moratorium on executions by the House of Delegates of the American Bar Association).[5] Nevertheless, objections on these grounds are largely irrelevant from my current perspective, because it is possible to imagine an ideal world of criminal justice in which such deep-seated flaws and costs would not arise or, if they did, could be remedied without abolishing the death penalty. In that case, we would still be left with the need to explain whether and why we nevertheless oppose all executions.[6]

II

I propose to look first at the most popular moral grounds on which ab-solute abolitionists rest their case and see whether they can bear the weight placed on them.

The Value of Life[7]   Some abolitionists hold that human life (if not all life) has infinite value or worth[8] and so must be respected and protected accordingly. It follows from this belief that death is the greatest disvalue and murder the gravest wrong. It also follows that even murderers must be treated in light of the value of their lives, a value not erased (even if severely marred) by the harm and injustice their lethal violence has caused the innocent. And that supposedly rules out the death penalty.

But does it? As an empirical claim in any ordinary sense of "value," the value of a murderer's life is often (though by no means always) open to question. How much value, or potentiality for value, can we reasonably assign to the future life of the worst murderers—the socio-pathic serial murderer, or the cold-hearted terrorist multiple murderer, or the unreformed and unreformable recidivist murderer—the Hanni-bal Lectors of fiction *(The Silence of the Lambs)* and the Ted Bundys and Timothy McVeighs of real life? (Henceforth I shall call all such of-fenders collectively the worst murderers—serial or multiple or recidi-vist killers—and their crimes the worst murders.) I think it extremely difficult, perhaps impossible, to make a convincing case that *all* such lives have value, based on their history, present condition, and future prospects—and that this value outweighs whatever benefits might be found (or harms avoided) in punishing them with death. The issue here is not whether the worst murderers find their lives worth living; it is rather whether society can reasonably view such murderers as having lives to live that are on balance more valuable than not.

I do not want to suggest, much less argue (although some might), that all or even most of the nearly four thousand persons currently on the death rows of American prisons[9] are persons whose lives are essen-tially worthless or valueless (that is, as judged by society). I wouldn't know how to carry out in a responsible manner a systematic measure-ment of the worth or value of any human life as judged from society's point of view, especially if doing so were to allow for the possibility that some lives turn out to be worthless or valueless. All but the most prejudiced observers will concede that some (perhaps most) murderers retain more than a shred of human dignity and that some can redeem themselves in their own eyes and in ours at least to some extent. But that is not enough for the purposes of the present argument. What must be shown is that this is true of *all* the worst murderers, and I hesitate to endorse any such sweeping empirical claim. Even if one grants (as I do) that convicted murderers do not cease to be persons by virtue of their terrible crimes,[10] this hardly seems enough to establish the value of the life of each such offender.

Of course, the doctrine that even the worst murderer's life has some value (enough to outweigh all its disvalue) may not be an empirical claim at all. Instead, it may be a disguised normative judgment expressing moral disapproval of all executions. In that case, there is only a verbal difference between asserting (1) *every murderer's life has some value* (and enough to outweigh all disvalues), and (2) *we ought not to execute even the worst of the murderers.* To be sure, assertion (2) looks like the conclusion of an argument in which assertion (1) figures as a premise. But if the two assertions differ only verbally, then an appeal to assertion (1) does not advance the argument for assertion (2); instead, it tacitly begs the question. The only way to tell whether there really is a difference in meaning between assertion (2) and assertion (1) is to defend the one without implicitly relying on the other; but that is a task too large to undertake here.

If we regard assertion (2) as a genuine empirical claim, then our task is to establish this claim in a convincing manner on a case-by-case basis. Whether that can be done I do not know.[11] I doubt that it is unreasonable to be cautious, if not skeptical. (Caution is especially recommended in light of what we know about the sociopathy of most of the worst murderers: about how they got that way, and what is necessary— albeit not always sufficient—to bring about fundamental change in their lives.)[12]

Pending the completion of that task in a persuasive manner, I suggest that the default position for abolitionists who wish to rely on the value or worth of all human life is to insist that this value—of each and

every person's life as judged by that person—puts the burden of argument on those who favor sentencing to death and killing persons
without their informed voluntary consent.[13] Imposing the burden of
argument in this manner is not only a minimalist strategy for the abolitionist; it is also fair and essential. The friends of the death penalty cannot reasonably reject or even contest this burden. Surely, there is no
question that those who favor deliberately killing other persons *always*
bear the burden of the argument. A serious discussion of life-and-death
issues is impossible on any other assumption. This means that we must
start from the somewhat paradoxical proposition that for the purposes
of punishment under law, society must assume everyone's life is valuable, and that our lives have equal value, even though some seem to
have little or no value.[14]

The Right to Life[15]   Some abolitionists (especially those influenced
by Amnesty International and other human rights organizations) would
say that we are morally forbidden to take the life of any murderer because even the murderer has an inalienable human right to life and that
sentencing to death and executing a person violates that right. This argument has the merit of leaving aside empirical questions of the sort
raised by the appeal to the value of human life. Instead, this argument
plainly rests on a normative proposition about our rights.

But is the argument sound? Defenders of the death penalty typically
reply (as John Locke did three centuries ago)[16] that even if the right to
life is "natural" and "inalienable," the murderer *forfeits* his life (or, in
some versions of this objection, his right to life), and so putting him to
death at most infringes—and does not violate—that right. Most friends
of the death penalty will agree that murderers, even if guilty and convicted, do not forfeit every right; they still have rights to due process of
law and to equal protection of the law. Hence, lynching a convicted
guilty murderer is itself a crime, even in a jurisdiction that authorizes
the death penalty. But murderers do forfeit the one right that really
matters, the right to life. Or so defenders of the death penalty will typically insist.

What reply do absolute abolitionists have to this objection? They
cannot attack the general idea that rights can be forfeited, because that

idea seems to be a perfectly ordinary even if tacit feature of any theory or doctrine of rights. For example, the Universal Declaration of Human Rights insists that everyone has a "right to liberty"; but it does not follow from this right that it is always wrong to deliberately deprive a person of liberty, as we do when we imprison a convicted offender. This amounts to conceding that under appropriate conditions persons can forfeit their right to liberty.[17]

Absolute abolitionists who resist the temptation to reject out of hand the doctrine of forfeiture of rights are likely to yield to the temptation to insist that whatever may be true of rights in general, the right to life cannot be forfeited—because it is an *absolute* right. That is, the right to life prevails over every other moral consideration that might be thought to compete with or override it. But here there is surely a problem. At best, I think, this is true only when we are referring to the right to life of the innocent. Consider the rationale of the use of lethal force in self-defense (or third-party defense).[18] Few abolitionists will deny that we have the right to act in self-defense to avoid becoming an undeserving victim of another's aggression. All but extreme pacifists will go on to grant that if the only way to prevent someone (oneself or another) from being the innocent victim of an unprovoked and uninvited act of apparently lethal intention is to use lethal force first, then in that sort of case one may kill the aggressor. Further, few abolitionists will insist that the police or other custodians of public order must never use lethal violence.

But once the use of lethal force is granted to be acceptable in such cases, the abolitionist is clearly not regarding the right to life as absolute. At most it is the right to life of the innocent that deserves unqualified respect, not the right to life of the guilty. Abolitionists who reason in this way thus cannot consistently use this right as a shield against deliberate and intentional lethal harm in all cases or as a stick with which to beat down claims by death penalty supporters who believe that even this right can be forfeited.[19]

Abolitionists, however, can reply that if there are any universal human rights at all, surely one of them is the right to life (no doubt in need of further specification). And they can go on to insist that, at the very least, this right puts the burden of argument on those who would kill or authorize others to kill persons (including the worst murderers) without their informed, voluntary consent. Thus, if there is a right to life, even if it is not an absolute right, part of its function is to locate the burden of argument. This requires the friends of the death penalty to explain why that punishment merely infringes the murderer's right to life but does not violate it.[20] And they should do this without over-reliance on the doctrine of forfeiture, because it turns out on closer inspection that forfeiture may be only a weak reed after all.[21]

Some absolute abolitionists currently want to argue that the right to life is too vague or abstract to be of much help in explaining the immorality of the death penalty in any case. They propose to appeal to a different right altogether, the right not to be executed.[22] Is this really an advance in thinking through the relevance of human rights to the death penalty controversy? To be sure, asserting that (3) *everyone has a right not to be executed* seems to be quite different from asserting that (4) *no one ought to be executed*, because invoking someone's rights is often a way of arguing what someone ought (or ought not) to do. Accordingly, assertion (4) looks like the conclusion for which assertion (3) is a plausible premise. I, of course, accept assertion (4), as do all absolute abolitionists. But I am not sure I accept assertion (3), and so I worry that, after all, there may be only a verbal difference between the two claims. In that case assertion (3) adds nothing to assertion (4).

Perhaps at this point some absolute abolitionists will want to shift from relying on rights to relying upon the sanctity of human life. Such a shift not only puts aside any worry about empirical questions concerning the value of human life; it also has the advantage of making it difficult and perhaps impossible to make sense of forfeiting the sanctity of one's life by committing a terrible crime (even a crime that violates the sanctity of the innocent victim's life). In this respect sanctity has the edge on rights. But these advantages are purchased at a price: The sanctity of human life can be explained and defended only within a sectarian religious framework; one cannot appeal to the sanctity of human life in isolation from a whole host of related ideas and beliefs that do not have universal appeal. What is needed, I suggest, is a secular norm of universal application, which is exactly what the value of human life and the right to life attempt to provide.

General Social Utility[23]   Some oppose the death penalty on utilitarian grounds, arguing that the general welfare is better served by adopting and acting on a rule that forbids killing anyone in the name of punishment. All of us, whether or not we are utilitarians, agree that some enforceable rule prohibiting deliberately killing persons is necessary; we all agree that homicide is a crime unless excused or justified; we also agree that the ideal civilized society is one in which all rational persons would live without anyone murdering anyone; and we also agree that government officials and their agents, as well as private citizens, have committed inexcusable and unjustifiable homicide. (Think, respectively, of the federal government's attack on the Waco compound of the Branch Davidians in 1993, and the bombing of the Federal Building in Oklahoma City in 1995.) Can these agreements best be recognized and enforced by utilitarian reasoning?

Perhaps they can, but they fall well short of what is necessary to rule out all recourse to the death penalty. A utilitarian is very likely to consider certain cases, given the facts, as exceptions to any rule that absolutely prohibits killing other human beings in the name of punishment. Even the abolitionist founders of utilitarianism, notably Jeremy Bentham[24] and (to a lesser degree) J. S. Mill,[25] thought that the death penalty was appropriate in a narrow range of cases; so did Cesare Beccaria[26] before them and the American pragmatist Sidney Hook[27] in our own day.

To see how a utilitarian (or a pragmatist) would reason, consider the following kind of case (variations on this argument were voiced by some who favored the death sentence for McVeigh). Terrorist acts causing great loss of innocent life have been committed against a tolerably just government, and the chief offenders have been captured, tried, convicted, and now await sentencing. There is every reason to believe that many of their coideologists remain at large, scattered across the nation, and that the leaders awaiting sentencing will continue to inspire terrorist attacks as long as they remain alive. Doesn't the most plausible reading of the political facts support putting these convicted terrorists to death (perhaps even by public execution), in order to reduce the likelihood of further rebellion and harmful disorder? Why risk society's precarious security just to avoid putting to death dangerous terrorists who are clearly guilty?[28] In the wake of September 11, 2001, would not most Americans reason in precisely this way regarding the terrorist bombers of that day?

Reasoning of this sort is bound to attract utilitarians; it is always just a question of time and circumstances before the utilitarian opponent of the death penalty caves in and agrees that, yes, in this or that special (hypothetical or genuine) case, we can reasonably predict worse overall consequences for society if we do not put convicted felons to death and instead keep them in prison until their natural death. Utilitarians can easily oppose most death penalty laws—and Beccaria, Bentham, Mill, and Sidney Hook did; but I doubt that any utilitarian (or pragmatist) can oppose such laws and their application in *all* cases.

Before moving on, we should notice that violent political radicals, such as Timothy McVeigh, present a very different problem from other kinds of murderers. No one seriously suggests that these other murderers if not executed are likely to become a rallying point for imitation. Thus, utilitarians have less reason to favor execution of the typical worst murderers, who are sociopaths, than they do the execution of dangerous ideologues, of whom McVeigh seems to have been one. J. S. Mill's parliamentary oration of 1868 in opposition to absolute abolition remains an instructive example of just such reasoning.[29] So does the careful review of the deterrent effect of the execution of Irish rebels in 1922 by the contemporary utilitarian philosopher Jonathan Glover.[30]

A minor chord in the theme discussed above emerged as the jury was deliberating McVeigh's sentence. Some in the public voiced their distress over the spectacle of McVeigh behind bars for life, spewing forth his perverse patriotism to the world over the Internet (as it was said the murderer Charles Manson has been doing from his prison cell in California).[31] As an argument for the death penalty, whether on utilitarian or other grounds, however, this worry seems singularly weak. Surely, an abuse of free speech fostered by excessively permissive prison regulations (if that is what Manson's behavior constitutes) does not have its only, much less its best, remedy in recourse to the death penalty.

Cruel and Unusual Punishment[32]   The Eighth Amendment in our Bill of Rights forbids "cruel and unusual punishment," and the Universal

Declaration of Human Rights similarly forbids "torture, cruel, inhumane, or degrading punishment." Most abolitionists regard the death penalty as a violation of these principles.[33] This is not the place to argue the point; let us suppose they are correct. Whence do these constitutional principles derive their authority? Why ought we to respect them, especially given the awful and boundlessly cruel nature of many crimes (especially those committed by the worst murderers)?

We can answer these questions in several ways. First, we might say we simply accept as intuitively sound the authority of these principles prohibiting cruelty; they are fundamental, nonderivative moral axioms governing our political thinking and our policy making. This answer will, of course, prove to have no persuasive effect on two groups of death penalty supporters: those who do not share this intuition in the first place; and those who do but who deny that these principles rule out the death penalty in all cases (especially if it is administered humanely and scrupulously).[34] Most of today's friends of the death penalty fall into the latter class. Few of them will seriously deny that we must accept some upper bound to permissible severity in punishment under law. But that still leaves considerable room for disagreement over just where to draw that upper bound—and in particular over which side of that boundary the death penalty falls.

Second, we might say that constitutional principles marking the upper bound of permissible severity in punishment are derived from something more fundamental. But what might that be? The value of human life, the right to life, the principle of greatest net social utility? Any route of derivation of the upper bound by appeal to a principle that rests on such foundations is likely to prove insufficient to protect all those guilty of the worst murder, as we have already seen.

Another strategy that may commend itself here is to consider whether a policy absolutely barring any death penalty on grounds of its cruelty, regardless of how that policy is administered, is one that a reasonably self-interested person would want adopted by society as a rational choice behind a veil of ignorance.[35] To decide this question requires us to take into account certain general facts about our society, chief among which is the fact that the risk for each of us of being convicted (guilty or innocent) of the worst murder, sentenced to death, and executed is almost certainly far less than is the risk of being a victim of the worst murder. But given these facts, this line of argument will prove to be a weapon in the hands of the friends of capital punishment, not of its opponents.

Of course, I have not exhausted all that moral reflection has to offer in defending a policy of absolute prohibition of the death penalty.[36] But perhaps I have said enough to cause some to conclude that absolute abolitionism is a policy insufficiently supported by sound moral principles (such as those reviewed above), reason, and experience. Those who believe this will view abolitionists as in the grip of an obsession against state authority to kill some prisoners and against exercising that authority in their names and on their behalf. This leads us to ask: Is it fair to impute stubborn irrationality and dogmatic sentimentality to those who are absolute abolitionists? I hope not, and I think not. There is another view to take of the prohibition against any killing as punishment, one that fastens on setting the upper bound of severity in punishment by reference to this question: Does the severity of the punishment under discussion exceed what is necessary to achieve whatever legitimate goals a system of punishment under law has in the first place? I think this question reorients the entire discussion in the right direction, and I now turn to the task of elaborating this perspective.

III

The argument I am about to present (and have mentioned in earlier chapters) is not an abstract or a priori argument (nor do I claim any originality for it), because it relies at several points on empirical generalizations about human behavior and our actual experience with abolition of the death penalty. Rather, the argument is consequentialist (without being utilitarian). Formulated in the context of American constitutional law, jurists would call it a "substantive due process" argument.[37] Political theorists will recognize its central principle as a familiar one in classic liberal political theory. The principle in question is that government must use "the least restrictive means to achieve a compelling state interest." In a somewhat fuller statement it can be formu-lated this way: Society, acting through the authority of its government, must not enact and enforce policies that impose more restrictive—invasive, harmful, violent—interference with human liberty, privacy, and autonomy than are absolutely necessary as the means to achieve legitimate and important social objectives. Anyone who takes this principle seriously, as I shall try to show, ought to oppose the death penalty in all cases because that penalty—at least in a society such as ours—violates this principle.

To reach that conclusion, one must accept the three propositions that constitute the argument. First, one must believe that the punish-ment of crime is a legitimate social objective, or (as I prefer) at least a necessary condition of achieving legitimate social objectives; otherwise, using severe sanctions and threatening serious deprivations in the name of punishment will not be warranted. Second, one must believe that the death penalty is much more severe, more invasive, less remediable, more violent than the usual alternative punishment, some form of long-term imprisonment. Third, one must believe that the death penalty is never necessary to achieve valid social objectives because other, less severe forms of punishment, such as constraints on an offender's liberty, privacy, and autonomy through long-term imprisonment, are sufficient.

These three propositions are of very different character. On what evidence and reasoning is each based? As to the first (punishment is a valid state objective), even opponents of current systems of imprison-ment agree that some form of punishment is appropriate for the gov-ernment to impose on convicted offenders, that the threat of punish-ment is an appropriate measure for society to use as a general deterrent, and that grave crimes call for severe punishment. Only the most radi-cally pacific opponents of the death penalty rest their opposition on a general repudiation of punishment under law. So the friends and the enemies of capital punishment ought to be able to agree on the first proposition.

They are likely to divide, however, on a neglected distinction in this context of some importance. Is punishment as such really a valid state objective? Does punishment (including the threat of punishment) for its own sake, quite apart from its consequences, constitute a goal or purpose of society? I suggest that it doesn't. I also suggest that punishment is generally thought to be a valid state objective because advocating punishment as a *means* to certain valid ends is confused with advocating punishment as an *end* in itself. The relevant and valid state objective is a society tolerably free of violent crime; so it is crime reduction, not punishment infliction, that ought to preoccupy our policy makers. If so, then severe punishment (including the threat thereof) is defensible only to the extent that it is necessary to that end. (On this point, utilitarians have always been correct.) Were other measures to suffice or be reasonably believed to suffice to control crime, punishment under law in a tolerably just constitutional democracy would immediately be put into question. It would be vulnerable to the objection that punishment serves no valid purpose and instead has become pointless cruelty.[38]

Retributivists, and especially retributivist friends of the death penalty, are certain to disagree, as their appeal to what they regard as the justly deserved punishment of criminals regardless of its costs testifies. How we are to resolve this disagreement rationally is not entirely clear; at the least, it would require an investigation into the adequacy of the retributive justification of punishment (about which I shall have a bit to say below).[39] As is true at prior stages of my argument, so here: I think the burden of argument falls on those who would defend punishment under law once it has been shown to be either futile or superfluous as an effective and necessary form of social control. At present, however, this issue is moot because society does not have at its disposal fully effective nonpunitive methods of social control, and so one cannot argue that punishment (including especially the credible threat thereof) is unnecessary.

As to the second proposition (death is a more severe punishment than long-term imprisonment), those in the best position to judge—prisoners on death row and prisoners under life sentence who were, or might have been, sentenced to death—show by their behavior that they overwhelmingly believe death is a worse punishment than prison. Very few death row prisoners dismiss their lawyers and reject appeals and clemency hearings;[40] very few death row prisoners try to commit suicide, and fewer still try until they succeed.[41] As for the judgment of others, defenders of capital punishment typically believe that it is both a better deterrent and a fitting retribution, because it is the more severe punishment of the two. Abolitionists also agree that death is the more severe punishment; few if any are on record favoring life in prison because the death penalty is not severe enough. So I suggest we agree about the relative severity of the two modes of punishment and accept the second of my three propositions.[42]

The third proposition (punishment by death is never necessary to achieve valid state objectives) is the one that is the most controversial. The argument for it must be an empirical one because the proposition itself is empirical. One source of disagreement here is lack of familiarity with the relevant evidence and unwillingness to accept the necessary inferences. (I shall ignore here the question of which side has the burden of argument and will proceed as if the abolitionist did.) The best version of the argument for this proposition goes like this: Anyone who studies the century and more of experience without the death penalty in American abolitionist jurisdictions must conclude that these jurisdictions have controlled criminal homicide and managed their criminal justice system, including their maximum security prisons with life-term violent offenders, at least as effectively as have neighboring death penalty jurisdictions. The public has not responded to abolition with riot and lynching; the police have not become habituated to excessive use of lethal force; prison guards, staff, and visitors are not at greater risk; surviving victims of murdered friends and loved ones have not found it more difficult to adjust to their grievous loss.[43]

If, in short, there is any argument for restoring the death penalty in America's abolition jurisdictions, it is not an argument rooted in the failures of long-term imprisonment as a general deterrent or incapacitation. It is not an argument from the insufficiency of retribution. It is not an argument from the destructive social behaviors inspired by abolition. And it is not an argument from the unmanageable dangers that a handful of the worst murderers present to public safety. So, what Michigan and Wisconsin did in abolishing the death penalty over a century ago, Ohio and Illinois could have done—and could do tomorrow if they wanted to. So could the rest of the nation.[44]

That completes the sketch of the general structure of the substantive due process argument against the death penalty; I think it carries the day.

IV

Die-hard friends of the death penalty can try to evade this conclusion in several ways. Perhaps the most obvious and attractive is to insist that the substantive due process argument is incomplete, because it ignores the role of revenge and retribution. Let us look more closely at this objection. "Revenge" and "retribution" are not synonyms, nor is the latter merely a euphemism for the former.[45] They can be deployed against my argument by defending either of two theses: (i) vicarious revenge is not only a legitimate motive, it is an essential motive, out of which the government ought to act in punishment generally and especially where the punishment of the worst murderers is in question; and (ii) the death penalty is the appropriate vehicle for retribution where murder is concerned and especially where the punishment of the worst murderers is in question. Attractive though some find these two propositions, I believe both ought to be rejected.

As to the second, anyone who is inclined to believe it must confront some unwelcome facts. First, it is worth noting that the criminal justice systems in many countries reject this appeal to retribution; or, if they accept the fittingness of death for murder, they have reasons for overriding this consideration, because they do not use the death penalty to punish any murderers.[46] Second, in our own country the vast majority (well over 90 percent) of all persons convicted of criminal homicide are never sentenced to death and executed.[47] Are we to infer that our prosecutors, juries, and judges are insufficiently retributive? It is more reasonable to infer that other considerations in practice overrule such retribution as only death is thought to provide. Third, on what basis do we attach any moral legitimacy to the idea that death is what murderers deserve, when we do not embrace (except in moments of extreme and thoughtless anger) the obvious parallels under the retributive principle that would require rapists to be raped, torturers to be tortured, and so on through the list of crimes and their matching retaliatory punishments? I suggest that the appeal to desert in order to decide how to punish murderers is largely a delusion; instead of constituting an appeal to a truly independent principle (a principle of retributive justice, presumably), asserting (5) *murderers deserve the death penalty* really differs only verbally from asserting (6) *murderers ought to be executed*, despite the fact that assertion (6) looks like the conclusion derivable from (5) as the premise.

As for the first proposition above (vicarious revenge is a legitimate motive for punishment under law), it too must be rejected. No reasonable liberal theory of constitutional government can accept the proposition that one of society's permanent, constitutional objectives is to punish the guilty by acting out of a motive of revenge.[48] Revenge is simply too untamed and volatile, too indifferent to the claims of justice to play a role in civilized society. The very idea of vicarious revenge as a motive for official punitive policy and its enforcement is frightening in its implications. Revenge may well be a motive out of which individual persons can and do sometimes act; as Nietzsche would have said, the thirst for revenge (and the desire to use punishment as a vehicle for revenge) is "all too human." But permitting, much less encouraging, officials to act out of vicarious revenge on behalf of society and the state is another matter entirely. More than two thousand years ago the *Oresteia* taught us to be wary of acting out of revenge, and so did the book of Genesis.[49]

Defenders of the death penalty might reject revenge as a motive and insist instead that they advocate only retribution.[50] Retribution is the form justice takes in punishment, and it is precisely what the criminal justice system is supposed to achieve. But (so the objection goes) since the substantive due process argument seems to ignore this, that argument is necessarily incomplete and inadequate.

By way of reply, it should be noted that any plausible system of punishment is retributive by its very nature; punishment aims to impose deprivations on all and only guilty convicted offenders because of their wrongdoing. So the proposition that offenders deserve to be punished (whatever else it is) is a truism of retributive justice.[51] But the issue here is what the punishment ought to be for a given offense—death, imprisonment, or something else altogether? Retributivists believe that the death penalty is necessary for retribution because it is the deserved punishment for some crimes. This requires that society can give practical effect to the idea of someone morally deserving to die as a punishment for his or her crimes. I stress moral desert, because retributivists obviously cannot be satisfied with desert as the law specifies it. One might well say that, of course, offenders deserve whatever punishment the law provides for the crimes of which they have been found guilty. But this trivializes the idea of desert because it has the consequence that in Michigan all convicted murderers deserve life imprisonment, whereas in Illinois some convicted murderers deserve death. Yet as soon as we leave the law behind and try to figure out what punishment a given offender morally deserves, we are out of our depth and caught in interminable disagreement. Instead, as I suggested earlier, invocation of desert in order to decide what ought to be the punishment for a given offender is really a delusion. At least in part it is fostered by the failure to keep clearly distinct the truism *that* offenders morally deserve to be punished from the unanswerable question of *what* they deserve as their punishment.[52]

I conclude from this brief investigation of revenge, retribution, and desert that the role of a system of punishment in a modern civilized society really is only as a means to the legitimate end of a society without criminal violence.

Let me restate some of the foregoing in another way. So long as we do not foolishly use a mere rebuke or a slap on the wrist as our considered punitive response to the convicted worst murderers, or employ any other mild sanction that amounts to an insult to the homicide victim, we are exacting retribution under law. Any suitable punishment lawfully meted out to those judged guilty is done in part at least as retribution. That is the nature of punishment in a constitutional democracy governed by liberal principles of justice.[53] But to try to go further and identify stable moral grounds on which to decide an offender's morally just deserts, seems to me an impossible task. The manifestly arbitrary nature of recent attempts to construct a penalty scale on grounds of moral desert confirms this judgment.[54] Thus, undermining the substantive due process argument against the death penalty by appeal to the role of retributive justice and morally deserved punishment seems to me a failure.

Another way to challenge the substantive due process argument is by attacking the empirical claim it makes, that is, by arguing that incapacitating the worst murderers by any punishment short of death cannot be reliably done. Here, too, I think the rebuttal fails. Keep in mind that we can identify a person as a worst murderer only *after* he has been arrested, tried, and convicted—and thus only after he has committed some terrible crime(s). We have no way to identify a worst murderer *prior* to his commiting the crimes that will make him a worst murderer. So we can classify him under that description only when he is (or only after he has been) securely in our custody and under our control. In principle at that point he is no more dangerous than any other offender behind bars with a history of prior violence.

At this point, the friends of the death penalty must ask themselves whether they advocate killing some convicted murderers because of the possibility that in the future they will become the worst killers. Does selective defense of the death penalty for these offenders really amount to endorsing executions as a preventive measure, and thus executing some convicted murderers not for what they have done but for what someone predicts they will (or could, or are likely to) do? (As an aside, is it fully appreciated that this is precisely what capital punishment in Texas involves, since every death sentence there rests on the trial jury's judgment that the convicted murderer constitutes "a continuing threat to society" because he or she would, if not executed, "commit criminal acts of violence"?)[55] Preventive *detention* (which in June 1997 received a strong endorsement from the Supreme Court)[56] may have its justifications. But preventive *execution* is another matter entirely. The argument for the death penalty for the worst murderers cannot be carried by nothing more than the bare assertion that incarceration is insufficient for public safety, because it can be made sufficient; the control of the worst convicted murderers in abolition states proves this. Nor can the argument be carried by pointing to existing cases of recidivist murder, since if such offenders could be identified before the fact while still in custody before they became recidivist killers, they could also be disabled in some lawful fashion well short of death and thus would not have become recidivists.

V

But the friends of the death penalty are not ready to throw in the towel, not yet. They will say, never mind that the worst murderers can be safely restrained; never mind that we cannot agree on which murderers deserve to die for their crimes; never mind that we cannot explain why any murderers morally deserve death rather than some lesser punishment. Leave all that to the side, and answer only this question: What possible *good* can come from not putting these offenders to death? What possible good could we obtain by running further risk from them, however slight? Why expend public resources on behalf of such persons when there are so many other productive uses to which those resources could be put?

The boldest way to address the first of these questions is to declare that it is not the right question and so does not need to be answered. Philosophers have argued for centuries that there is a fundamental difference between doing the *right* thing and bringing about *good* (better or best) results.[57] There is, in general, no easy way to connect the two concepts, and in the argument over absolute abolition we have a good example of their disconnection. Throughout, my argument has been that abolishing the death penalty for all offenders is the right policy, quite apart from whatever good it may achieve. On the view I have been defending, absolute abolition rather than any alternative follows from the fundamental principle on which I have relied (offical punishment policy ought to impose the minimal violence necessary to achieve its valid ends) when taken in conjunction with the best account of all the relevant facts. Asking for more than this in the argument against the death penalty is unreasonable.

Nevertheless, there are a few ancillary comments to be made in a last effort to make that argument more convincing.

First, the complaint about the expenditure of public resources on behalf of the worst citizens in our society—a complaint now often expressed in the angriest of language—is a red herring. For one thing, estimates of relative costs show that our current death penalty systems are far more expensive than systems in which long-term imprisonment is the severest sanction.[58] For another, the refusal to expend public resources to imprison the worst murderers for life instead of executing them opens the door to reducing or withdrawing entirely other resources in the criminal justice system because they, too, are spent on the indigent, the guilty, the undeserving. Setting our feet down that path is guaranteed to aggravate social problems rather than alleviate them.

Second, it is important to realize that the worst killers we are talking about are mostly sociopaths or psychopaths who belong under detention because they are dangerous both to others and to themselves. It may be that the best we can do for such offenders and for us is to imprison them for life, despite the fact that it is doubtful whether any sentence of punishment is morally appropriate in these cases. The picture of such offenders as autonomous rational serial, multiple, or recidivist killers is largely if not entirely a fictional portrait.[59] Timothy McVeigh may be the exception; he appears to have been no ordinary sociopath, and his responsibility for his terrorist act (assuming his guilt) was neither diminished nor in doubt.

Third, where recidivist murderers are concerned, the failure of our prison system (a failure that the public seems uninterested in trying to remedy) to tame if not reeducate them when they were in our custody spreads the responsibility onto the rest of society for the harm they later cause. We had them fully in our control, we knew they were dangerous, and we failed to take appropriate measures to protect others from falling prey to their violent intentions. This failure on our part to moralize and socialize them cannot simply be ignored when the time comes to assess their responsibility as recidivists.

Fourth, it is desirable to close the door tightly against state-sanctioned killing of prisoners, including the worst murderers, lest further exceptions worm their way through the crack and into the law. If, as I believe, liberals and conservatives alike accept the principle that government must not use more force than necessary to achieve society's legitimate objectives, then abolishing the death penalty for all crimes ought to have strong appeal. It is impossible to teach respect for human life by acts of unnecessary and to that extent unjustifiable lethal violence. But this is exactly what the death penalty represents. In no other area of government authority is it so easy to bring sanctioned violence to an immediate end as it is by abolishing outright the death penalty without exceptions.

Finally, such good as there is in not executing the worst murderers is the abstract and negative good of not doing the wrong thing—more precisely, not causing (or permitting others to cause) more harm to persons (in this case, offenders) than is necessary to accomplish legitimate social goals. This good is not lessened when it goes unappreciated by a convicted murderer who "volunteers" for execution or who commits suicide while on death row, or by those whose job it is to operate prisons efficiently and humanely, or by the angry and grieving survivors of the murder of a loved one. Nonetheless, as a society we are better when we act better, and we act better whenever we reject unnecessary lethal violence. We need to uproot the mentality of murder, especially when it is clothed in political authority, carried out under official auspices in cool detachment, and known to be unnecessary. As Albert Camus memorably wrote, let us try to live in a world without becoming either anyone's victim or anyone's executioner.[60]

EPILOGUE

I

Public interest in capital punishment thrives in part because of our susceptibility to the pornography of death—the murder and the grisly crime scene; the search for the fugitive; the arrest, trial, and sentencing (with all their flaws); the struggle of the accused to escape a death sentence; the usually futile appeals to higher courts; the perfunctory clemency hearing; the death watch; the clamor outside the prison walls; the execution itself; the disposal of the prisoner's body. The drama is even greater, of course, when there is reason to believe that the convicted prisoner is innocent.

Although a majority of Americans continue to favor the death penalty, as they have since 1967, the level of support has dropped from nearly 80 percent in 1994 to 66 percent as of February 2000. The chief factor in that drop seems to be public concern over the frightening possibility that innocent persons will be executed—a concern shared by supporters of capital punishment. A November 1998 conference in Chicago on wrongful death penalty convictions brought this issue sharply into focus. Organized by Professor Larry Marshall of Northwestern University Law School, the conference was attended by hundreds of students, lawyers, journalists, anti–death penalty activists, and ex–death row prisoners.

The most striking moment of the conference was an unprecedented public display in the main auditorium with 1,500 in attendance. Thirty men and one woman from several death penalty jurisdictions, each an exonerated death row inmate, walked one by one from the wings onto center stage. Each introduced himself, saying: "If the State of [Florida, Texas, Illinois, and so forth] had gotten its way, I'd be dead today." The unadorned eloquence of their message and their collective presence, as they stood shoulder to shoulder across the stage, was stunning. Here was personified and incontrovertible evidence of the worst failures of our criminal justice system—the worst, short of the actual execution of innocents.

Several of the most egregious cases were from Illinois and had received considerable publicity (local and national) before the conference opened. One was the case of Gary Gauger, sent to death row in 1994 for the murder of his parents and released two years later when it was established that the police had no reason to arrest him in the first place. The Gauger case and others in Illinois where first-degree murder convictions were overturned (thirteen between 1987 and 2000), as well as the publicity surrounding the Northwestern conference, helped to encourage Illinois Governor George Ryan two months later (in January 2000) to declare the nation's first moratorium on executions, pending reforms of the system to reduce the likelihood of more such errors. Two years later, after receiving the report of the special commission appointed to advise him on desirable reforms in death penalty jurisprudence, Ryan granted clemency to all of Illinois's death row prisoners: 4 outright pardons and 167 commutations of sentence from death to life in prison.

Procedural reforms in capital cases, of course, are not a guarantee against convicting and executing the innocent. But such reforms—pertaining to the conduct of investigations, admissible evidence, and greater support for defense attorneys in capital cases—can reduce the likelihood of such errors. The issue is not a new one. Reform proposals emerged as early as 1932, but few have been incorporated into American law. Congress made a first step in addressing this problem with the

Innocence Protection Act of 2001, championed by Senator Patrick Leahy of Vermont and cosponsored by two dozen senators and more than two hundred representatives. It focuses on providing routine DNA testing for death row inmates in the federal system. (As of this writing the bill is still in committee and its future is uncertain.) That bill, however, reflects only a small part of a movement and a growing body of literature that takes a new approach to death penalty reform and abolition.

II

This naturally leads us to inquire about recent proposed reforms aimed at reducing the likelihood of convicting the innocent. We now have at our disposal at least four independent sources of advice. Frequently recommended are two reforms: Obtain DNA evidence wherever possible, and exempt the mentally retarded from liability to a death sentence. This latter recommendation has become law under the Supreme Court's ruling in June 2002 in *Atkins v. Virginia*.

Professor James S. Liebman and his associates, authors of *A Broken System* (2000, 2002)—an outstanding piece of empirical research into the patterns of reversal of death penalty convictions and sentences—confined their reform recommendations to a modest ten. Although one of these—abolishing judicial override of the jury's sentencing decision—has become law, thanks to the Supreme Court's ruling in June 2002 in *Ring v. Arizona*, some of their other recommendations may have a longer and rougher road to adoption. These include requiring proof of guilt "beyond *any* doubt" in a capital case; insulating sentencing and appellate judges who deal with capital cases from "political pressure"; and increasing compensation for capital defense lawyers to provide incentives for "well-qualified lawyers" to do the work.

Mandatory Justice: Eighteen Reforms to the Death Penalty was released in 2001 by the Constitution Project, part of Georgetown University's Public Policy Institute. Among its recommendations are these four: Adopt a better standard for incompetence of defense counsel than is provided by *Strickland v. Washington*; enact life without parole (LWOP) as the alternative to the death sentence; conduct proportionality review of all capital convictions and sentences; treat the jury's "lingering doubt" over the defendant's guilt as a mitigating circumstance in the sentencing phase.

In their book, *Actual Innocence: Five Days to Execution and Other Dispatches from the Wrongly Convicted* (2000), attorneys Barry Scheck and Peter Neufield and journalist Jim Dwyer open with a reminder for their readers of the shockingly complacent remark of former Attorney General Edwin Meese III: "If a person is innocent of a crime, then he is not a suspect." They offer a list of forty proposed reforms. Seven would restrict the admissibility of eyewitness testimony. Fourteen others are devoted to controlling the evidence tendered by "jailhouse snitches." Another fourteen would constrain forensic laboratories and the use of their findings. Two of their proposed reforms would be relatively easy to implement: Use sequential rather than simultaneous presentation of suspects in police lineups, and videotape all interrogations.

The report of Governor Ryan's Commission on Capital Punishment (2002) has produced by far the greatest number of recommendations— no fewer than eighty-five. Nineteen are addressed to police and pretrial practices; the commission also joins Scheck et al. in endorsing video-taping of interrogations and favoring a sequential lineup. Seven of their recommendations address the role of forensic evidence, and of course they urge wider use of DNA testing. Prosecutorial selection of which homicide cases are to be tried as capital cases—one of the most troubling and unregulated areas in capital punishment jurisprudence—is the subject of three proposed reforms. Ten of the recommendations are aimed at overhauling pretrial proceedings, including the use by the prosecution of testimony by informants in custody (jailhouse snitches). The commission would not bar such testimony; instead, it would require that the defense be fully informed of the prosecution's intention to use such testimony, and that the uncorroborated testimony of such a witness "may not be the sole basis for imposition of a death penalty." The commission also agreed with Liebman et al. in favoring "adequate compensation" for trial counsel (although their Recomendation 80 is unfortunately unclear about comparable compensation for defense counsel in post-conviction litigation).

What are we to make of these 150 recommendations (some of which overlap with each other)? Could we imagine a high-level conference of lawyers and judges devoted to achieving a consensus on reform in which, say, fifteen or twenty of these proposals received unanimous endorsement? Could the Supreme Court be persuaded to adopt some if not all of these reforms, just as it adopted two new rules in *Ring* and *Atkins* in the spring of 2002? Could state legislatures and Congress take it upon themselves to enact some of these reforms, without waiting for the Supreme Court or a panel of distinguished jurists to act? We should have answers to these questions within the next few years. Perhaps one conclusion is already obvious. Friends of the death penalty can hardly complain if adopting these reforms narrows the range of death-eligible defendants and increases the economic cost of the entire system. By the same token, abolitionists can hardly complain if good-faith adoption of these reforms breathes new life into our current "broken" and deregulated death penalty system.

III

Miscarriages of justice in capital cases result in large part from the ill-equipped defense counsel available to defendants and the all-but-overwhelming burden placed on even the most talented lawyers in such cases (recall the discussion in Chapter 3). To appreciate the obstacles faced by defense counsel in a modern capital case, one cannot do better than to study *The Wrong Man* (2001), Michael Mello's account of a Florida death penalty case. Mello, now a professor at Vermont Law School, was a young public defender in Florida when the story began. In 1983, he became defense counsel on appeal for Joseph "Crazy Joe" Spaziano. Spaziano had been on Florida's death row since 1976, after being convicted of murdering one victim in 1973 and raping another in 1974; he would remain there for twenty years. During that time, five death warrants would be signed for his execution; each would eventually be vacated by court order. Today, Spaziano is still in prison, serving a sentence for rape; oddly enough, his conviction for that crime was based on the same testimony that, when later recanted, secured a reversal of his conviction for murder.

Mello gives the reader virtually a day-by-day account of his imaginative and relentless efforts on his client's behalf. The briefs drafted, the evidence presented to appellate courts, the race to meet filing deadlines, letters and memoranda, documents and journal entries—these, the detritus of the case, make up the bulk of the book. As Mello says, they acquaint the reader with "some of the chaos and uncertainty of daily life in deathwork." For anyone unfamiliar with modern death penalty cases, Mello's account provides a detailed and disturbing education.

The Spaziano case shows dramatically that convicted innocents are frequently vindicated not by the system but in spite of it. Crucial to getting Spaziano off death row was Mello's success in persuading editors at the *Miami Herald* to examine the case afresh. (Florida has an unenviable record of miscarriages of justice in capital cases, and the *Herald* staff has more than once established the innocence of a death row prisoner.) Spaziano had already been on the row for seven years and was facing execution in a few weeks when the *Herald* concluded that he was not guilty of murder. Only when the *Herald*'s investigation received nationwide publicity did the Florida authorities finally take notice.

Mello is no friend of the death penalty. But like several other volumes under discussion here, his book is not an argumentative brief against it either. Rather, as he explains,

> In this book I tell a story; I don't make an argument. This book is not a polemic on capital punishment; I use capital punishment as a frame of reference and as a window into how the human spirit responds to extreme circumstances. What interests me is not the moral issue of the death penalty, but the world of capital punishment as it exists as a legal system. Joe Spaziano's case is a microcosm of everything that is wrong with capital punishment as a legal institution: rogue cops, rabid prosecutors, inept defense lawyers, cowardly, tunnel-visioned judges, and politicians who play the politics of death with perfect pitch.

Whether Mello's book or other death penalty case narratives can supplant more sustained argument is doubtful, though such accounts undeniably provide indispensable supplements to more argumentative texts. They may be of particular importance in moving public opinion.

IV

Arbitrariness in sentencing is a second large problem that, along with execution of the innocent, plagues capital punishment. We gain some insight into the roots of such arbitrariness from what is perhaps the most important research project on the death penalty currently under way—the Capital Jury Project, initiated in 1990, funded by the National Science Foundation, under the direction of William J. Bowers at Northeastern University. Its purpose is to study why some capital trial juries award death sentences while others don't and whether these sentencing practices are reasonable under prevailing law. Over a thousand interviews with former jurors have so far established two principal findings: juries rarely understand the judge's instructions that are supposed to guide them in choosing between a death and a prison sentence, and when they do understand, they disregard those instructions in favor of their own predilections.

This research (by no means complete, with only fragments available in print in scattered law review articles) has also shown that jurors in capital trials are quite reluctant to take personal responsibility for sending the condemned prisoner to death. But if the trial jurors won't accept responsibility, who will? Psychiatrist Robert J. Lifton and his co-author Greg Mitchell searched for an answer and titled their book *Who Owns Death?* (2000). In the course of their inquiry they interviewed a wide variety of respondents, "scholars and activists, prosecutors and defense attorneys, religious figures . . . judges and jurors, murder victims' families, wardens and guards, and witnesses to executions." It turns out that jurors are not alone in shunning personal responsibility for the death sentences they impose: "No one feels responsible for the killing. Decision makers (prosecutors, judges, jurors, and governors) remain aloof from the execution itself as they ambivalently contemplate legal arguments or make judgments from afar while hands-on executioners simply 'do their job.' " As for the men and women on the execution teams who have the duty to carry out the death warrant, they are engaged in an unhealthy occupation. Lifton and Mitchell report that depression, anxiety, and psychic numbness often afflict the team members and occasionally result in an end to a career in corrections.

The authors also address the pursuit of "closure"—the alleviation of anger, frustration, and helplessness that the execution of the murderer is supposed to offer the victim's relatives. The desire for closure and the failure of an execution to achieve it were brought to public attention a few years ago in the book and film *Dead Man Walking*, by Sister Helen Prejean. Lifton and Mitchell agree. "Psychologically speaking," they write, " 'closure' is an illusion. Family members' sense of horror, pain, and loss may gradually diminish over time, but no outcome can enable them to be free of such feelings. They remain death-haunted survivors throughout their lives." In this connection, the authors mention the important work being done by Murder Victims Families for Reconciliation (MVFR), headquartered in Cambridge, Massachusetts, a national organization of survivors that offers extensive support and counseling services. The three pages devoted to the stories of MVFR members are among the most significant and constructive in the book; they address the questions of reparation and healing without fostering illusions of "closure" where none is to be had.

V

The death penalty is not simply a law on the books: it is part of a broader culture, and some of the most striking criticisms come from individuals deep inside the culture—from wardens who have had to supervise executions of which they did not approve to prison chaplains who had to provide spiritual comfort during a condemned man's last hours. Carroll Pickett, formerly a Texas prison chaplain, presents an intimate look at day-to-day life in the Death House of Huntsville in his book *Within These Walls* (2002). Not surprisingly, fifteen years of chaplaincy there (during which he attended ninety-five executions) have left their mark on him. "I am among those growing voices who believe it is time that lawmakers and peacekeepers, members of the greatest society in the world, come to the civilized realization that the cruel act of revenge—however cloaked in legal terms—nets us nothing and diminishes us all," writes Pickett. As for "closure," he echoes Lifton and Mitchell:

> In those dark early mornings following an execution, I spoke with the loved ones of crime victims—husbands and wives; mothers, fathers, and children—and almost without exception found that the feeling of relief so long anticipated was not realized. A death, however horrible and senseless, cannot be erased by another death, however quick and humane.

Pickett was in attendance at the December 1982 execution of Charles Brooks, Jr., the first in Texas after the nationwide moratorium on executions ended in 1977 with the death by firing squad of Gary Gilmore in Utah. Pickett devotes some two dozen pages to Brooks's story and his death by lethal injection, the first execution by that method in the nation.

> The execution had, as promised, taken only minutes—seven to be exact—and so far as I could tell, it had been as painless and as merciful as possible. As I stood there, I was vaguely aware of the witnesses quietly filing out. If there were tears, I did not see them; if there were sobs of grief, they did not reach my ears. All that remained was an air of stunned silence—testimony to the fact that none of those who had witnessed penal history being made had really been prepared for what they had seen.

To judge by the silence of the *New York Times*, which covered the execution, there was no significant protest marking the inauguration of this new "humane" way of death.

One perhaps expects prison chaplains to be against the death penalty, much as one expects a more ambiguous posture from most of the prison guards and officials who manage America's death rows and carry out our executions. The nature of that ambiguous response is evident in journalist Ivan Solotaroff's account of his visits to death rows in the "Death Belt" that stretches from Florida to Texas. Many writers have, like Pickett, chronicled life on death row, but none has done so with more patience and intimacy than Solotaroff. One of his interviews was with Donald Cabana, former warden of Mississippi's Parchman State Prison and supervising official there at the gas chamber execution of Edward Earl Johnson in 1987. Cabana, author of *Death at Midnight: The Confession of an Executioner* (1996), is one of those rare corrections officials who resigned his post largely because of moral scruples about his job.

In his book *The Last Face You'll Ever See* (2001), Solotaroff quotes Cabana on the issue of "who owns death" in a manner that recalls Lifton and Mitchell:

> I really don't know what the motive behind the penalty is, or who the *real* executioner is. . . . I teach criminal justice for a living, and I know that the penalty comes in watersheds and thresholds that politicians build and open, just on or about election day. You can call them your real executioners and get no argument from me, particularly in times like this, when everyone from the county courthouse to the White House wants to milk the law-and-order vote. And once you've done that, you can say: It's the people that elect them; that the yous and mes that pull the ballot box levers are the hands that pull the switch.

Like several of the other authors under discussion here, Solotaroff presents himself as neutral on the great moral issues raised by the death penalty. Early on in his book he states flatly that he has "made no attempt . . . in this book" to address the moral dilemma of capital punishment. But he later compromises this avowed neutrality: "Like mid-nineteenth-century slavery, [the death penalty] is rather our 'peculiar institution'—and . . . the will to enslave and the will to execute are either the same or remarkably similar." In the epilogue, Solotaroff stands back and concludes: "We execute to exert power over what horrifies us most supremely, and we execute imperfectly—randomly, cruelly, unusually—because murder itself seems exactly so to civilized eyes." One might well take issue with Solotaroff here; our "imperfect" executions are better explained not—as he explains them—by deliberate cruelty in executions, inspired by the cruelty of murders, but by the various forms in which society shields itself from too close an exposure to the realities of the death penalty culture.

Criticisms of that culture from insiders raise a question about the wider society: How firmly are we in the grip of a death penalty culture today? What are the prospects for a sea change in that culture? Austin Sarat, professor of political science at Amherst College, is not optimistic. In his recent book, *When the State Kills* (2001), he writes:

> Americans today live in a killing state in which violence is met with violence, and the measure of our sovereignty as a people is found in our ability both to make laws carrying the penalty of death and to translate those laws into a calm, bureaucratic bloodletting. . . . [T]he killing state will be a regular feature of the landscape of American politics for a long time to come.

The evidence certainly supports such a disheartening conclusion. Sarat's final judgment on the death penalty is equally uncompromising:

> [S]tate killing contributes to some of the most dangerous features of contemporary America. Among them are the substitution of a politics of revenge and resentment for sustained attention to the social problems responsible for so much violence today; . . . the erosion of basic legal protections and legal values in favor of short-term political expediency; the turning of state killing into an invisible . . . act.

These conclusions rest on an argument that begins by examining the case of Timothy McVeigh and the "demonization" of offenders. Sarat then turns to examine the victims' rights movement and the ambiguity of its motives: "Victim politics looks like vengeance pure and simple. Yet it is also a symptom of frustration and cynicism with our public institutions." Next he charts the crooked path from hanging to the electric chair (1888), to the gas chamber (1923), to lethal injection (1977), in society's search for a reliable method of "painless" and "humane" state killing. The middle chapters of the book are devoted to case histories that illustrate the badly flawed current administration of the death penalty and to the role that narratives of the capital defendant's life can play in presenting to the jury, during the sentencing phase of a capital trial, the human qualities of even the worst murderer.

In response to the question whether we should be allowed to watch an execution "live" on television, Sarat argues, as have many opponents of the death penalty, that "the survival of capital punishment in America depends, in part, on its relative invisibility." He believes that making executions "visible to a mass audience would as likely reveal the sadism that is at the heart of the state's tenacious attachment to capital punishment as reveal and invite the 'bad taste' of its viewers. For me the possibility of the former is well worth the risk of the latter."

Two demurrers. First, "sadism" is excessive. Sarat offers no evidence of sadism on the part of those who actually carry out executions (any more than Solotaroff and Pickett do). Second, I am less confident than he is about the public reaction to executions on television. Although a strong argument on First Amendment grounds can be made for permitting some form of public display of executions, it also seems likely that over time, such displays, viewed in the comfort of one's living room (or during the distractions of feeding the children their supper), will coarsen public taste and eventually have a numbing effect. Balancing the gains and losses to be expected from any manner of return to public executions by means of modern technology is not easy. In any case, no pictures of an execution are worth a thousand words of effective argument and analysis that explore and explain what precedes the event itself in the life of the prisoner.

VI

Thanks to the work of capital defense lawyers—several of whom (Stephen Bright, David Bruck, Bryan Stevenson, Ronald Tabak, Franklin Zimring, and especially Anthony Amsterdam) are well known through their lectures and writings—other lawyers and the law review–reading public have been thoroughly educated in the woefully unsatisfactory practices of the defense, the prosecution, and the judiciary in their handling of capital cases at trial and on appeal. This mismanagement, plus the overwhelming evidence that the part of the nation where a death penalty culture is most entrenched is in the southern states of the old "slaveocracy," has sparked interest in the connection between yesterday's unlawful lynchings and today's lawful executions. So far, however, to the best of my knowledge, the only published attempt to connect lynching and the death penalty is to be found in passing references by sociologists James W. Marquart, Sheldon Ekland-Olson, and Jonathan R. Sorenson in their monograph, *The Rope, the Chair, and the Needle: Capital Punishment in Texas, 1923–1990* (1994). Nowhere is the connection of the two practices more provocatively brought to public attention than in the title of the recent book *Legal Lynching: The Death Penalty and America's Future* (2001), by Jesse Jackson, his son Jesse, Jr., and journalist Bruce Shapiro.

Legal Lynching is a convenient vade mecum on the death penalty, descriptive as well as critical. The authors round up all the usual objections to death sentences and executions in a spirited manner—their racist administration, lack of superior marginal deterrence, risk of convicting the innocent, excessive costs, approval from misguided Supreme Court rulings, uncertain foundation in biblical writ, and the tenuous support of public opinion. Though it is a useful compendium of arguments, the book contains little or nothing that is new; the authors have relied heavily on compressing and digesting the writings of others, as their frequent quotations indicate.

Taken strictly, of course, "legal lynching" is an oxymoron, and it is tempting to dismiss the whole idea out of hand as a distorting exaggeration. But to do so would be a grave mistake. First, the mentality that once tolerated—indeed, demanded—lynching a century ago can be seen today in the mentality that tolerates—indeed, demands—continuation of our badly flawed death penalty system. Second, the states that historically were the sites of the most frequent lawless executions—lynchings—are also the states with the greatest frequency of lawful executions today.

Third, the complete disregard for due process of law and the rule of law manifest in a lynching survives in the indifference and disrespect for law as the instrument of justice to be found in many (most?) capital cases. Fourth, just as the paradigmatic lynchings in American history were carried out by white mobs on helpless black men as a popular racist method of ruthless social control, so the death penalty is to a troubling extent a socially approved practice of white-on-black violence, especially where the crimes involved are black male–on–white female. Fifth, many of those who opposed lynching in the South relied on the argument that the death penalty could do under cover of law what lynching did lawlessly—and the record of abandonment in capital cases of any but the thinnest pretense of due process proved the point. Sixth, in cases where a posse was formed to run down an accused with the intention of killing him on the spot, rather than taking him into custody for a trial later on, it is virtually impossible to tell whether such a killing should be judged murder by a mob or a summary execution. Finally, just as the defense of lynching a century ago was predicated on states' rights and vigorous resistance to federal interference with local self-government, the attack on federal habeas corpus for state capital defendants takes refuge, to some extent, in the same hostility to judicial intervention from Washington, D.C. (This is obscured by the Supreme Court's own inconsistent attempts to regulate the nation's death penalty system, which often puts judicial self-restraint, respect for federalism, and deference to the legislative branch ahead of substantive justice under the Bill of Rights.) One way to view the current moratorium movement, insofar as it is supported by those who seek to defend the death penalty, is to see it as the latest nationwide effort to erase the many disturbing parallels between the lynching practices of a century ago and the death penalty practices of our own day.

Possibly the most valuable contribution of the Jackon-Jackson-Shapiro book is its appendix. There we have the complete text of House Bill 1038, the National Death Penalty Moratorium Act of 2001, filed in Congress by the younger Jackson in March 2001. (His sponsorship of this bill puts him in tandem with Governor Ryan; both are from Illinois.) The bill lays out in thorough detail the structure of the argument in support of a national moratorium and the creation of a National Commission on the Death Penalty to review "the fairness of the imposition of capital punishment." (Back in 1980, at the end of President Carter's administration, Amnesty International and other anti–death penalty organizations took initial steps to obtain both a moratorium and a study commission, to be established in Carter's second term. But of course there was no such term.) The current mood of Congress is not friendly to such proposals, despite the overwhelming evidence accumulated over the past generation that shows the "new" (post-1972) American death penalty system to be a disgraceful mess.

VII

Moral criticism of the death penalty falls into two main categories. One category focuses on the well-known flaws in its actual administration, the social and political objections explored by the Jacksons. The other category responds to more abstract questions. At their root they ask this: Suppose all the administrative flaws in the death penalty were corrected, on what ground would you then oppose this punishment—or would you oppose it? Is the death penalty morally objectionable because it is "the same as murder"? Do we need executions in order to "show respect" for the murdered victims? Is capital punishment justified because "murderers deserve death"? Was the Supreme Court right in ruling that the death penalty is not a "cruel and unusual punishment"? Is the death penalty justified because it expresses a legitimate "desire for vengeance"? In his sustained, sharply focused, and well-informed critique of the death penalty, *An Eye for an Eye: The Immorality of Punishing by Death* (2001), Stephen Nathanson, a professor of philosophy at Northeastern University, gives each of these basic questions a thorough airing and concludes that none can be correctly answered in the affirmative.

This new edition of his book (first published in 1987) offers a philosopher's stalking horse for friends of the death penalty, a "knockdown argument" that he thinks trumps other arguments about the fate of this form of punishment. Addressed to a defender of the death penalty, the argument goes like this:

1. You accept justice and respect for human life as fundamental values.
2. The death penalty is inconsistent with these values.
3. Therefore, based on your own values, you ought to reject the death penalty.

The argument is certainly valid—if the premises are true, the conclusion is established. But are they true? Nathanson is well aware of how difficult it is to provide a knock-down philosophical argument on any question of social policy. In this instance, he seems to me to be obviously vulnerable to this counter-argument:

A. You (abolitionist) accept justice and respect for human life as fundamental values.
B. The death penalty is essential to uphold these values.
C. Therefore, based on your own values, you ought to accept the death penalty.

What is at issue, obviously, is the truth of the second premise in each argument. I happen to agree with Nathanson's defense of his argument; the evidence he marshals on behalf of both of his premises seems to me convincing. That evidence consists principally of the now-familiar truths about the maladministration of capital punishment, with no real improvements in sight (the relevant evidence can be found in the Jacksons' book). But resourceful defenders of the death penalty such as Walter Berns, Ernest van den Haag, Louis Pojman, and Tom Sorell are confident that "justice and respect for human life" are more coherently protected by policies based on their assumptions than on Nathanson's (or mine). Even if Nathanson fails to carry the day with his argument—and I do agree with the argument—he does focus the debate on the essential moral questions. Here, as elsewhere, we can use a formal argument as a tool of inquiry even if we can't use it as a bludgeon to finish off those who disagree.

VIII

Nathanson's book is the latest in a long line of moral criticisms of the death penalty. To be sure, in our day constitutional and political considerations have had an influence quite unlike their insignificant role in earlier centuries. Just the reverse is true regarding religious criticisms of the death penalty; even the best of these (such as the 1995 papal encyclical *Evangelium Vitae*) now rely heavily on empirical considerations regarding deterrence, racism, and miscarriages of justice. This contrast between the past and the present can now be seen with great clarity, thanks to U.C.L.A. law professor Stuart Banner and his comprehensive book, *The Death Penalty: An American History* (2002).

American historians have been slow to undertake anything like a full-scale study of the subject, comparable, for example, to what Richard Evans has done for the death penalty in Germany and Peter Linebaugh and V. A. C. Gatrell have done for the death penalty in England. As early as the 1940s, a scattering of articles began to appear in professional journals, providing us with bits and pieces of our history. In more recent years, Philip English Mackey, Louis Masur, and Michael Meltsner, among others, have told portions of the story at book length. But great gaps remained, and Banner's book does much to fill them. It is an important and comprehensive, even if not encyclopedic or flawless, treatment of the topic.

The essence of the story he tells is straightforward. The American abolition movement began with scattered protests against the death penalty by Quakers in the seventeenth century and by political leaders in post-Revolutionary Philadelphia. These protests led to widespread efforts in the first half of the nineteenth century to persuade state legislatures to end public executions, introduce the distinction between first- and second-degree murder, repeal all capital statutes except for first-degree murder, and give juries discretionary sentencing authority. Few of these efforts made much headway. As for complete abolition, it was confined to no more than a dozen or so states at any given time. The story in the South is quite different. There, the death penalty is rooted in popular culture, even to the present. As Banner notes,

> [M]ost of the northern debate over eliminating capital punishment completely was absent from the South. No committee of any antebellum southern state legislature recommended complete abolition. The issue was never part of any legislative agenda. . . . By the time of the Civil War the North had been through decades of debate over capital punishment. The South had not.

After the Civil War it was not until the Progressive Era that abolitionists made any headway; within a few years, eight states saw fit to end the death penalty. The great transformation in the struggle for abolition began in the 1950s, when the federal courts increased the frequency with which they reviewed state death penalty convictions and sentences. This led, in the 1970s, to what Banner calls "the constitutionalizing of capital punishment." During the subsequent three decades, as he points out, the Supreme Court has taken over the responsibility from the states and their courts and legislatures in order to manage the national death penalty system—refusing to abolish it entirely and willing to regulate it only sporadically. The result is our current deregulated system, deplored by friends and enemies of the death penalty alike.

What emerges from Banner's account is how disorganized, fragmentary, and impulsive the American struggle over the death penalty has been. But then, what else could we expect, given the federal nature of our government, the sovereign authority retained by the states to act or not as they see fit, and the hesitancy of the Supreme Court to intervene in the affairs of the states? Repeal of the death penalty has rarely been on the political agenda of the states and never on the national agenda of the federal government. (I learned from Banner, to my surprise, that President Roosevelt in 1933 said he "would like to see capital punishment abolished throughout this country"—a sentiment never publicly shared by any of his successors.) Save for the quarter-century struggle over the constitutionality of the death penalty (1963 to 1987), there has never been a national focus on abolition.

Banner's work addresses a variety of questions about the history of the death penalty in this country. For example: What were the rea-

sons the traditional mandatory death penalty gave way to jury sentencing discretion (death or prison)? What accounts for the steady decline in
death sentences and executions from 1940 to 1965? How private were
executions after they ceased to be carried out in public places? Where
and when have capital trial juries refused to convict because they could
not otherwise avoid a death sentence they thought undeserved? Were
politicians always as prominent in protecting and extending the death
penalty as they are now—and not only in the South? What accounts for
this politicization of the death penalty since the 1960s? Could the
Supreme Court have abolished capital punishment in 1972, instead
of rendering its temporizing decision in *Furman v. Georgia*? How, if
at all, is the death penalty in the South today connected with the erstwhile practice of lynching? Have the innocent not only been convicted
of capital crimes and sentenced to death, but also executed? Why have
some states abolished the death penalty, only to reinstate it—while
other states either never abolished it or never reinstated it? Have various reforms, such as the end to mandatory death penalties and the
adoption of "painless" and "humane" lethal injection, entrenched what
remains of capital punishment? Banner offers compelling and detailed
answers to many of these questions—answers that will reward anyone
who makes a close study of the book. On a few of the larger issues,
he seems to have ignored a significant amount of the published research. Though publications he neglects that I am aware of do not con-
tradict his conclusions, they do contain useful details that he leaves un-
mentioned. That cavil aside, Banner has done a prodigious amount of
research—especially on the eighteenth and nineteenth centuries—and
all subsequent historical studies on this subject will begin where he
left off.

It does not fall to Banner, of course, to suggest what the future will
hold for the death penalty in our country. But in the wake of September 11, with all the attendant concerns about security and our unde-
clared war on "the axis of evil," it is hard not to speculate. Does that
large-scale tragedy constitute a new baseline for the future of our death
penalty? Some signs are ominous. The Bush administration, right from
the start, seized on the threat of execution both as a deterrent and as
suitable retribution; the president also proposed placing this weapon in

the hands of special tribunals that would be created to deal with accused terrorists. Whether those kangaroo courts (if they ever come to
pass) or the regular federal courts will have recourse to the death
penalty remains to be seen, but it seems likely. Meanwhile, several
states (including three traditional abolition jurisdictions—Iowa, Rhode
Island, and Wisconsin) have drafted bills to make terrorism a capital
crime. We should not be surprised if many erstwhile opponents of the
death penalty now find themselves willing to make exceptions for per-
petrators of attacks like those of September 11. Some abolitionists re-
acted this way to the bombing of the Murrah Federal Building in Oklahoma City, for which Timothy McVeigh was executed in June 2001,
even though that disaster—grim as it was—pales by comparison with
September 11. Still, a politically minded abolitionist might say that
if the friends of the death penalty would be willing to confine its application to terrorist acts of mass murder, we abolitionists ought to be
able to live with that, provided all the other convicted murderers were
(re)sentenced to prison. It's not such a bad compromise because it
would empty our death rows of upwards of 99 percent of their current
occupants. Whether abolitionists will have this or some other compromise available only the future will tell.

If the past three decades of struggle over the future of capital punishment in this country have taught us anything, it is this: The appellants in *Gregg v. Georgia* (1976) were right and the Supreme Court was
wrong. The reforms enacted by state and federal legislatures in the
wake of *Furman* (1972) have turned out to be, to a disturbing extent,
merely cosmetic—precisely as the appellants said they were. Astute observers of the system argued even then that it was impossible to design
reforms that would be effective in bringing fairness into the death
penalty system and still serve rational grounds of deterrence, incapacitation, and retribution. Whether the death penalty system that would
be created if the new proposed reforms are enacted will prove to be
otherwise cannot be foretold. What can be predicted is that pressure
for complete abolition will not vanish or even subside.

In his concurring opinion in *Furman*, Justice Thurgood Marshall remarked that the American people have a very incomplete understanding
of the death penalty—its history and current practice—and that if they

were not so ignorant they would oppose it. In the thirty years since Marshall made that observation, abolitionists have often said that they have won the battle of words, even if they have yet to prevail in the courts, the legislatures, and the hearts and minds of the public. The nine volumes discussed here add much of value to the already burgeoning literature on the death penalty. Is it too much to hope that a future generation will seize on the moral, political, and constitutional objections to capital punishment and bring it to a long-overdue end?

NOTES

CHAPTER 2

1. New York Times, Jan. 6, 1993.
2. Boston Globe, Jan. 6, 1993.
3. Spokane Spokesman Review, Jan. 6, 1993.
4. Helen Prejean, Dead Man Walking, 214 (1993).
5. *Id.* at 226.
6. *Id.* at 235.
7. J. Germond and J. Witcover, Whose Broad Stripes and Bright Stars: The Trivial Pursuit of the Presidency (1988).
8. The [Village] Voice, Mar. 1992, at 2.
9. Austin-American Statesman, Dec. 14, 1976, at B-1.
10. Dallas Morning News, Jan. 5, 1977, editorial page.
11. Dallas Morning News, Jan. 6, 1977, at 1.
12. Boston Globe, Mar. 13, 1984, at 20.
13. W. M. Thackeray, *Going to See a Man Hanged* (1842), *reprinted in* The Death Penalty: A Literary and Historical Approach (E. G. McGehee and W. H. Hildebrand eds., 1964).
14. Nat Hentoff, *Execution in Your Living Room*, The Progressive 16–17 (Nov. 1991).
15. Boston Globe, Mar. 20, 1984, at 20.
16. *Supra* note 14.
17. *Supra* note 14.
18. David A. Kaplan, *Live, From San Quentin . . .* Newsweek, Apr. 1, 1991, at 61.
19. *Supra* note 18.
20. Michael Kroll, *I Oppose Existing Executions*, San Francisco Examiner, Mar. 22, 1991, at A-23.
21. Lockett v. Ohio, 438 U.S. 586, 604 (1978).
22. Booth v. Maryland, 482 U.S. 496, 502 (1987); *cf.* South Carolina v. Gathers, 490 U.S. 805, 810 (1989).
23. Payne v. Tennessee, 501 U.S. 808 (1991) at 814.
24. *Id.* at 826.
25. *Id.* at 822.
26. *Id.* at 834.

27. *Id.* at 856.

28. *Id.* at 844.

29. VIVIAN BERGER, *Payne and Suffering: A Personal Reflection and a Victim-Centered Critique*, 20 FLA. ST. U. L. REV. 21 (1992).

30. FRANKLIN ZIMRING & GORDON HAWKINS, CAPITAL PUNISHMENT AND THE AMERICAN AGENDA (1986).

CHAPTER 3

1. See American Bar Ass'n, *Whatever You Think About the Death Penalty, A System That Will Take Life Must First Give Justice: A Report from the IR&R Death Penalty Committee*, 24 W.T.R. HUM. RTS. 22 (1997).

2. *See id.* at 22–24.

3. *See* MICHAEL L. RADELET ET AL., IN SPITE OF INNOCENCE (1992) [hereinafter RADELET ET AL., INNOCENCE]; Hugo Adam Bedau & Michael L. Radelet, *Miscarriages of Justice in Potentially Capital Cases*, 40 STAN. L. REV. 21 (1987); Michael L. Radelet et al., *Prisoners Released from Death Rows Since 1970 Because of Doubts About Their Guilt*, 13 T.M. COOLEY L. REV. 907 (1996) [hereinafter Radelet et al., *Doubts*].

4. For a discussion of some recent research on the issue of wrongful convictions in capital cases, see the Epilogue.

5. *See, e.g.*, C. RONALD HUFF ET AL., CONVICTED BUT INNOCENT: WRONGFUL CONVICTION AND PUBLIC POLICY (1996); RADELET ET AL., INNOCENCE, *supra* note 3; Bedau & Radelet, *supra* note 3; Radelet et al., *Doubts, supra* note 3.

6. For example, see the case of William Henry Anderson, in RADELET ET AL., INNOCENCE, *supra* note 3, at 282. In a five-month period in 1945 in Ft. Lauderdale, Anderson, who was black, was arrested for rape, tried, found guilty, sentenced to death, and executed. Much evidence indicates that the relationship between Anderson and the "victim," who was white, was consensual.

7. *See* RADELET ET AL., INNOCENCE, *supra* note 3, at 269–70.

8. As far as we know, the last execution that was later officially acknowledged to have been in error occurred in Illinois in 1887, when four Haymarket defendants were hanged in Illinois. A fifth defendant took his own life on the eve of the scheduled executions. Six years later, Governor John Altgeld pardoned the three surviving codefendants because all eight "had been wrongfully convicted and were innocent of the crime. . . ." PAUL AVRICH, THE HAYMARKET TRAGEDY 423 (1984). On August 21, 1993, Governor Walter D. Miller formally apologized for the wrongful hanging of Thomas Egan in 1882. *See generally* C. JOHN EGAN, JR., DROP HIM TILL HE DIES (1994).

9. "Defendants are acquitted for many reasons, the least likely being innocence." Louis B. Schwartz, *"Innocence"—A Dialogue with Professor Sundby*, 41 HASTINGS L.J. 153, 154 (1989).

10. 1 STAFF OF THE SUBCOMM. ON DIV. AND CONST. RIGHTS, OF THE HOUSE COMM. ON THE JUDICIARY, 103D CONG., REPORT ON INNOCENCE AND THE DEATH PENALTY: ASSESSING THE DANGER OF MISTAKEN EXECUTIONS 13 (Subcomm. Print 1993).

11. Our most recent work extends those parameters slightly by including three cases in which the defendant, initially sentenced to death, was later able to show that the homicide was committed in self-defense. *See* Radelet et al., *Doubts, supra* note 3, at 912.

12. *See* Michael L. Radelet & Barbara A. Zsembik, *Executive Clemency in Post-*Furman *Capital Cases*, 27 U. RICH. L. REV. 289, 309 (1993).

13. *See* Radelet et al., *Doubts, supra* note 3, at 933–34.

14. *See id.* at 948.

15. *See, e.g.*, Stephen B. Bright, *Counsel for the Poor: The Death Sentence Not for the Worst Crime but for the Worst Lawyer*, 103 YALE L.J. 1835 (1994) [hereinafter Bright 1994]; Stephen B. Bright, *In Defense of Life: Enforcing the Bill of Rights on Behalf of Poor, Minority and Disadvantaged Persons Facing the Death Penalty*, 57 MO. L. REV. 849 (1992) [hereinafter Bright 1992]; Stephen B. Bright, *The Politics of Crime and the Death Penalty: Not "Soft on Crime," but Hard on the Bill of Rights*, 39 ST. LOUIS U. L.J. 479 (1995) [hereinafter Bright 1995].

16. *See* Fred W. Friendly, *A Crime and Its Aftershock*, N.Y. TIMES MAG., Mar. 21, 1976, at 16.

17. *See Man Guilty of Oklahoma Murders; Defendant in Nebraska Acquitted*, N.Y. TIMES, Oct. 18, 1979, at 16.

18. Rick Bragg, *A Killer Racked by Delusions Dies in Alabama's Electric Chair*, N.Y. TIMES, May 13, 1995, at A7.

19. Andrew L. Shapiro, *An Insane Execution*, N.Y. TIMES, May 11, 1995, at A29.

20. *See* KENT S. MILLER & MICHAEL L. RADELET, EXECUTING THE MENTALLY ILL (1993); Dorothy Otnow Lewis et al., *Psychiatric, Neurological, and Psychoeducational Characteristics of 15 Death Row Inmates in the United States*, 143 AM. J. PSYCHIATRY 838 (1986).

21. CHARLES L. BLACK, JR., CAPITAL PUNISHMENT: THE INEVITABILITY OF CAPRICE AND MISTAKE 17–18 (2d ed. 1981).

22. *See* DAVID C. BALDUS ET AL., EQUAL JUSTICE AND THE DEATH PENALTY: A LEGAL AND EMPIRICAL ANALYSIS 22 & n.* (1990).

23. *See* Michael L. Radelet & Glenn L. Pierce, *Choosing Those Who Will Die: Race and the Death Penalty in Florida*, 43 FLA. L. REV. 1, 20 (1991).

24. *See* Michael Mello, *On Metaphors, Mirrors, and Murders: Theodore Bundy and the Rule of Law*, 18 N.Y.U. REV. L. & SOC. CHANGE 887, 900 (1990–91).

25. *See* Kenneth B. Noble, *Prosecutor in Simpson Case Won't Seek Death Penalty*, N.Y. TIMES, Sept. 10, 1994, at A6.

26. He later recanted and said his sister had actually died from choking on food.

27. Dobbert v. Wainwright, 468 U.S. 1231, 1246 (1984).

28. *See* GEN. GOV'T DIV., U.S. GEN. ACCOUNTING OFFICE, REP. GGD-90-57, DEATH PENALTY SENTENCING: RESEARCH INDICATES PATTERN OF RACIAL DISPARITIES (Feb. 26, 1990); AMNESTY INTERNATIONAL U.S.A, THE MACHINERY OF DEATH: A SHOCKING INDICTMENT OF CAPITAL PUNISHMENT IN THE UNITED STATES (1995); BALDUS ET AL., *supra* note 22; HUGO ADAM BEDAU, THE CASE AGAINST THE DEATH PENALTY 11–16 (1997); INTERNATIONAL COMMISSION OF JURISTS, ADMINISTRATION OF THE DEATH PENALTY IN THE UNITED STATES: REPORT OF A MISSION (1996); David C. Baldus & George Woodworth, *Race Discrimination and the Death Penalty: An Empirical and Legal Overview, in* AMERICA'S EXPERIMENT WITH CAPITAL PUNISHMENT: REFLECTIONS ON THE PAST, PRESENT, AND FU-

TURE OF THE ULTIMATE PENAL SANCTION 385 (James R. Acker et al. eds., 1998); Bright 1994, *supra* note 15.

29. *See generally* Bright 1995, *supra* note 15; Bright 1994, *supra* note 15; Bright 1992, *supra* note 15.

30. *See* Radelet & Pierce, *supra* note 23, at 21.

31. *See* BALDUS ET AL., *Supra* note 22; SAMUEL R. GROSS & ROBERT MAURO, DEATH AND DISCRIMINATION: RACIAL DISPARITIES IN CAPITAL SENTENCING (1989).

32. *See* Radelet & Pierce, *supra* note 23, at 28.

33. William S. Geimer & Jonathan Amsterdam, *Why Jurors Vote Life or Death: Operative Factors in Ten Florida Death Penalty Cases*, 15 AM. J. CRIM. L. 1, 28 (1987–88).

34. *See* Michael L. Radelet et al., *Families, Prisons, and Men with Death Sentences: The Human Impact of Structured Uncertainty*, 4 J. FAM. ISSUES 593 (1983); Margaret Vandiver, *The Impact of the Death Penalty on the Families of Homicide Victims and of Condemned Prisoners, in* AMERICA'S EXPERIMENT WITH CAPITAL PUNISHMENT, *supra* note 28, at 477.

35. *See* Phoebe C. Ellsworth & Samuel R. Gross, *Hardening of the Attitudes: Americans' Views on the Death Penalty*, 50 J. SOC. ISSUES 19 (1994), *reprinted in* THE DEATH PENALTY IN AMERICA: CURRENT CONTROVERSIES 90, 95–98 (Hugo Adam Bedau ed., 1997).

36. *See* David Margolick, *25 Wrongfully Executed in U.S., Study Finds*, N.Y. TIMES, Nov. 14, 1985, at A19.

37. In the 1972 case of *Furman v. Georgia*, 408 U.S. 238, the Supreme Court (in effect) invalidated all existing death penalty statutes in the United States. Thereafter, states drew up new capital laws and procedures, making *Furman* the demarcation of the "modern" era of the death penalty in the United States.

38. *See* Carl J. Seneker, *Governor Reagan and Executive Clemency*, 55 CAL. L. REV. 412 (1967).

39. *See* Stephen J. Markman & Paul G. Cassell, *Protecting the Innocent: A Response to the Bedau-Radelet Study*, 41 STAN. L. REV. 121 (1988); *see also* Hugo Adam Bedau & Michael L. Radelet, *The Myth of Infallibility: A Reply to Markman and Cassell*, 41 STAN. L. REV. 161 (1988).

40. Two other similar distortions of academic scholarship on the death penalty deserve mention. In 1975, when Solicitor General Robert Bork submitted an *amicus* brief in *Fowler v. North Carolina*, 428 U.S. 904 (1976), he asserted that all research that concluded the death penalty had no deterrent effect was severely flawed, and that the research of Isaac Ehrlich, which found that each execution deterred seven murders, provided "a reliable basis for judging whether the death penalty has a deterrent effect." David C. Baldus & James W. L. Cole, *A Comparison of the Work of Thorsten Sellin and Isaac Ehrlich on the Deterrent Effect of Capital Punishment*, 85 YALE L.J. 170 (1975). The inadequacies and inconclusiveness of Ehrlich's research have been extensively demonstrated. *See, e.g.,* William C. Bailey & Ruth D. Peterson, *Murder, Capital Punishment, and Deterrence: A Review of the Literature, in* THE DEATH PENALTY IN AMERICA, *supra* note 35, at 135, 141–43; Ruth D. Peterson & William C. Bailey, *Is Capital Punishment an Effective Deterrent for Murder? An Examination of Social Science Research, in* AMERICA'S EXPERIMENT WITH CAPITAL PUNISHMENT, *supra* note 28, at 157, 165–66. In 1972, Henry Peterson, an assistant attorney general in the Nixon administration, testified before Congress to the effect that a "study" by the ABA showed that the death penalty was an effective deterrent. No such

ABA study existed. *See* Hugo Adam Bedau, *The Nixon Administration and the Deterrent Effect of the Death Penalty*, 34 U. PITT. L. REV. 557 (1973).

41. *See, e.g.*, Wendy Kaminer, *The Wrong Men*, ATLANTIC, Dec. 1992, at 147; Lawrence C. Marshall, *Book Review*, 85 J. CRIM. L. & CRIMINOLOGY 261 (1994).

42. *See* Stephen J. Markman, *Innocents on Death Row?*, NAT'L REV., Sept. 12, 1994, at 72.

43. Callins v. Collins, 510 U.S. 1141, 1145 (1994) (Blackmun, J., dissenting from denial of *certiorari* to Callins v. Collins, 998 F.2d 269 [5th Cir. 1993]).

44. *See* Jenny Staletovich, *Justice Raising Voice to Bury Death Penalty*, PALM BEACH POST, Jan. 19, 1998, at A1, A8. Kogan is the former chief of the capital crimes unit for the Dade County State Attorney's Office.

45. "[W]e have found no instance in which the government has officially acknowledged that an execution carried out under lawful authority was in error." Bedau & Radelet, *supra* note 3, at 25.

46. In an extremely important article, Professor Samuel Gross argued that both the probability of erroneous conviction and the odds of erroneous convictions being ignored by appellate courts and clemency officials are higher in capital than in noncapital cases. *See* Samuel R. Gross, *The Risks of Death: Why Erroneous Convictions Are Common in Capital Cases*, 44 BUFF. L. REV. 469 (1996).

47. *See* Ellen McGarrahan, *3 Jolts Used to Execute Killer*, MIAMI HERALD, May 5, 1990, at A1.

48. *See* Jacobs v. Singletary, 952 F.2d 1282 (11th Cir. 1992).

49. The made-for-television show was entitled *In the Blink of an Eye*, and aired in the spring of 1996.

50. *See, e.g.*, Cynthia Barnett, *New Evidence Might Have Spared Killer*, GAINESVILLE SUN (Fla.), Nov. 21, 1992, at A1.

51. For an excellent discussion of why American criminal procedures do not protect the innocent from erroneous conviction, see Daniel Givelber, *Meaningless Acquittals, Meaningful Convictions: Do We Reliably Acquit the Innocent?*, 49 RUTGERS L. REV. 1317, 1358–93 (1997).

52. Radelet et al., *Doubts, supra* note 3. A later report based on our research was issued by the Death Penalty Information Center. *See* DEATH PENALTY INFORMATION CENTER, INNOCENCE AND THE DEATH PENALTY: THE INCREASING DANGER OF EXECUTING THE INNOCENT (1997). This report received extensive national and international publicity. *See, e.g.*, Terry Carter, *Numbers Tell the Story*, 83 A.B.A.J. 20 (Oct. 1997).

53. *See* Carter, *supra* note 52, at 20.

54. *See* RADELET ET AL., INNOCENCE, *supra* note 3, at 67–69.

55. *See* Radelet et al., *Doubts, supra* note 3, at 950–51.

56. *See* RADELET ET AL., INNOCENCE, *supra* note 3, at 318.

57. For two dozen cases in which innocent prisoners came to within seventy-two hours of executions, see *id.* at 276; Bedau & Radelet, *supra* note 3, at 72.

58. On July 1, 2002, the exact number of prisoners on America's death rows stood at 3,718. *See* NAACP LEGAL DEFENSE & EDUCATIONAL FUND, DEATH ROW U.S.A., Summer 2002, at 1.

59. *See generally* Markman & Cassell, *supra* note 39.

60. *See* RADELET ET AL., INNOCENCE, *supra* note 3, at 176–88.

61. *See id.* at 23–39.

62. *See id.* at 326.

63. *See* Radelet et al., *Doubts, supra* note 3, at 926–27.

64. *See* Schlup v. Delo, 513 U.S. 298 (1995).

65. *See id.* at 313 n.27.

66. *See* Don Terry, *Despite New Evidence, a Prisoner Faces Death*, N.Y. Times, Nov. 15, 1993, at A12.

67. *See Schlup*, 513 U.S. at 298.

68. *Id.*

69. *See* Daniel T. Kobil, *The Evolving Role of Clemency in Capital Cases, in* America's Experiment with Capital Punishment, *supra* note 28, at 531.

70. *See* Radelet & Zsembik, *supra* note 12, at 297–99; *cf.* Hugo Adam Bedau, *The Decline of Executive Clemency in Capital Cases*, 18 N.Y.U. Rev. L. & Soc. Change 255, 263 (1990–91). These two sources cite different commutation totals for the years in question because I relied upon adjusted Bureau of Justice Statistics (which include some appellate court-ordered resentencing), whereas Radelet and Zsembik's more accurate figures were derived from examining records of all death sentences imposed in the United States since 1972 (primarily in the files of the NAACP Legal Defense Fund).

71. *See* Radelet & Zsembik, *supra* note 12, at 300. Since this research was published, four more death row inmates have had their sentences commuted to life imprisonment because of doubts about guilt: Earl Washington, Jr. (Virginia, Jan. 15, 1994), Don Paradis (Idaho, May 24, 1996), Joseph Payne (Virginia, Nov. 7, 1996), and Henry Lee Lucas (Texas, June 26, 1998).

72. *See id.* at 313.

73. *See* John Dvorak, *Kansas Approves Death Penalty After 22 Years; Governor Says She Won't Fight Law*, Times-Picayune (New Orleans), Apr. 9, 1994, at A15.

74. *See* James Dao, *Death Penalty in New York Reinstated After 18 Years; Pataki Sees Justice Served*, N.Y. Times, Mar. 8, 1995, at A1.

75. *See* Adrian Walker & Doris Sue Wong, *No Death Penalty, by One Vote*, Boston Globe, Nov. 7, 1997, at 1.

76. *See generally* Radelet et al., Innocence, *supra* note 3, at 282–358; Marty I. Rosenbaum, *Inevitable Error: Wrongful New York State Homicide Convictions, 1965–1988*, 18 N.Y.U. Rev. L. & Soc. Change 807 (1990–91).

77. *See* N.Y. Correct. Law §§ 650–662 (McKinney Supp. 1997).

78. *See* Ian Fisher, *The 1994 Campaign: Clamor over Death Penalty Dominates Debate on Crime*, N.Y. Times, Oct. 9, 1994, at A45.

79. *See* Elkan Abramowitz & David Paget, *Executive Clemency in Capital Cases*, 39 N.Y.U. L. Rev. 136, 170 (1964).

80. *See* Lis Wiehl, *A Program for Death-Row Appeals Is Facing Elimination*, N.Y. Times, Aug. 11, 1995, at B16.

81. Pub. L. No. 104–132, §§ 101–8, 110 Stat. 1214, 1217–26 (codified at 28 U.S.C. §§ 2244–2266 [Supp. II 1996]).

82. *See* Marcia Coyle, *Law: Innocent Dead Men Walking?*, Nat'l L.J., May 20, 1996, at 1; Ronald J. Tabak, *Habeas Corpus as a Crucial Protector of Constitutional Rights: A Tribute Which May Also Be a Eulogy*, 26 Seton Hall L. Rev. 1477 (1996); Ronald J. Tabak, *Panel Discussion: Capital Punishment: Is There Any Habeas Left in This Corpus?*, 27 Loy. U. Chi. L.J. 523, 538 n.119 (1996); Panel Discussion, *Dead Man Walking Without Due Process? A*

Discussion of the Anti-Terrorism and Effective Death Penalty Act of 1996, 23 N.Y.U. REV. L. & SOC. CHANGE 163 (1997) (remarks of Ronald J. Tabak, moderator).

83. Alex Gallup & Frank Newport, *Death Penalty Support Remains Strong*, 309 GALLUP POLL MONTHLY 40, 42 (June 1991).

84. *See id.*

85. Among those executed in recent years despite doubts about their guilt are James Adams (Florida, May 10, 1984), Edward Earl Johnson (Mississippi, May 20, 1987), Jimmy Wingo (Louisiana, June 16, 1987), Willie Darden (Florida, Mar. 15, 1988), Roger Keith Coleman (Virginia, May 20, 1992), Leonel Herrera (Texas, May 12, 1993), Jesse DeWayne Jacobs (Texas, Jan. 4, 1995), and David Wayne Spence (Texas, Apr. 3, 1997).

86. *See* Furman v. Georgia, 408 U.S. 238, 360–63 (1972) (Marshall, J., concurring).

87. *But see* Robert M. Bohm, *American Death Penalty Opinion: Past, Present, and Future, in* AMERICA'S EXPERIMENT WITH CAPITAL PUNISHMENT, *supra* note 28, at 25, 31–41; Robert M. Bohm et al., *Knowledge and Death Penalty Opinion: A Test of the Marshall Hypothesis*, 28 J. RES. CRIME & DELINQ. 360 (1991); Austin Sarat & Neil Vidmar, *Public Opinion, the Death Penalty, and the Eighth Amendment: Testing the Marshall Hypothesis*, 1976 WIS. L. REV. 171.

88. *See* Michael L. Radelet, *Sociologists as Expert Witnesses in Capital Cases: A Case Study, in* EXPERT WITNESSES: CRIMINOLOGISTS IN THE COURTROOM 119, 127–31 (Patrick R. Anderson & L. Thomas Winfree, Jr., eds., 1987).

89. *See generally* American Bar Ass'n, *supra* note 1.

90. *American Bar Ass'n*, Section of Individual Rights and Responsibilities, *Toward Greater Awareness: The American Bar Association Call for a Moratorium on Executions Gains Ground* 55, 99 (Aug. 2001).

91. The Moratorium Campaign newsletter (summer 2001).

92. For a discussion of America's ambivalence about the death penalty, see Franklin E. Zimring, *Ambivalence in State Capital Punishment Policy: An Empirical Sounding*, 18 N.Y.U. REV. L. & SOC. CHANGE 729 (1990–91).

93. *See* Rex L. Carter, *Letter to the Editor*, HOUSTON POST, Nov. 13, 1994, at C2.

94. *See Ex parte* Gary Graham, 853 S.W.2d 565 (Tex. Crim. App. 1993).

95. *See* Susan Blaustein, *The Executioner's Wrong: Texas Will Execute Gary Graham for a Murder He Almost Certainly Didn't Commit*, WASH. POST, Aug. 1, 1993, at C1.

96. Carter, *supra* note 93.

97. We are reminded of the scene in *Dr. Strangelove* in which Joint Chief of Staff Chairman General Buck Turgidson (played by George C. Scott) tells the president (Peter Sellars) that a forty-megaton nuclear bomb is about to be dropped in error on a target in Russia:

> President: General Turgidson, when you instituted the human reliability tests you assured me there was no possibility of such a thing ever occurring.
>
> General Turgidson: Well, ahh, I don't think it's quite fair to condemn the whole program because of a single slipup.

Dr. Strangelove or: How I Learned to Stop Worrying and Love the Bomb (Columbia 1964).

98. *See* Sam Howe Verhovek, *When Justice Shows Its Darker Side*, N.Y. TIMES, Jan. 8, 1995, at D6.

99. *See id.*

100. Ernest van den Haag, *Why Capital Punishment?*, 54 ALBANY L. REV. 501, 512 (1990).

101. *See generally* THE DEATH PENALTY IN AMERICA, *supra* note 35, at 95–98; BEDAU, *supra* note 28.

102. *See* Radelet et al., *Doubts, supra* note 3, at 271–81.

CHAPTER 4

1. *Matthew* 27:15–26; *Mark* 15:6–15; *Luke* 23:13–25; *John* 18:28–40.

2. *Mark* 15:6–15. For further discussion of the crucifixion of Jesus, see S. BRANDON, THE TRIAL OF JESUS OF NAZARETH (1968), and W. WILSON, THE EXECUTION OF JESUS (1970).

3. P. LAGERKVIST, BARABBAS (A. Blair trans., 1951).

4. Address by former New York State Senator James Donovan (Apr. 7, 1978), *quoted in* H. BEDAU, THE DEATH PENALTY IN AMERICA 305 n.1 (3d ed. 1982).

5. *Genesis* 4:1–16.

6. For a general discussion of the history of executive clemency, see Ringold, *The Dynamics of Executive Clemency*, 52 A.B.A. J. 240 (Mar. 1966), *reprinted in* T. SELLIN, CAPITAL PUNISHMENT 226, 236 (1967). *See also* Note, *Executive Clemency in Capital Cases*, 39 N.Y.U. L. REV. 136 (1964).

7. NATIONAL INSTITUTE OF CORRECTIONS, U.S. DEP'T OF JUSTICE GUIDE TO EXECUTIVE CLEMENCY AMONG THE AMERICAN STATES (1988) [hereinafter DEP'T OF JUSTICE GUIDE]. Unfortunately, no special section is devoted to clemency in capital as opposed to other cases, nor is there any index to the legal provisions governing this aspect of the topic.

8. NAACP LEGAL DEFENSE AND EDUCATIONAL FUND, INC., DEATH ROW U.S.A. 1 (July 2002) (reporting 3,718 persons on death rows of two federal and thirty-seven state jurisdictions).

9. Note, *Reviving Mercy in the Structure of Capital Punishment*, 99 YALE L.J. 389, 392 n.16 (1989) ("governors (as opposed to pardon boards) have the final clemency discretion in 22 of the 37 death penalty states," eleven states require concurrence of another body with the governor, and the remaining four death penalty states vest the entire power in a board of pardons).

10. *See* Leavy, *A Matter of Life and Death: Due Process Protection in Capital Clemency Proceedings*, 90 YALE L.J. 889, 891 (1981).

11. *Id.* at 893–94.

12. Rockefeller, *Executive Clemency and the Death Penalty*, 21 CATH. U.L. REV. 94, 96 (1971).

13. K. MOORE, PARDONS: JUSTICE, MERCY, AND THE PUBLIC INTEREST (1989).

14. *Id.* at 50, 51, 132, 193, 212.

15. Note, *supra* note 6, at 177; *see also* K. MOORE, *supra* note 13, at 50, 193.

16. Ringold, *supra* note 6, at 236.

17. United States v. Wilson, 32 U.S. (7 Pet.) 150 (1833).

18. *Id.* at 160.

19. Rockefeller, *supra* note 12, at 95.

20. *Ex parte* Grossman, 267 U.S. 87, 120–21 (1925).

21. K. MOORE, *supra* note 13.

22. *See* M. Gardner, *The Renaissance of Retribution—An Examination of Doing Justice*, 1976 WIS. L. REV. 781; F. Kellog, *From Retribution to Desert: The Evolution of Criminal Punishment*, 15 CRIMINOLOGY 179 (1977); *Symposium: The New Retributivism*, 75 J. PHIL. 601 (1978).

23. K. MOORE, *supra* note 13, at 9.

24. *Id.* at 89.

25. *Id.* at 199 (emphasis in original).

26. For an example of commutation as an act of free grace, see the story of the commutations granted by Governor Coleman Blease in 1912 in South Carolina, as reported in K. MOORE, *supra* note 13, at 3. For an example of commutation for special reasons, see Rockefeller, *supra* note 12, and for an example of commutation as retribution (even though not described that way), *see* Commutation Statement of Governor Robert Meyner in New Jersey in 1960, *reprinted in* Bedau, *Death Sentences in New Jersey 1907–1960*, 19 RUTGERS L. REV. 1, 54–55 (1964) [hereinafter *Death in New Jersey*].

27. Moore is sympathetic to such a development. *See* K. MOORE, *supra* note 13, at 175–77, 223.

28. *See* Reiman, *Justice, Civilization, and the Death Penalty: Answering van den Haag*, 14 PHIL. & PUB. AFF. 115 (1985); Pugsley, *A Retributivist Argument Against Capital Punishment*, 9 HOFSTRA L. REV. 1501 (1981). I am not persuaded that the retributive critique of the death penalty is the best critique; *see* Chapters 6–9 and H. BEDAU, DEATH IS DIFFERENT: STUDIES IN THE MORALITY, LAW, AND POLITICS OF CAPITAL PUNISHMENT 38–42, 55–63 (1987) [hereinafter DEATH IS DIFFERENT].

29. The authors of Note, *supra* note 6, at 159–77, list thirteen different reasons, but make no attempt to assess the relative frequency with which each is cited in the commutation statements examined. For the results of a recent survey citing reasons for commutation in capital, and non-capital, cases see DEP'T OF JUSTICE GUIDE, *supra* note 7, at 169 (table 5).

30. Bedau & Radelet, *Miscarriages of Justice in Potentially Capital Cases*, 40 STAN. L. REV. 21, 139–40 (1987).

31. F. STRAUSS, WHERE DID THE JUSTICE GO? viii (1970); *see also* Bedau & Radelet, *supra* note 30, at 117–18.

32. *Death in New Jersey*, *supra* note 26, at 54–55.

33. Bedau, *The 1964 Death Penalty Referendum in Oregon: Some Notes from a Participant-Observer*, 26 CRIME & DELINQ. 528, 535 (1980) [hereinafter *Death Penalty Referendum*]. These three commutations in November 1964 were not tallied as among those between 1903 and 1964. *See infra* notes 45–46 and accompanying text; Bedau, *Capital Punishment in Oregon, 1903–64*, 45 OR. L. REV. 1, 6 (table 1) (1965) [hereinafter *Capital Punishment in Oregon*].

34. Note, *supra* note 6, at 170.

35. N.Y. TIMES, Oct. 20, 1976, at 25, col. 6.

36. *Id.* Several years later, Professor Charles L. Black, Jr., argued that despite the Supreme Court's judgment in *Gregg v. Georgia*, in which it ruled that the death penalty is not per se a "cruel and unusual punishment," state governors are lawfully free to commute all death sentences under their jurisdiction if they believe that the death penalty is, in fact, unconstitutional. C. Black, *Governors' Dilemma*, NEW REPUBLIC, Apr. 25, 1979, at 12–13.

37. N.Y. TIMES, June 13, 1971, at 53, col. 3.

38. H. BEDAU, THE DEATH PENALTY IN AMERICA 563 (1st ed., 1964).

39. *See* Rockefeller, *supra* note 12, at 25. For Governor Holmes's views, see *Death Penalty Referendum, supra* note 33, at 529–30. For Governor Peabody's views, see Note, *supra* note 6, at 173 n. 135.

40. *See* John Wilgoren, *Citing Issue of Fairness, Governor Clears Out Death Row in Illinois*, N.Y. TIMES, Jan. 12, 2003, at 1.

41. REPORT OF THE GOVERNOR'S COMMISSION ON CAPITAL PUNISHMENT 1 (Apr. 15, 2002).

42. Scott, *The Pardoning Power,* 284 ANNALS 95, 99 (Nov. 1952) (citing BUREAU OF THE CENSUS, U.S. DEP'T COMMERCE, PRISONERS IN STATE AND FEDERAL PRISONS AND REFORMATORIES [annual reports for 1940–46]).

43. *Id.* at 99.

44. *Compare* BUREAU OF PRISONS, U.S. DEP'T OF JUSTICE, NATIONAL PRISONER STATISTICS 26 (March 1961) (commutation statistics for the year 1960 are disclosed in Figure A, Movement of Prisoners Under Sentence of Death by Offense: 1960) *with* FEDERAL BUREAU OF PRISONS, U.S. DEP'T OF JUSTICE, NATIONAL PRISONER STATISTICS 23 (February 1960) (commutation statistics for the year 1959 are not disclosed).

45. There is some question about the reliability of the commutation statistics in the 1980s as reported in Table 1. See *infra* note 46. Efforts by the NAACP Legal Defense and Educational Fund researchers to identify commutations outside Texas in 1982 and 1983 were unsuccessful. *See also* Letter from Richard Brody, Director of Research, Capital Punishment Project at NAACP Legal Defense Fund, to Hugo Bedau (Aug. 20, 1985). Nevertheless, the Justice Department reported such commutations, including two in Virginia in 1982. *See* BUREAU OF JUSTICE STATISTICS, U.S. DEP'T OF JUSTICE, CAPITAL PUNISHMENT 1982, at 40 (table 17). For subsequent years, the Department of Justice did not publish statistics on a state by state basis but rather published only aggregate national totals of annual death sentence commutations. *See* BUREAU OF JUSTICE STATISTICS, U.S. DEP'T OF JUSTICE, CAPITAL PUNISHMENT 1983, at 4, col. 3, and subsequent issues.

46. Numbers for the years 1973–2000 are from U.S. DEPT. OF JUSTICE, BUREAU OF JUSTICE STATISTICS, CAPITAL PUNISHMENT 2000, appendix table 1, at 13 (Dec. 2001). Numbers for the years 1961–67 are from NATIONAL PRISONER STATISTICS, CAPITAL PUNISHMENT 1971–72, table 4, at 20 (Dec. 1974). Numbers for the years 1968–72 are from NATIONAL PRISONER STATISTICS, CAPITAL PUNISHMENT 1979, table 6, at 20 (Dec. 1980).

47. Numbers for the years 1973–2000 are from U.S. DEP'T OF JUSTICE, *supra* note 46, at 13 (Dec. 2001). Numbers for the years 1961–70 are from NATIONAL PRISONER STATISTICS, CAPITAL PUNISHMENT 1930–1970, table 2, at 9 (Aug. 1971). No commutations as such were reported by the Bureau of Justice Statistics for the years 1971–72.

48. During the period extending from June 1967 (subsequent to the execution in Colorado of Luis Monge) to January 1977 (prior to the execution of Gary Gilmore in Utah), the courts stayed all executions as a result of a national litigation campaign to abolish the death penalty on constitutional grounds. *See generally* H. BEDAU, THE COURTS, THE CONSTITUTION, AND CAPITAL PUNISHMENT (1977) [hereinafter COURTS, CONSTITUTION, AND CAPITAL PUNISHMENT]; M. MELTSNER, CRUEL AND UNUSUAL: THE SUPREME COURT AND CAPITAL PUNISHMENT (1973); B. WOLFE, PILEUP ON DEATH ROW (1973).

49. I am indebted to S. Adele Shank, Ohio Public Defender Commission, for provoking discussion on the point that follows in the text.

50. 428 U.S. 153, *reh'g denied*, 429 U.S. 875 (1976).

51. NAACP Legal Defense and Educational Fund, Inc., Execution Update (July 2000) (lists 93 of the 784 prisoners executed between 1977 and January 2002 as having been "volunteers").

52. Note, *supra* note 6, at 191–92 (citing commutation data from several states but giving no sources for the data).

53. Subcommittee of the Judiciary Comm. on Capital Punishment, Problems of the Death Penalty and Its Administration in California, 20 Assembly Interim Comm. Reps. No. 3, at 14 (Table IX) (1955–57); and E. Brown, Public Justice, Private Mercy: A Governor's Education on Death Row xiii (1989).

54. D. von Drehle, *Clemency Exists Only in Theory*, Miami Herald (special reprint of a four-part series originally published July 10–13, 1988), at 8. These fifty-seven cases represented 21.3 percent of 268 clemency applications reviewed. The total death sentences for the period were not reported.

55. Bentele, *The Death Penalty in Georgia: Still Arbitrary*, 62 Wash. U.L.Q. 573, 628–29 (1985). Seven clemency applications are reported during this decade; total death sentences for the period are not reported.

56. Legislative Council of Maryland, Report of the Comm. On Capital Punishment 10 (1962).

57. Commonwealth of Massachusetts Rep. and Recommendations of the Special Comm'n Established for the Purpose of Investigating and Studying the Abolition of the Death Penalty in Capital Cases, Mass. H. Rep. No. 2575, at 29 (1958).

58. *Death in New Jersey*, *supra* note 26, at 7 (table I).

59. Scott, *supra* note 42, at 99 (citing Select Committee on Capital Punishment, Minutes of Evidence 551 [1930]).

60. Johnson, *Selective Factors in Capital Punishment*, 36 Soc. Forces 165, 166 (1957).

61. Ohio Legislative Service Comm'n, Capital Punishment, Staff Research Rep. No. 46, at 62 (table 14) (1961).

62. *Capital Punishment in Oregon*, *supra* note 33, at 6 (table I).

63. Wolfgang, Nolde, & Kelly, *Comparison of the Executed and the Commuted Among Admissions to Death Row*, 53 J. Crim. L. & Criminology 301 (1962).

64. Koeninger, *Capital Punishment in Texas, 1924–68*, 15 Crime & Delinq. 132, 135, 140 (1969).

65. 408 U.S. 238 (1972).

66. D. von Drehle, Among the Lowest of the Dead 35 (1995), quoting David Kendall.

67. 428 U.S. 153, *reh'g denied*, 429 U.S. 875 (1976).

68. D. von Drehle, *supra* note 54, at 8.

69. *Id.*

70. *Id.*

71. Radelet, *Rejecting the Jury: The Imposition of the Death Penalty in Florida*, 18 U.C. Davis L. Rev. 1409, 1427–30 (1985).

72. D. von Drehle, *supra* note 54, at 8.

73. W. Bowers, Executions in America 76 n.b. (1974); Scott, *supra* note 42, at 99.

74. Note, *supra* note 9, at 393.

75. *See* H. Bedau, *supra* note 4, at 247.

76. *Id.*

77. Maxwell v. Bishop, 398 F.2d 138 (8th Cir. 1968), *vacated and remanded*, 398 U.S. 262 (1970).

78. Amnesty International, United States of America: The Death Penalty 102–3 (1987).

79. F. Zimring & G. Hawkins, Capital Punishment and the American Agenda 100 (1986).

80. "Apparent" because various surveys indicate that the level of public support for the death penalty drops dramatically as soon as various follow-up questions to the facile question of whether they support the death penalty are asked, notably when respondents are presented with the alternative punishment of life imprisonment without parole. *See* Fox, Radelet, & Bonsteel, *Death Penalty Opinion in the Post-Furman Years*, 18 N.Y.U. Rev. L. & Soc. Change 499, 511–15 (1990–91); Bowers, *The Death Penalty's Shaky Support*, N.Y. Times, May 28, 1990 (editorial), at A21, col. 2.

81. *See, e.g.*, Bedau, *The Politics of Capital Punishment*, San Francisco Recorder, Mar. 26, 1990, Special Pullout Section, at ii; Dingerson & Rust-Tierney, *Politicians and Death*, Lifelines: Newsletter of the National Coalition to Abolish the Death Penalty, Mar.–Apr. 1990, at 1; Goodavage, *Cover Story: Death Penalty Politics*, USA Today, Mar. 29, 1990, at 1; Lacayo, *The Politics of Life and Death*, Time, Apr. 2, 1990, at 18; *The Death Penalty and Politics in 1990*, 2 National Legal Aid & Defender Ass'n Capital Report, Jan.–Feb. 1990, at 8; Oreskes, *The Political Stampede on Execution*, N.Y. Times, Apr. 4, 1990, at A16, col. 1.

82. Governor Edmund "Pat" Brown attributes his loss to Ronald Reagan in the gubernatorial campaign of 1966 in part to his handling of the Caryl Chessman case in the late 1950s. *See* E. Brown, Public Justice, Private Mercy: A Governor's Education on Death Row xiii, 51–52, 121 (1989); *see also* B. Wolfe, *supra* note 48; Culver, *The Politics of Capital Punishment in California*, in The Political Science of Criminal Justice 14–26 (S. Nagel, E. Fairchild, & A. Champagne eds., 1983).

83. Death Is Different, *supra* note 28, at 149–53.

84. Sumner v. Shuman, 483 U.S. 66 (1987); Woodson v. North Carolina, 428 U.S. 280 (1976).

85. Gregg v. Georgia, 428 U.S. 153, *reh'g denied*, 429 U.S. 875 (1976).

86. Lockett v. Ohio, 438 U.S. 586 (1978).

87. *See* Radelet, *supra* note 71.

88. Goodpaster, *Judicial Review of Death Sentences*, 74 J. Crim. L. & Criminology 776 (1983); Davis, *The Death Penalty and Current State of the Law*, 14 Crim. L. Bull. 7, 15 (1978). *But see* Whitmore v. Arkansas, 110 S. Ct. 1717, 1729 (1990) (Marshall, J., dissenting) (Supreme Court refused to invalidate an Arkansas death sentence "even though no appellate court ha[d] reviewed the validity of [the capital] conviction or [death] sentence").

89. On the development of federal appeals in capital cases, see H. Bedau, *supra* note 4, at 18–21.

90. Federal habeas corpus litigation in federal appeals of state-imposed death sentences alone "result in as many as half of all death sentences being overturned." Greenhouse, *Judicial Panel Urges Limit on Appeals by Death Row Inmates*, N.Y. Times, Sept. 22, 1989, at B20, col. 3.

91. *See* Lardent & Cohen, *The Last Best Hope: Representing Death Row Inmates*, 23 Loy.

L.A.L. REV. 213 (1989); Mello, *Facing Death Alone: The Post-Conviction Attorney Crisis on Death Row*, 37 AM. U.L. REV. 513 (1988); Stout, *The Lawyers of Death Row*, N.Y. TIMES, Feb. 14, 1988 (Magazine), at 46.

92. Note, *supra* note 9, at 394.

93. Weisberg, *Deregulating Death*, 8 SUP. CT. REV. 305 (1983).

94. Bentele, *supra* note 55; Tabak, *The Death of Fairness: The Arbitrary and Capricious Imposition of the Death Penalty in the 1980s*, 14 N.Y.U. REV. L. & SOC. CHANGE 797 (1986).

95. *New Threat to Adequate Federal Review of Death Sentences*, LEGAL DEFENSE FUND NEWS, Winter 1989, at 1; Kaufman, *Speedy Justice—At What Cost?*, N.Y. TIMES, May 1, 1990, at A23, col. 1; Greenhouse, *Chief Justice Is Off Cue as Curtain Is Lifted*, N.Y. TIMES, Mar. 16, 1990, at A12, col. 5; Greenhouse, *Vote Is a Rebuff for Chief Justice*, N.Y. TIMES, Mar. 15, 1990, at A16, col. 4; Greenhouse, *The Court Cuts Off Another Exit from Death Row*, N.Y. TIMES, Mar. 11, 1990, at E5, col. 1; *The Court's Deadly New Rules*, N.Y. TIMES, Mar. 10, 1990, at 24, col. 1; Greenhouse, *Justices Limit Path to U.S. Courts for State Prisoners on Death Row*, N.Y. TIMES, Mar. 6, 1990, at A1, col. 1; Office of the Governor of Florida, Press Release: Governor Calls for Reform of Federal Criminal Appeals to Reduce Capital Punishment Delays (Feb. 1, 1990) [hereinafter Governor of Florida Press Release].

96. In Gregg v. Georgia, 428 U.S. 153, 188, *reh'g denied*, 429 U.S. 875 (1976), the plurality acknowledged that "the penalty of death is different in kind from any other punishment imposed under our system of criminal justice," a sentiment echoed in many later opinions by several members of the Court. For articles questioning whether the Court still believes that "death is different," *see* WHITE, THE DEATH PENALTY IN THE EIGHTIES: AN EXAMINATION OF THE MODERN SYSTEM OF CAPITAL PUNISHMENT (1987); Tabak, *supra* note 94, Weisberg, *supra* note 93.

97. There is evidence that Governor Jerry Brown's refusal to commute any of California's death row prisoners after his defeat for reelection was owing to the desire "not [to] prejudice his future in public life with this sort of dramatic and controversial act." Letter from Henry Schwarzschild, on the ACLU staff, to Signers of the Commutation Plea Addressed to Governor Jerry Brown of California (Dec. 20, 1982).

98. Note, *supra* note 9, at 395 ("For all practical purposes, mercy is no longer available from the executive branch"); D. von Drehle, *supra* note 54 ("Clemency exists only in theory, like UFOs and Bigfoot").

99. Tabak, *supra* note 94, at 846.

100. For a partial scorecard evaluating progress in abolishing the death penalty as measured from various temporal baselines *see* Chapter 1.

101. *See* Note, *Life-Without-Parole: An Alternative to Death or Not Much of a Life at All?* 43 VAND. L. REV. 529 (1990). Except for the fact that it may be politically expedient as a step in abolishing the death penalty, I have never advocated life imprisonment without the possibility of parole. *See* Chapter 5.

102. *See* Fox, Radelet, & Bonsteel, *supra* note 80; Bowers, *supra* note 80.

103. *See* Spangenberg & Walsh, *Capital Punishment or Life Imprisonment? Some Cost Considerations*, 23 LOY. L.A.L. REV. 45 (1989).

104. In particular, see articles by Linda Greenhouse, *supra* note 95 (views of Chief Justice Rehnquist), Governor of Florida Press Release, *supra* note 95 (view of Governor Martinez), and Powell, *Commentary: Capital Punishment*, 102 HARV. L. REV. 1035 (1989) (views of retired Associate Justice Lewis F. Powell, Jr.). Unlike the Chief Justice and the

governor, former Justice Powell has threatened to throw down the gauntlet to the legislatures if the appellate review system is not drastically streamlined: "If capital punishment cannot be enforced even where innocence is not an issue, and the fairness of the trial is not seriously questioned, perhaps Congress and the state legislatures should take a serious look at whether the retention of a punishment that is being enforced only haphazardly is in the public interest." *Id.* at 1046.

105. On annual death sentences in the last forty years, *see* Table 1, *supra* notes 45–47 and accompanying text.

106. For critiques of the death penalty from the moral point of view, see DEATH IS DIFFERENT, *supra* note 28, at 9–63, 92–128, 238–47; S. NATHANSON, AN EYE FOR AN EYE? THE MORALITY OF PUNISHING BY DEATH 2d ed. (2001).

CHAPTER 5

1. *See* H. Bedau, *Retribution and the Theory of Punishment*, 75 J. PHIL. 601 (1978) (noting that retribution is increasingly the rationale in advocating punishment for criminals).

2. *Cf.* THE PHILOSOPHICAL LEXICON (D. Dennett & K. Lambert eds., 1978) (a collection of words and their definitions, which, if used uniformly, would immensely aid public understanding of philosophical doctrines and methods of argument; I believe it is a model that is badly needed throughout all the fields of human knowledge).

3. L. SHELEFF, ULTIMATE PENALTIES: CAPITAL PUNISHMENT, LIFE IMPRISONMENT, PHYSICAL TORTURE (1987).

4. *Id.* at 285–325.

5. *Id.* at 117–50.

6. *See* Note, *Life-Without-Parole: An Alternative to Death or Not Much of a Life at All?*, 43 VAND. L. REV. 529 (1990) [hereinafter Note, *Life-Without-Parole*] (discussing the differences and effectiveness in application of LWOP sentences). *See also* Cheatwood, *The Life-Without-Parole Sanction: Its Current Status and a Research Agenda*, 34 CRIME & DELINQ. 43 (1988) (examining the nature of life-without-parole sanctions and the possible problems associated with these sentences, concluding that further study is needed).

7. L. SHELEFF, *supra* note 3, at 115–50.

8. J. AUSTIN, PHILOSOPHICAL PAPERS 125 (1961). *See* L. SHELEFF, *supra* note 3, at 132.

9. C. BECCARIA, ON CRIMES AND PUNISHMENTS (D. Young trans., 1986).

10. Sellin, *Beccaria's Substitute for the Death Penalty*, in CRIMINOLOGY IN PERSPECTIVE: ESSAYS IN HONOR OF ISRAEL DRAPKIN 3, 4 (S. Landau & L. Sebba eds., 1977).

11. *See* C. BECCARIA, *supra* note 9, at 48–50.

12. *Id.* at 48.

13. *Id.*

14. For further discussion on the forfeiture of the natural right to life, see H. BEDAU, DEATH IS DIFFERENT: STUDIES IN THE MORALITY, LAW, AND POLITICS OF CAPITAL PUNISHMENT 55–59 (1987).

15. *See* C. BECCARIA, *supra* note 9, at 51.

16. *Id.*

17. For my own discussion of this issue, *see* Bedau, *Thinking of the Death Penalty as a Cruel and Unusual Punishment*, 18 U.C. DAVIS L. REV. 873 (1985), *revised and reprinted in* H. BEDAU, *supra* note 14, at 92–128.

18. *See* C. BECCARIA, *supra* note 9, at 51.

19. *Id.*

20. *See* Sellin, *supra* note 10, at 6.

21. *See* J. MILL, UTILITARIANISM 8 (G. Sher ed., 1979).

22. *See* A. MILLER & J. BOWMAN, DEATH BY INSTALLMENTS: THE ORDEAL OF WILLIE FRANCIS (1988).

23. *See* Bedau, *The Right to Die by Firing Squad*, HASTINGS CENTER REP., Feb. 1977, at 5, *reprinted in* H. BEDAU, THE COURTS, THE CONSTITUTION, AND CAPITAL PUNISHMENT 121–25 (1977).

24. L. SHELEFF, *supra* note 3, at 140.

25. *Id.* at 132.

26. J. BENTHAM, PRINCIPLES OF PENAL LAW: PART II—RATIONALE OF PUNISHMENT, *reprinted in* 1 THE WORKS OF JEREMY BENTHAM 441–50 (J. Bowring ed., 1843).

27. *See id.* at app. 525–32.

28. *See* Bedau, *Bentham's Utilitarian Critique of the Death Penalty*, 74 J. CRIM. L. & CRIMINOLOGY 1033 (1983), *revised and reprinted in* H. BEDAU, *supra* note 14, at 64–91.

29. J. BENTHAM, *supra* note 26, at 450.

30. *See* P. HILL, MAKING DECISIONS: A MULTIDISCIPLINARY INTRODUCTION 120–27 (1979).

31. For an illustration of how the decision matrix works, see *id.*

32. *See* J. BENTHAM, *supra* note 26, at 444.

33. *Id.* at 444–45.

34. *Id.* at 445–49.

35. *See id.* at 444–50.

36. *See* Bedau, *Capital Punishment*, in MATTERS OF LIFE AND DEATH 148–82 (T. Regan ed., 1980) [hereinafter Bedau, *Capital Punishment*], *revised and reprinted in* H. BEDAU, *supra* note 14, at 9–45. *See also* Radin, *The Jurisprudence of Death: Evolving Standards for the Cruel and Unusual Punishments Clause*, 126 U. PA. L. REV. 989, 1022 (1978) (arguing that because death is irrevocable, courts need to consider the risk of error in their decisions on the death penalty, and concluding that because both society and the courts remain divided on the issue of the death penalty, executions should not be allowed).

37. *See* Bedau, *Capital Punishment*, *supra* note 36, at 163–64, *revised and reprinted in* H. BEDAU, *supra* note 14, at 26–28.

38. NAACP LEGAL DEFENSE & EDUCATIONAL FUND, INC., DEATH ROW U.S.A., 1–5 (July 1, 2002).

39. U.S. DEP'T OF JUSTICE, BUREAU OF JUSTICE STATISTICS, annually, 1991 through 2000.

40. For a discussion of United Nations sanctions regarding the punishment and treatment of offenders, *see* P. SIEGHART, THE INTERNATIONAL LAW OF HUMAN RIGHTS 125–92 (1983).

41. *See* L. SHELEFF, *supra* note 3, at 131.

42. *See* Bedau, *Death as a Punishment*, in THE DEATH PENALTY IN AMERICA 214–31 (H. Bedau, 1st ed. 1964).

43. L. LAWES, MAN'S JUDGMENT OF DEATH (1924).

44. *Id.* at 27–29.

45. For a review of how some states have applied the LWOP sanction, *see* Note, *Life-Without-Parole, supra* note 6, and Cheatwood, *supra* note 6.

46. For an explanation of the current punishment schedule for federal crimes, see U.S. SENTENCING COMM'N, FEDERAL SENTENCING GUIDELINES MANUAL—1991 Edition (1990).

CHAPTER 6

1. RONALD DWORKIN, FREEDOM'S LAW: THE MORAL READING OF THE AMERICAN CONSTITUTION (1996).

2. *Id.* at 2.

3. *Id.* at 2–7, 11.

4. 347 U.S. 483 (1954).

5. DWORKIN, *supra* note 1, at 10.

6. *See* ROBERT H. BORK, THE TEMPTING OF AMERICA: THE POLITICAL SEDUCTION OF THE LAW (1990).

7. RAOUL BERGER, DEATH PENALTIES: THE SUPREME COURT'S OBSTACLE COURSE (1982). For a review of this work, *see* Hugo Adam Bedau, *Berger's Defense of the Death Penalty: How Not to Read the Constitution*, 81 MICH. L. REV. 1152 (1983).

8. DWORKIN, *supra* note 1, at 13.

9. *See id.* at 18–19.

10. *See, e.g.*, JUDITH JARVIS THOMSON, THE REALM OF RIGHTS 1–33 (1990).

11. DWORKIN, *supra* note 1, at 15.

12. *Id.*

13. *Id.* at 15–16.

14. *Id.* at 17.

15. *Id.*

16. *Id.*

17. U.S. CONST. amend. VIII.

18. U.S. CONST. amend. XIV, § 1.

19. 408 U.S. 238 (1972).

20. *See id.* at 240–57 (Douglas, J., concurring), 257–306 (Brennan, J., concurring), 306–10 (Stewart, J., concurring), 310–14 (White, J., concurring), 314–73 (Marshall, J., concurring).

21. *See id.* at 375–405 (Burger, C.J., dissenting), 405–14 (Blackmun, J., dissenting), 414–65 (Powell, J., dissenting), 465–70 (Rehnquist, J., dissenting).

22. *See id.* at 257–306 (Brennan, J., concurring).

23. *Id.* at 270.

24. *Id.* at 271.

25. *Id.* at 273.

26. *Id.* at 274.

27. *Id.* at 277.

28. *Id.* at 279.

29. 428 U.S. 153 (1976).

30. 428 U.S. 280 (1976).

31. *See Furman*, 408 U.S., at 314–74 (Marshall, J., concurring). Justice Marshall's argument is also explicitly structured around four "standards" or "principles," but they overlap only in part with Brennan's (and none makes any reference to "human dignity," so prominent in Brennan's formulation). *Id.* at 277, 330, 371. Justice Marshall argues that a punishment violates the Eighth Amendment if it violates the principle that punishments must not be too painful to be tolerated, or the principle that bizarre punishments must not be enacted, or the principle prohibiting severity in excess of what is necessary to serve a valid legislative purpose, or the principle that a punishment must not be abhorred by popular sentiment. *See id.* at 330–32. For the purposes of his argument against the death penalty, Justice Marshall dropped any further reference to the first two principles and relied exclusively on the second pair. *See id.* at 332–33. He then argued that the empirical facts show the death penalty is subject to conclusive criticism under these two principles. *See id.* at 342–59.

Thus, Justices Brennan and Marshall share the same populist principle (viz., Marshall's fourth is equivalent to Brennan's third). *See supra* note 27 and accompanying text. Also, Justice Marshall's reliance on Justice Brennan's third principle, as he rightly points out, brings his Eighth Amendment argument into "parallel" with a Fourteenth Amendment substantive due process argument. *See id.* at 359 n.141; *see also infra* Part VIII.

32. Justice Stewart in effect endorsed only the second of Justice Brennan's four principles. *See Furman*, 408 U.S., at 309–10.

33. Justice White also implicitly endorsed Justice Brennan's second principle, and he gave somewhat implicit and indirect support to Justice Brennan's fourth principle. *See id.* at 313–14.

34. Justice Douglas also endorsed Justice Brennan's second principle. *See id.* at 245, 249, 253, 256.

35. 217 U.S. 349 (1910).

36. *See, e.g.*, Michael Davis, To Make the Punishment Fit the Crime 69–97 (1992); R. A. Duff, Trials and Punishments 279 (1986); Christopher Harding & Richard W. Ireland, Punishment: Rhetoric, Rule, and Practice 107 (1989); H. L. A. Hart, Punishment and Responsibility: Essays in the Philosophy of Law 25 (1968); Nicola Lacey, State Punishment: Political Principles and Community Values 194 (1988); David A. J. Richards, The Moral Criticism of Law 229–31 (1977); C. L. Ten, Crime, Guilt, and Punishment: A Philosophical Introduction 153 (1987); Andrew von Hirsch, Doing Justice: The Choice of Punishments 66–76 (1976); Nigel Walker, Why Punish? 96–105 (1991).

37. *See Furman*, 408 U.S., at 393 n.18 (Burger, C.J., dissenting).

38. *See Gregg v. Georgia*, 428 U.S. 153, 158–207 (1976) (Stewart, Powell, Stevens, JJ., plurality opinion).

39. Justice Brennan does mention proportionality, but he dismisses it as being of secondary importance to his more inclusive fourth principle. *See Furman*, 408 U.S., at 280 (Brennan, J., concurring).

40. *Id.* at 277.

41. *Id.* at 279 (emphasis added); *cf. id.* at 300 (stating that society's view of a severe punishment is determined by "what society does with it").

42. *Id.* at 300.

43. *Id.* at 299.

44. *Id.* at 332 (Marshall, J., concurring).

45. *Id.* at 360.

46. *See id.* at 361 n.144 (citing Witherspoon v. Illinois, 391 U.S. 510, 520 [1968]).

47. *Furman*, 408 U.S., at 361 n.145.

48. *See* MICHAEL MELTSNER, CRUEL AND UNUSUAL: THE SUPREME COURT AND CAPITAL PUNISHMENT 106–15, 126–48 (1974).

49. *See infra* Part V, under "The Marshall Hypothesis."

50. *Furman*, 408 U.S., at 386–87 (Burger, C.J., dissenting).

51. *See id.* at 309–10 (Stewart, J., concurring) (concluding that the Eighth and Fourteenth Amendments will not permit imposition of the death penalty in a wanton or freakish fashion).

52. *See id.* at 256 (Douglas, J., concurring) (stating the death penalty should not be "sparsely, selectively, and spottily" applied).

53. *See id.* at 291–95 (Brennan, J., concurring) (stating that death is only "freakishly" or "spectacularly" imposed in most cases warranting the death penalty).

54. *See id.* at 313 (White, J., concurring) (concluding "the death penalty is exacted with great infrequency").

55. *Id.* at 388 (Burger, C.J., dissenting).

56. *Id.* at 389.

57. *See* Briefs for Petitioners at Appendix F, Aikens v. California, 406 U.S. 813 (1972) (No. 68–5027), Furman v. Georgia, 408 U.S. 238 (1972) (No. 69–5003), Jackson v. Georgia, 408 U.S. 238 (1972) (No. 69–5030).

58. *See* Gregg v. Georgia, 428 U.S. 153, 158–207 (1976). Elsewhere I have offered a more comprehensive criticism of Justice Stewart's opinion in *Gregg*. *See* Hugo Adam Bedau, Gregg v. Georgia *and the "New" Death Penalty*, 4 CRIM. JUST. ETHICS, Summer/Fall 1985, at 3, *reprinted in* HUGO ADAM BEDAU, DEATH IS DIFFERENT: STUDIES IN THE MORALITY, LAW, AND POLITICS OF CAPITAL PUNISHMENT 164 (1987).

59. *Gregg*, 428 U.S. at 179–80.

60. *Id.* at 181.

61. *Id.* at 181–82.

62. *See id.* at 181 n.25.

63. *See* Brief for the N.A.A.C.P. Legal Defense and Educational Fund, Inc., as *Amicus Curiae*, Gregg v. Georgia, 428 U.S. 153 (1976) (No. 74–6257).

64. This and the following eight paragraphs are taken from HUGO ADAM BEDAU, THE DEATH PENALTY IN AMERICA: CURRENT CONTROVERSIES (Hugo Adam Bedau ed., 1997).

65. *See* PLAYBOY ENTERPRISES, INC., THE PLAYBOY REPORT ON AMERICAN MEN 46 (1979).

66. A-T-O, INC., THE FIGGIE REPORT PART II: THE CORPORATE RESPONSE TO FEAR OF CRIME (1980).

67. Julie Lewin, *Figgie II: Crime Fear in the Suites*, NATION, July 4, 1981, at 8, 8.

68. Robert D. McFadden, *Poll Indicates Half of New Yorkers See Crime as City's Chief Problem*, N.Y. TIMES, Jan. 14, 1985, at A1.

69. *See Poll Finds Broad Support for Executions*, STATE (S.C.), Jan. 31, 1985, at A1.

70. Lawrence Kilman, *Part I: Support for Death Penalty High Despite Fairness Question*, ASSOCIATED PRESS, Jan. 27, 1985.

71. *See* Woodson v. North Carolina, 428 U.S. 280 (1976); Roberts v. Louisiana, 428 U.S. 325 (1976).

72. *See* Kilman, *supra* note 70.

73. Lynn Minton, *What's Up This Week: Readers Respond on Capital Punishment*, Parade Mag., Jan. 25, 1987, at 10, 10.

74. Maggie Rivas, *Most in Poll Favor Capital Punishment*, Dallas Morning News,
Nov. 15, 1988, *available in* 1988 WL 5310268.

75. *See id.*

76. *See* Alexander W. Astin et al., The American Freshman: Twenty Year Trends,
1966–1985, at 98 (1987).

77. *See id.*

78. *See* Alexander W. Astin et al., The American Freshman: National Norms for
Fall 1991, at 26 (1991).

79. *See* Rene Sanchez, *Students Seen as Apathetic to Politics*, Boston Globe, Jan. 9,
1995, at 3.

80. *See* George Gallup, Jr., The Gallup Poll: Public Opinion 1994, at 148–49 (1995).

81. *See* Fox Butterfield, *Seeds of Murder Epidemic: Teen-Age Boys with Guns*, N.Y.
Times, Oct. 19, 1992, at A8.

82. *See* Fox Butterfield, *States Revamping Laws on Juveniles as Felonies Soar*, N.Y.
Times, May 12, 1996, at 1.

83. Phoebe C. Ellsworth & Samuel R. Gross, *Hardening of the Attitudes: Americans'
Views on the Death Penalty*, 50 J. Soc. Issues 19, 40 (1994).

84. Jeffrey M. Jones, *Slim Majority of Americans Say Death Penalty Applied Fairly*,
Gallup News Service, May 20, 2002, at 1–6.

85. *See* Furman v. Georgia, 408 U.S. 238, 360–69 (1972) (Marshall, J., concurring).

86. *Id.* at 361.

87. *Id.* at 361–62.

88. Austin Sarat & Neil Vidmar, *Public Opinion, the Death Penalty, and the Eighth
Amendment: Testing the Marshall Hypothesis*, reprinted in Capital Punishment in the
United States 190, 205–6 (Hugo Adam Bedau & Chester M. Pierce eds., 1976).

89. Phoebe C. Ellsworth & Lee Ross, *Public Opinion and Capital Punishment: A
Close Examination of the Views of Abolitionists and Retentionists*, 29 Crime & Delinq. 116,
147 (1983).

90. *Id.* at 135.

91. *Id.* at 161.

92. On the problems of retributivism, see Hugo Adam Bedau, *Retribution and the
Theory of Punishment*, 75 J. Phil. 601 (1978). On the history of retributivism, see Marvin
Henberg, *Retribution: Evil for Evil in Ethics, Law, and Literature* (1990). Elsewhere, I have
acknowledged a limited role for retribution in justifying punishment. *See* Hugo Adam
Bedau, *Justice and Punishment: Philosophical Basics, in* The Socio-Economics of Crime and
Justice 19–36 (Brian Forst ed., 1993).

93. *See, e.g.*, Michael L. Radelet et al., In Spite of Innocence: Erroneous Convictions in Capital Cases (1992); Hugo Adam Bedau & Michael L. Radelet, *The Myth
of Infallibility: A Reply to Markman and Cassell*, 41 Stan. L. Rev. 161 (1988); Hugo Adam
Bedau & Michael L. Radelet, *Miscarriages of Justice in Potentially Capital Cases*, 40 Stan. L.
Rev. 21 (1987).

94. Death Penalty Info. Ctr., Sentencing for Life: Americans Embrace Alternatives to the Death Penalty 6 (1993).

95. Andrew H. Malcolm, *Capital Punishment Is Popular, but So Are Its Alternatives,* N.Y. TIMES, Sept. 10, 1989, at E4.

96. James Alan Fox et al., *Death Penalty Opinion in the Post-Furman Years,* 18 N.Y.U. REV. L. & SOC. CHANGE 499, 514 (1990–91).

97. *See id.* at 525 fig.5.

98. William J. Bowers, *The Death Penalty's Shaky Support,* N.Y. TIMES, May 28, 1990, at 21.

99. *Id.*

100. Joe Davidson, *Poll Finds Death-Penalty Support Isn't as Strong as It Might Appear,* WALL ST. J., Apr. 19, 1993, at B2.

101. William J. Bowers et al., *A New Look at Public Opinion on Capital Punishment: What Citizens and Legislators Prefer,* 22 AM. J. CRIM. L. 77, 79 (1994).

102. *See* LEON SHASKOLSKY SHELEFF, ULTIMATE PENALTIES: CAPITAL PUNISHMENT, LIFE IMPRISONMENT, PHYSICAL TORTURE (1987).

103. CESARE BECCARIA, ON CRIMES AND PUNISHMENT (David Young trans., 1986) (1764).

104. *See* JEREMY BENTHAM, THE RATIONALE OF PUNISHMENT (1830); *see also* Hugo Adam Bedau, *Bentham's Utilitarian Critique of the Death Penalty,* 74 J. CRIM. L. & CRIMINOLOGY 1033 (1983).

105. *See* BECCARIA, *supra* note 103, at 51; BENTHAM, *supra* note 104, at 1044–45.

106. Elsewhere I have proposed as the punishment for first-degree murder a fixed minimum term without parole eligibility followed by an indeterminate sentence with parole eligibility. *See* Hugo Adam Bedau, *Death as a Punishment, in* THE DEATH PENALTY IN AMERICA: AN ANTHOLOGY 214, 228–31 (Hugo Adam Bedau ed., 1964); Hugo Adam Bedau, *Imprisonment vs. Death: Does Avoiding Schwarzschild's Paradox Lead to Sheleff's Dilemma?* 54 ALB. L. REV. 481, 493–95 (1990), Chapter 5 in this volume.

107. Mary Brown Parlee, *Pinning Down Vague Talk About the Death Penalty,* PSYCHOL. TODAY, Jan. 1979, at 13, 13.

108. DAVID C. BALDUS ET AL., EQUAL JUSTICE AND THE DEATH PENALTY: A LEGAL AND EMPIRICAL ANALYSIS 235 (1990).

109. *See* TRACY L. SNELL, U.S. DEP'T OF JUSTICE, CAPITAL PUNISHMENT 2000, at 10 table 1 (2001).

110. I have discussed this problem at somewhat greater length in Chapter 5.

111. SNELL, *supra* note 109, at 1.

112. Gregg v. Georgia, 428 U.S. 153, 182 (1976).

113. *See* Ursula Bentele, *The Death Penalty in Georgia: Still Arbitrary,* 62 WASH. U. L.Q. 573, 585–88 (1985).

114. *See* Vivian Berger, *Rolling the Dice to Decide Who Dies,* N.Y. ST. B.J., Oct. 1988, at 32, 33.

115. For unsympathetic portraits of those on death row, see *Death Row* (1995), an annual volume published by Glenn Hare Publications.

116. *See* Stephen B. Bright, *Counsel for the Poor: The Death Sentence Not for the Worst Crime but for the Worst Lawyer,* 103 YALE L.J. 1835 (1994).

117. *See id.* at 1835–48.

118. *See* William J. Bowers, *The Capital Jury Project: Rationale, Design, and Preview of Early Findings,* 70 IND. L.J. 1043 (1995).

119. *See* Michael Mello & Ruthann Robson, *Judge Over Jury: Florida's Practice of Imposing Death Over Life in Capital Cases,* 13 FLA. ST. U. L. REV. 31 (1985).

120. DEATH PENALTY INFO. CTR., CHATTAHOOCHEE JUDICIAL DISTRICT: BUCKLE OF THE DEATH BELT (1991); *see* Stephen B. Bright, *Discrimination, Death and Denial: The Tolerance of Racial Discrimination in Infliction of the Death Penalty,* 35 SANTA CLARA L. REV. 433 (1995).

121. *See* Tina Rosenberg, *The Deadliest D.A.,* N.Y. TIMES, July 16, 1995, § 6 (magazine), at 1.

122. *See* Michael L. Radelet & Barbara A. Zsembik, *Executive Clemency in Post-Furman Capital Cases,* 27 U. RICH. L. REV. 289 (1993); Hugo Adam Bedau, *The Decline of Executive Clemency in Capital Cases,* 18 N.Y.U. REV. L. & SOC. CHANGE 255 (1990–91).

123. *See also* Conference, *The Death Penalty in the Twenty-First Century,* 45 AM. U. L. REV. 239 (1995).

124. *See* Furman v. Georgia, 408 U.S. 238, 386–89 (1972) (Burger, C.J., dissenting).

125. Gregg v. Georgia, 428 U.S. 153, 182 (1976).

126. Callins v. Collins, 510 U.S. 1141, 1145 (1994) (Blackmun. J., dissenting).

127. *See* Robert Weisberg, *Deregulating Death,* 8 SUP. CT. REV. 305 (1983).

128. *Gregg,* 428 U.S. at 198.

129. Bedau, *supra* note 110, at 164.

130. 381 U.S. 479 (1965).

131. *See* WILLIAM A. SCHABAS, THE ABOLITION OF THE DEATH PENALTY IN INTERNATIONAL LAW (1993).

132. Furman v. Georgia, 408 U.S. 238, 279 (1972) (Brennan, J., concurring).

133. *Id.* at 331 (Marshall, J., concurring).

134. *See* EDWARD KEYNES, LIBERTY, PROPERTY, AND PRIVACY: TOWARD A JURISPRUDENCE OF SUBSTANTIVE DUE PROCESS (1996). Unfortunately, Keynes completely avoids reviewing the use by Justices Brennan and Marshall of the substantive due process argument in *Furman* in particular, and on the constitutionality of the death penalty in general.

135. *See Furman,* 408 U.S. at 331 (Marshall, J., concurring).

136. Exactly what punishment is the *least* restrictive means to the relevant valid ends where the crime of murder is concerned is, of course, controversial. What ought not to be in dispute is that long-term imprisonment is clearly a far *less* restrictive means to those ends than is the death penalty. For a substantive due process argument, that is sufficient.

137. Retribution is hardly acknowledged by Justice Brennan or Justice Marshall as a legitimate goal or objective of the criminal justice system. *See Furman,* 408 U.S., at 257–306 (Brennan, J., concurring), 342–45 (Marshall, J., concurring).

138. For a sharply drawn contrast between legitimate retribution and illegitimate revenge, see ROBERT NOZICK, PHILOSOPHICAL EXPLANATIONS 366–70 (1981).

139. *See Furman,* 408 U.S., at 342, 359 n.141 (Marshall, J., concurring); *see also* Michael H. Marcus & David S. Weissbrodt, *The Death Penalty Cases,* 56 CAL. L. REV. 1268, 1270, 1325, 1343–64 (1968) (suggesting that substantive due process shows the death penalty is unconstitutional). Some years ago, I sketched what amounted to a substantive due process argument against the death penalty. *See* Hugo Adam Bedau, *The Courts, the Constitution, and Capital Punishment,* 1968 UTAH L. REV. 201, 225–36 (1968), *reprinted in* HUGO ADAM BEDAU, THE COURTS, THE CONSTITUTION, AND CAPITAL PUNISHMENT 32–41 (1977). I am indebted to Deborah Rosenthal for bringing forcefully to my attention the

importance and relevance of a straightforwardly substantive due process argument against the death penalty.

140. *See* KEYNES, *supra* note 134, at x–xi, 131, 133–35, 153, 205, 215. Substantive due process arguments may have been abandoned by the Court in regard to economic issues, but they thrive where other "preferred" or more "fundamental" rights of personal liberty, privacy, and autonomy (e.g., concerning reproductive issues) are concerned. *Id.* Whether and why substantive due process arguments have not been comparably persuasive over the past several decades in scrutinizing legislatively enacted penal policies Keynes does not explore.

CHAPTER 7

1. On autonomy *see, e.g.*, THE INNER CITADEL: ESSAYS ON INDIVIDUAL AUTONOMY (John Christman ed., 1989); GERALD DWORKIN, THE THEORY AND PRACTICE OF AUTONOMY (1988); and LAURENCE HAWORTH, AUTONOMY: AN ESSAY IN PHILOSOPHICAL PSYCHOLOGY (1986). On privacy *see, e.g.*, PHILOSOPHICAL DIMENSIONS OF PRIVACY: AN ANTHOLOGY (Ferdinand D. Schoeman ed., 1984); PRIVACY: NOMOS XIII (J. Roland Pennock & John Chapman eds., 1971).

2. Roe v. Wade, 410 U.S. 113 (1972); Eisenstadt v. Baird, 405 U.S. 438 (1972); Griswold v. Connecticut, 381 U.S. 479 (1967).

3. For criticism of the death penalty by moral philosophers *see, e.g.*, STEPHEN NATHANSON, AN EYE FOR AN EYE: THE MORALITY OF PUNISHING BY DEATH (2d ed. 2001); Jeffrey H. Reiman, *Justice, Civilization, and the Death Penalty: Answering van den Haag*, 14 PHIL. & PUB. AFFAIRS 115 (1985); Richard A. Wasserstrom, *Capital Punishment as Punishment: Theoretical Issues and Objections*, 3 MIDWEST STUD. IN PHIL. 473 (1982); JEFFRIE G. MURPHY, RETRIBUTION, JUSTICE, AND THERAPY 223 (1979); Hugo Adam Bedau, DEATH IS DIFFERENT: STUDIES IN THE MORALITY, LAW, AND POLITICS OF CAPITAL PUNISHMENT (1987); and *see* Chapters 8 and 9 in this volume.

4. See the discussion of the Blanquist-Marxist slogan as a "precept of justice" in JOHN RAWLS, THEORY OF JUSTICE 305 (1971).

5. This is how Raoul Berger dismisses reference to human dignity in the interpretation of the Eighth Amendment; *see* his DEATH PENALTIES: THE SUPREME COURT'S OBSTACLE COURSE 118 (1982).

6. I borrow this term from Joel Feinberg; *see* his HARM TO SELF xvi (1986) and HARM TO OTHERS 187–88 (1984).

7. IMMANUEL KANT, GROUNDING FOR THE METAPHYSICS OF MORALS 40–45 (James W. Ellington trans., 1981); and THE METAPHYSICAL ELEMENTS OF JUSTICE 98, 132n. (John Ladd trans., 1965).

8. *See* especially the essay by Pico della Mirandola, *Oration on the Dignity of Man* (ca. 1486) *in* THE RENAISSANCE PHILOSOPHY OF MAN 223 (Ernst Cassirer et al. eds., 1948).

9. *See* Herbert Chanan Brichto, *The Hebrew Bible on Human Rights, in* ESSAYS ON HUMAN RIGHTS: CATEGORIES, ISSUES, AND JEWISH PERSPECTIVES 215, 217–18 (David Sidorsky ed., 1979).

10. On Kant's defense of the death penalty, *see* TOM SORELL, MORAL THEORY AND

CAPITAL PUNISHMENT 129 (1987). For an argument that Kant's defense of the death penalty was faithless to his own idea of human dignity, *see* Stephen Schwarzschild, *Kantianism and the Death Penalty (and Related Social Problems)*, 71 ARCHIV FÜR RECHTS- UND SOZIALPHILOSOPHIE 343 (1985).

11. *See* DAVID RIESMAN, THE LONELY CROWD: A STUDY OF THE CHANGING AMERICAN CHARACTER (1950).

12. Perhaps the best-known recent attack on the notion that persons have *dignity* is to be found in B. F. SKINNER, BEYOND FREEDOM AND DIGNITY 44 (1971). Skinner never explains what dignity is, but it is clear that he attacks it because it is implicated with "autonomy," and he is convinced that human autonomy is an illusion. For reasons to conclude that Skinner's arguments utterly fail to establish this conclusion, *see* D. C. DENNETT, *Skinner Skinned, in* BRAINSTORMS: PHILOSOPHICAL ESSAYS ON MIND AND PSYCHOLOGY 53 (1978); and my review essay *Beyond Skinner*, WORLDVIEW 45 (Apr. 1972).

13. Probably the best-known current version of this essentially Kantian position is to be found in JOHN RAWLS, THEORY OF JUSTICE. But human dignity as such plays a very small explicit role in the pages of this book. It is somewhat more evident in the equally Kantian moral theory of Alan Gewirth; see his HUMAN RIGHTS: ESSAYS ON JUSTIFICATIONS AND APPLICATIONS (1982). Gewirth argues against trying to "derive" any human rights from human dignity (see 27–30), and I agree with his objection that such a "derivation" is circular. That Kant's conception of human dignity as presented in his own writings is not beyond criticism is shown by Joel Feinberg in his HARM TO SELF, *supra* note 6, at 94–97.

14. Furman v. Georgia, 408 U.S. 238, 270 (1972).

15. *See* LARRY CHARLES BERKSON, THE CONCEPT OF CRUEL AND UNUSUAL PUNISHMENT 9 (1975).

16. The contribution by constitutional commentators to the analysis of human dignity in the setting of the Eighth Amendment has, so far, been slight; *see, e.g.*, Gerald H. Gottlieb, *Testing the Death Penalty*, 34 S. CAL. L. REV. 268, 277–78 (1961); Malcolm E. Wheeler, *Toward a Theory of Limited Punishment II: The Eighth Amendment after* Furman, 25 STAN. L. REV. 62, 67–71 (1972); and Margaret Jane Radin, *Cruel Punishment and Respect for Persons: Super Due Process for Death*, 53 S. CAL. L. REV. 1143, 1173–85 (1980).

17. *Furman*, at 271, and *cf.* 281.

18. *Id.* at 273.

19. *Id.* at 274.

20. *Id.* at 277.

21. *Id.* at 279.

22. *Id.* at 282, 286.

23. Gregg v. Georgia, 428 U.S. 253, 187 (1976); also IGOR PRIMORATZ, JUSTIFYING LEGAL PUNISHMENT 163–64 (1989).

24. *See* John Cottingham, *Punishment and Respect for Persons, in* LAW, MORALITY AND RIGHTS 423, 430 (M. A. Stewart ed., 1973); also Igor Primoratz, *Murder Is Different*, 8 CRIM. JUST. ETHICS 46, 51 (1989).

25. *Furman*, at 385–91 (Burger, C.J., dissenting)

26. *Gregg*, at 179–82, citing "objective indicia that reflect the public attitude" toward the death penalty.

27. I have discussed these indicia elsewhere; *see* BEDAU, *supra* note 3, at 169–70.

28. *Furman*, at 300.

29. Gregg, at 179–80.

30. *Id.* at 181–82.

31. During the 1980s public opinion surveys reported considerably more support for the death penalty than during the 1960s or 1970s. What should be inferred from these polls about public attitudes, however, is more controversial. *See* Hans Zeisel and A. M. Gallup, *Death Penalty Sentiment in the United States,* 5 J. of Quant. Crim. 285–96 (1989); and P. W. Harris, *Oversimplification and Error in Public Opinion Surveys on Capital Punishment,* 3 JUST. Q. 429 (1986).

32. *See* WILLIAM J. BOWERS, LEGAL HOMICIDE: DEATH AS PUNISHMENT IN AMERICA, 1864–1982, at 25–32, 49–58 (1984).

33. Indeed, I am inclined to think that this criterion was introduced (consciously or otherwise) in order to put an equal protection spin on the whole argument.

34. The crude populist abuse to which (what amounts to) this third principle can be put is well illustrated in the opinion for the Court by Justice Antonin Scalia in the death penalty case of Stanford v. Kentucky, 492 U.S. 361 (1989).

35. A parallel argument has been made by David Dolinko, *Foreword: How to Criticize the Death Penalty,* 77 J. OF CRIM. L. & CRIMINOLOGY 546, 596, n.252 (1986).

36. Trop v. Dulles, 356 U.S. 86, 100–101 (1958).

37. *See* Vivian Berger, *Justice Delayed or Justice Denied?—A Comment on Recent Proposals to Reform Death Penalty Habeas Corpus,* 90 COLUM. L. REV. 1665 (Oct. 1990); DAVID C. BALDUS ET AL., EQUAL JUSTICE AND THE DEATH PENALTY (1990); Ronald J. Tabak and J. Mark Lane, *The Execution of Injustice: A Cost and Lack-of-Benefit Analysis of the Death Penalty,* 23 LOY. L.A. L. REV. 59, 62–98 (1989); and BEDAU, *supra* note 3, at 164–84, 195–237.

David Dolinko's criticism of arguments against the death penalty that rest on such "procedural" facts suggests that he thinks it is incorrect to interpret the meaning of the prohibition against "cruel and unusual punishments" by reference to principles—such as Justice Brennan's second and third principles—to which facts of this sort are relevant; *see* Dolinko, *supra* note 35, at 571–601. What principles (if any) it would be appropriate to use to interpret this constitutional provision, aside from Justice Brennan's first and fourth principles ("a punishment must not be so severe as to be degrading to the dignity of human beings" and "a severe punishment must not be excessive"), remain unclear.

38. This and the next section are a revised version of an argument that appears in my book DEATH IS DIFFERENT, *supra* note 3, at 123–28, itself a revised version of my essay *Thinking about the Death Penalty as Cruel and Unusual Punishment,* 18 U.C. DAVIS L. REV. 873, 917–23 (1985).

39. *See* Judith Shklar, *Putting Cruelty First,* in her book ORDINARY VICES 7–44 (1984).

40. *In re* Kemmler, 136 U.S. 436 (1890); Malloy v. South Carolina, 237 U.S. 180 (1915).

41. Amnesty International USA, *What's Your Idea of Cruel and Unusual?* (poster, distributed 1989).

42. On the history of electrocution as a "humane" advance in methods of execution, *see* RICHARD MORAN, EXECUTIONER'S CURRENT (2002).

43. Thus, Walter Berns concedes that carrying out the death penalty by drawing and quartering and disemboweling would be cruel and unusual punishment; *see* his FOR CAPITAL PUNISHMENT: CRIME AND THE MORALITY OF THE DEATH PENALTY 32 (1979). *Cf.* Raoul Berger on the death penalty by crucifixion or boiling in oil, in his DEATH PENAL-

TIES, *supra* note 5, at 41; and Ernest van den Haag on the death penalty for only "the gravest crimes in their most aggravated form, e.g., not for rape, but for rape-murder," in his PUNISHING CRIMINALS: CONCERNING A VERY OLD AND PAINFUL QUESTION 227 (1975). For a list of the "degrading," "shocking," and "horrible" punishments that have been described over the years in Supreme Court dicta as "cruel and unusual punishments," *see* BERKSON, *supra* note 15, at 10.

44. PHILLIP P. HALLIE, THE PARADOX OF CRUELTY 90 (1969).

45. *Id.* at 34.

46. *See* Primoratz, *supra* note 23, at 50.

47. ERVING GOFFMAN, ASYLUMS: ESSAYS ON THE SOCIAL SITUATION OF MENTAL PATIENTS AND OTHER INMATES (1961); TOTAL INSTITUTIONS (Samuel E. Wallace ed., 1971).

48. This is of course not to deny that observers across two centuries, from Cesare Beccaria (an opponent of the death penalty) to Jacques Barzun (a defender), have claimed that life imprisonment is the more severe punishment or that imprisonment can be and often is turned into a living hell.

49. Perhaps the most persuasive argument against life imprisonment on the ground that it violates human rights is to be found in LEON SHASKOLSKY SHELEFF, ULTIMATE PENALTIES: CAPITAL PUNISHMENT, LIFE IMPRISONMENT, PHYSICAL TORTURE 58–59, 117–50 (1987). I have explained in Chapter 5 why life imprisonment, even without parole, is not essentially as severe or as cruel as death. Sheleff's critique was not addressed to my argument and left untouched the points I had made. As to why incarceration does not in practice or in theory necessarily take life-destroying forms, *see, e.g.,* ROBERT JOHNSON, HARD TIME: UNDERSTANDING AND REFORMING THE PRISON (1987); MICHAEL SHERMAN & GORDON HAWKINS, IMPRISONMENT IN AMERICA: CHOOSING THE FUTURE (1981); and NORVAL MORRIS, THE FUTURE OF IMPRISONMENT (1974).

50. On the interpretation of "unusual" by the Supreme Court, see *Furman* at 277 (Brennan, J., concurring opinion) and 376–79 (Burger, C. J., dissenting). I have discussed the matter further in BEDAU, *supra* note 3, at 96–98.

51. Herbert Morris, *A Paternalistic Theory of Punishment*, AM. PHIL. Q. 263, 270 (1981). Morris does not discuss the relevance of this right to the moral or constitutional status of the death penalty.

A rather different argument from mine has been offered by Jeffrie G. Murphy, *Cruel and Unusual Punishments, in* LAW, MORALITY AND RIGHTS, *supra* note 24, at 373, 386, 389, 391–97; a briefer version appears in Murphy, *supra* note 3, at 223–49. Murphy's argument rests mainly on "the right not to be dealt with negligently by one's government" and "the right not to have one's basic interests threatened in casual and irresponsible ways."

52. *See, e.g.* JOHN LOCKE, *The Second Treatise of Government* (1690), *in* TWO TREATISES OF GOVERNMENTS, §§23, 172 (Peter Laslett ed., 1963). It is a curious feature of historical studies of natural rights theories that little or nothing has been said about the role of forfeiture of such rights: *see, e.g.,* RICHARD TUCK, NATURAL RIGHTS THEORIES (1979). For further discussion, see Hugo Adam Bedau, *Right to Life*, 63 THE MONIST 550 (1967); and Bedau, *supra* note 3, at 55–59.

53. A possible exception to my claim that waiver of this fundamental right is impossible is the case of the death row prisoner who "volunteers" for execution, i.e., who does not permit his attorneys to pursue every possible avenue for relief, or who dismisses his attorneys before such relief has been pursued. Such a "volunteer" could, and I think

would more accurately, be described as someone who acquiesced in an infringement of his rights, viz., to due process and equal protection of the laws. In Gilmore v. Utah, 429 U.S. 1012 (1976), Justice White agreed, at least to the extent of arguing that the defendant was " 'unable' as a matter of law to waive the right to state appellate review" (1018). However, the majority of the Court in effect held otherwise, and Gilmore was executed. For discussion and argument on constitutional grounds against the Court's position, *see* W. S. White, *Defendants Who Elect Execution*, 48 U. PITT. L. REV. 853 (1987).

54. *See, e.g.,* THE HUMAN SIDE OF HOMICIDE (Bruce Danto et al. eds., 1982); DOUG MAGEE, SLOW COMING DARK: INTERVIEWS ON DEATH ROW (1980); ROBERT JOHNSON, CONDEMNED TO DIE: LIFE UNDER SENTENCE OF DEATH (1981); BRUCE JACKSON & DIANE CHRISTIAN, DEATH ROW (1980); Michael Radelet et al., *Families, Prisons, and Men with Death Sentences: The Human Impact of Structured Uncertainty*, 4 J. OF FAM. ISSUES 593 (1983); Margaret Vandiver, *Coping with Death: Families of the Terminally Ill, Homicide Victims, and Condemned Prisoners, in* FACING THE DEATH PENALTY (M. L. Radelet ed., 1989).

55. Walter Berns, *Defending the Death Penalty*, 26 CRIME & DELINQ. 507 (1980).

56. Gregory Vlastos, *Justice and Equality*, in SOCIAL JUSTICE 48 (Richard B. Brandt ed., 1962).

57. I have explored this point somewhat further in Bedau, *supra* note 3, at 55–59.

58. On these criteria, *see* D. C. Dennertt, *Conditions of Personhood*, reprinted in BRAINSTORMS, *supra* note 12, at 267–85. *See*, in general, WHAT IS A PERSON? (Michael Goodman ed., 1988); THE CATEGORY OF THE PERSON (Michael Carrithers ed., 1985); and THE IDENTITIES OF PERSONS (A. O. Rorty ed., 1976).

59. *See* Bedau, *supra* note 3, at 51–53.

60. *Id.* at 39–40, 60–62, 171–72. For arguments against the death penalty on retributivist grounds, see Reiman, *supra* note 3; and Murphy, RETRIBUTION, JUSTICE, AND THERAPY, *supra* note 3, at 223.

CHAPTER 8

1. Lawrence R. Klein et al., *The Deterrent Effects of Capital Punishment: An Assessment of the Estimates, in* DETERRENCE AND INCAPACITATION: ESTIMATING THE EFFECTS OF CRIMINAL SANCTIONS ON CRIME RATES 336 (Alfred Blumstein et al. eds., 1978). See, however, the as yet unpublished research by faculty in economics at Emory University purporting to show a deterrent effect of executions in recent years in the United States.

2. DAVID C. BALDUS ET AL., EQUAL JUSTICE AND THE DEATH PENALTY: A LEGAL AND EMPIRICAL ANALYSIS (1990).

3. Hugo Adam Bedau & Michael Radelet, *Miscarriages of Justice in Potentially Capital Cases*, 40 STAN. L. REV. 21 (1987).

4. THE DEATH PENALTY IN AMERICA 173–80 (Hugo Adam Bedau ed., 3d ed. 1982).

5. Gregg v. Georgia, 428 U.S. 153 (1976); Profitt v. Florida, 428 U.S. 242 (1976); Jurek v. Texas, 428 U.S. 262 (1976).

6. Marvin E. Wolfgang & Marc Riedel, *Rape, Racial Discrimination, and the Death Penalty, in* CAPITAL PUNISHMENT IN THE UNITED STATES 99 (Hugo Adam Bedau & Charles M. Pierce eds., 1976).

7. *See, e.g.*, JOHN RAWLS, A THEORY OF JUSTICE (1971), and H. L. A. HART, PUNISH-MENT AND RESPONSIBILITY: ESSAYS IN THE PHILOSOPHY OF LAW (1968).

8. *Cf.* RONALD DWORKIN, TAKING RIGHTS SERIOUSLY 22–23, 169–71 (1977).

9. Furman v. Georgia, 408 U.S. 238 (1972).

10. See Hugo Adam Bedau, *Bentham's Utilitarian Critique of the Death Penalty* 74 J. CRIM. L. & CRIMINOLOGY 1033 (1983), *reprinted in* HUGO ADAM BEDAU, DEATH IS DIF-FERENT: STUDIES IN MORALITY, LAW, AND POLITICS OF CAPITAL PUNISHMENT 64 (1987).

11. WALTER BERNS, FOR CAPITAL PUNISHMENT: CRIME AND THE MORALITY OF THE DEATH PENALTY (1979).

12. Hugo Adam Bedau, *Capital Punishment, in* MATTERS OF LIFE AND DEATH 159–60 (Tom Regan ed., 1980); *reprinted in* Bedau, DEATH IS DIFFERENT, *supra* note 10, at 24.

13. Ernest van den Haag, *The Ultimate Punishment: A Defense*, 99 HARV. L. REV. 1662, 1665 ff.

14. See Bedau & Radelet, *supra* note 3, at 78–81, 83–85.

15. Vivian Berger, *Justice Delayed or Justice Denied?—A Comment on Recent Proposals to Reform Death Penalty Habeas Corpus*, 90 COLUM. L. REV. 1665 (Oct. 1990); Anthony G. Amsterdam, *The Supreme Court and Capital Punishment*, 14 HUM. RTS. Q. 1, 14–18 (1987); Ronald J. Tabak, *The Death of Fairness: The Arbitrary and Capricious Imposition of the Death Penalty in the 1980s*, 14 N.Y.U. REV. L. & SOC. CHANGE 797 (1986); Hugo Adam Bedau, Gregg v. Georgia *and the "New" Death Penalty*, 4 CRIM. JUST. ETHICS 2, 3–17 (1985); Robert Weisberg, *Deregulating Death*, S. CT. REV. 305 (1984); and BALDUS ET AL., *supra* note 2.

16. Bedau, DEATH IS DIFFERENT, *supra* note 10, at 45.

17. Karl Marx, CAPITAL PUNISHMENT (1853), *reprinted in* BASIC WRITINGS ON POLITICS AND PHILOSOPHY: KARL MARX AND FREDERICK ENGELS 485–86 (Lewis Feuer ed., 1959).

18. BEDAU, DEATH IS DIFFERENT, *supra* note 10, at 123–28.

CHAPTER 9

1. Coker v. Georgia, 433 U.S. 584 (1977), and Eberhard v. Georgia, 433 U.S. 917 (1977). The constitutionality of nonhomicidal capital crimes as defined in the Anti-Terrorism and Effective Death Penalty Act, enacted by Congress in 1995, has yet to be decided.

2. Woodson v. North Carolina, 428 U.S. 280 (1976), and Sumner v. Shuman, 483 U.S. 66 (1987).

3. Phoebe C. Ellsworth & Samuel R. Gross, *Hardening of Attitudes: Americans' Views on the Death Penalty*, 50 J. SOC. ISSUES 19–52 (1994), *reprinted in* THE DEATH PENALTY IN AMERICA: CURRENT CONTROVERSIES (Hugo Adam Bedau ed., 1997).

4. *See* Bedau, *supra* note 3; also INTERNATIONAL COMMISSION OF JURISTS, ADMINIS-TRATION OF THE DEATH PENALTY IN THE UNITED STATES (1996); RAYMOND PATERNOSTER, CAPITAL PUNISHMENT IN AMERICA (1991); WELSH S. WHITE, THE DEATH PENALTY IN THE NINETIES: AN EXAMINATION OF THE MODERN SYSTEM OF CAPITAL PUNISHMENT (1991); and AMNESTY INTERNATIONAL, UNITED STATES OF AMERICA: THE DEATH PENALTY (1987).

5. *See* N.Y. TIMES, Feb. 4, 1997, at A20.

6. *See* David Dolinko, *Foreword: How to Criticize the Death Penalty*, 77 J. CRIM. L. & CRIMINOLOGY 546 (1986), where this point is forcefully made.

7. For a general discussion of the value of human life, *see* JOHN KLEINIG, VALUING LIFE (1991). Kleinig does not address the question of differential valuation of human lives or of how to measure the value of a person's life (nor does he dismiss these questions as unanswerable or as nonsense).

8. Immanual Kant distinguished between the "relative worth" or "price" and the "intrinsic worth" or "dignity" of all persons. The former could vary from person to person and from time to time, but not the latter; all rational creatures were forever equal in dignity. *See* KANT, GROUNDING FOR THE METAPHYSICS OF MORALS 40–41 (1785; trans. J. W. Ellington, 1981). This did not prevent Kant from arguing that murderers must be put to death; for a critical discussion, *see* MARVIN HENBERG, RETRIBUTION: EVIL FOR EVIL IN ETHICS, LAW, AND LITERATURE 158 (1990).

9. NAACP LEGAL DEFENSE AND EDUCATIONAL FUND, INC., DEATH ROW U.S.A. (Winter 1998), reports 3,365 person awaiting execution of a death sentence.

10. *See* Hugo Adam Bedau, *Thinking about the Death Penalty as a Cruel and Unusual Punishment*, 18 U.C. DAVIS L. REV. 873, 921–23 (1985), *reprinted in* HUGO ADAM BEDAU, DEATH IS DIFFERENT: STUDIES IN THE MORALITY, LAW, AND POLITICS OF CAPITAL PUNISHMENT 126–27 (1987).

11. Jeffrie Murphy discusses the possibility of human beings who are not moral persons because of their sociopathy; *see* his *Moral Death: A Kantian Essay on Psychopathy*, 82 ETHICS 284 (1972), *reprinted in* his RETRIBUTION, JUSTICE, AND THERAPY 128–43 (1979). Murphy does not confuse clarifying this concept with arguing for its application in actual cases.

12. *See in general* JOHN GILLIGAN, VIOLENCE: OUR DEADLY EPIDEMIC AND ITS CAUSES (1996).

13. I insert this qualification so as to leave open the possibility that forms of euthanasia or assisted suicide may be morally acceptable.

14. The Supreme Court's decision in *Payne v. Tennessee*, 501 U.S. 808 (1991), which permits victim impact testimony during the sentencing phase of a capital trial, in effect repudiates this assumption of moral equality, because it invites testimony designed to show that the victim is someone exceptional, and so the killer deserves the exceptional punishment of death.

15. The right to life has yet to receive the lengthy treatment that it deserves. For some recent suggestions, *see* SUSAN UNIACKE, PERMISSIBLE KILLING: THE SELF-DEFENSE JUSTIFICATION OF HOMICIDE 209–18 (1994).

16. JOHN LOCKE, *The Second Treatise of Government* (1690), *in* TWO TREATISES OF GOVERNMENTS, §§ 23, 172 (Peter Laslett ed., 1963). For an influential modern moralist who takes the same line (without expressly leaning on Locke), *see* W. D. ROSS, THE RIGHT AND THE GOOD 60 (1934).

17. Neglect by contemporary defenders of human rights to face the problems raised by traditional and commonplace claims that any right can be forfeited is nothing short of astounding; for further discussion see my article *The Precarious Sovereignty of Rights*, PHIL. EXCHANGE 5–16 (1997–98), and UNIACKE, *supra* note 15.

18. For a general discussion of self-defense and related issues, *see* UNIACKE, *supra* note 15.

19. For fuller discussion of the issues in this paragraph, *see* Bedau, *supra* note 17.

20. I borrow from Judith Jarvis Thomson the distinction between infringing a right

(failing to act in accordance with someone's right, but for adequate reasons) and violating a right (failing to act in accordance with someone's right, and for inadequate reasons). *See* her THE REALM OF RIGHTS (1990).

21. *Id.* at 367.

22. *See* ROUTES TO ABOLITION: THE LAW AND POLITICS OF THE DEATH PENALTY (Peter Hodgkinson et al. eds., 2004).

23. For representative contemporary utilitarian moral theory, see GEOFFREY SCARRE, UTILITARIANISM (1996); RICHARD B. BRANDT, MORALITY, UTILITARIANISM, AND RIGHTS (1992); ANTHONY QUINTON, UTILITARIANISM (2d ed. 1989); J. J. C. SMART & BERNARD WILLIAMS, UTILITARIANISM: FOR AND AGAINST (1973). None of these sources, however, offers any extended discussion of a utilitarian theory of punishment.

24. JEREMY BENTHAM, THE RATIONALE OF PUNISHMENT (1830), *reprinted in* 1 THE WORKS OF JEREMY BENTHAM 388 (John Bowring ed., 1838). *See also* my *Bentham's Utilitarian Critique of the Death Penalty*, 74 J. CRIM. L. & CRIMINOLOGY 1033 (1983), *reprinted in* my DEATH IS DIFFERENT, *supra* note 10, at 64–91.

25. J. S. Mill, *Speech in Favor of Capital Punishment* (1868), *reprinted in* PHILOSOPHICAL PERSPECTIVES ON PUNISHMENT 271 (Gertrude Ezorsky ed., 1972).

26. CESARE BECCARIA, ON CRIMES AND PUNISHMENTS AND OTHER WRITINGS (1764; Richard Bellamy ed., 1995).

27. Sidney Hook, *The Death Sentence, in* THE DEATH PENALTY IN AMERICA: AN ANTHOLOGY 146 (Hugo Adam Bedau ed., 1964).

28. For my part, I reject this argument for reasons well stated by Thomas Perry Thornton, *Terrorism and the Death Penalty, reprinted in* THE DEATH PENALTY IN AMERICA 181 (Hugo Adam Bedau ed., 3d ed. 1982), and by James Corcoran, *McVeigh Gets a Last Chance: To Be a Martyr,* BOSTON GLOBE, June 22, 1997, at D4. The position of the Catholic Church as set out in the papal encyclical *Evangelium Vitae* (1995) contemplates the possibility of the need to make a terrorist exception to complete abolition of the death penalty, but it implies that in actual fact modern nations do not need to do it.

29. *See* Mill, *supra* note 25.

30. JONATHAN GLOVER, CAUSING DEATH AND SAVING LIVES 240–42 (1977).

31. *See* Adolphe V. Bernotas, *Expert on Terrorism: McVeigh Must Die,* VALLEY [Lebanon, N.H.] NEWS, June 8, 1997, at B1.

32. Unfortunately, there is no comprehensive study of this clause in the Eighth Amendment. LARRY CHARLES BERKSON, THE CONCEPT OF CRUEL AND UNUSUAL PUNISHMENT (1975), provides little more than a digest of cases and statutes, when what is needed is a much deeper and broader theoretical account. For a fuller discussion of Berkson's book, see my review in 68 J. CRIM. L. & CRIMINOLOGY 167–68 (1977).

33. Why the death penalty is a violation of the Eighth Amendment has yet to receive the thorough treatment it needs. Raoul Berger, in his DEATH PENALTIES: THE SUPREME COURT'S OBSTACLE COURSE (1982), vigorously argued against that idea and thereby provoked vigorous criticism among most of his reviewers. See, for example, my review in 81 MICH. L. REV. 1152 (Mar. 1983). *See also* my *Thinking about the Death Penalty, supra* note 10. On the death penalty as a violation of the UDHR and related norms of international law, *see* WILLIAM A. SCHABAS, THE DEATH PENALTY AS CRUEL TREATMENT AND TORTURE: CAPITAL PUNISHMENT CHALLENGED IN THE WORLD'S COURTS (1996).

34. Today, lethal injection is widely defended on these grounds; it may well be true

that this method of execution is superior to the legal alternatives (lethal gas, hanging, firing squad, electrocution) and yet still open to objection. For a recent discussion, see Schabas, *supra* note 33, at 197–200.

35. Reasoning from behind a veil of ignorance to establish fair and reasonable fundamental principles of political organization is in the spirit of John Rawls; see his book A THEORY OF JUSTICE 136–42 (1972). For an application of such reasoning in the theory of punishment, see NORVAL MORRIS, THE FUTURE OF IMPRISONMENT 81–83 (1974).

36. For other discussions of the morality (or, rather, the immorality) of capital punishment, see my *Capital Punishment, in* MATTERS OF LIFE AND DEATH: NEW ESSAYS IN MORAL PHILOSOPHY 160 (Tom Regan ed., 3d ed. 1993), and my earlier essay *Objections to the Death Penalty from the Moral Point of View*, 58 REV. INTERNAT. DE DROIT PENAL 557 (1987). *See also* Jeffrey Reiman, *Justice, Civilization, and the Death Penalty*, 14 PHIL. & PUB. AFFAIRS 115 (1985), *reprinted in* his CRITICAL MORAL LIBERALISM: THEORY AND PRACTICE (1997); CARL WELLMAN, MORALS AND ETHICS 244 (2d ed. 1988); STEPHEN NATHANSON, AN EYE FOR AN EYE: THE MORALITY OF PUNISHING BY DEATH (1987); Richard Wasserstrom, *Capital Punishment as Punishment: Some Theoretical Issues and Objections*, 7 MIDWEST STUD. IN PHIL. 473 (1982); Thomas Hurka, *Rights and Capital Punishment*, 21 DIALOGUE 647 (1982); and H. L. A. Hart, *Murder and the Principles of Punishment: England and the United States*, 52 Nw. U. L. REV. 433 (1957), *reprinted in* his PUNISHMENT AND RESPONSIBILITY: ESSAYS IN THE PHIOSOPHY OF LAW (1968).

37. Elsewhere I have suggested that this argument has merit as an interpretation of the Eighth Amendment; *see* Chapter 6.

38. Elsewhere I have explored further the issues of this paragraph; *see* my *Punitive Violence and Its Alternatives, in* JUSTICE, LAW, AND VIOLENCE 193 (James B. Brady & Newton Garver eds., 1991).

39. Elsewhere I have explored and criticized the retributive theory of punishment (without, however, repudiating it entirely); see my *Retribution and the Theory of Punishment*, 75 J. PHIL. 601 (1978), and my *Justice and Punishment: Philosophical Basics, in* THE SOCIO-ECONOMICS OF CRIME AND JUSTICE, 19 (Brian Forst ed., 1993).

40. NAACP LEGAL DEFENSE FUND, *supra* note 9, at 7–15, reporting forty-seven "volunteers" for execution between 1973 and 1997. The total number of persons sentenced to death during these years is not less than five thousand.

41. *Id.*, reporting fifty-one suicides among death row convicts from 1973 through 1997. Attempted suicides are not reported.

42. I have explored in greater detail the reasons why it is rational to regard the death penalty as a more severe punishment than life imprisonment in Chapter 5.

43. We lack generally available reports and discussions of the prison behavior of life-term convicted murderers in the prisons of American abolition jurisdictions. In taking the position I do in the text, I am relying mainly on the absence of evidence to the contrary. Thus, at the symposium to celebrate 150 years without the death penalty in Michigan, held in May 1996 at the Thomas M. Cooley Law School in Lansing, Michigan, the state officials and local scholars who spoke on the occasion made no mention of problems in prison management that they believed would have been solved if only Michigan had had the death penalty. *See especially* Eugene G. Wanger, *Historical Reflections on Michigan's Abolition of the Death Penalty*, 13 THOMAS M. COOLEY L. REV. 755 (1996).

44. Is it reasonable to believe that the death penalty could be abolished tomorrow in

the Death Belt across the South (from the Carolinas to Arizona) without troubling social repercussions? One might well doubt that it could be. There is no sign in these states of the political leadership needed to make abolition acceptable to the general public as a humane and rational change in punitive policy. The political climate for the past generation, in which the death penalty has received rabid support, makes legislative or judicial abolition (or extensive executive clemency) all but impossible in these jurisdictions. In other death penalty states it is a different story. In New York, for example, beginning in 1977 gubernatorial vetos of death penalty legislation prevented its revival, and without public disorder, until 1995. Were New York's legislature or highest court tomorrow to repeal the death penalty or declare it unconstitutional under the state constitution (either is highly unlikely), I am confident the return to abolition could be managed without adverse social effects.

45. Retribution is not a motive, whereas revenge is; revenge knows no upper limits, whereas retribution does; revenge is personal, whereas retribution can be impersonal. For the best discussion, to which I am indebted, of the differences between these two concepts, see ROBERT NOZICK, PHILOSOPHICAL EXPLANATION 366–70 (1981). For a general discussion of retribution and revenge, *see* HENBERG, *supra* note 8.

46. For a list of abolitionist nations as of 1996, see the report from Amnesty International reprinted in BEDAU, *supra* note 3, at 78–83. I do not pursue here the strategy that allows us to grant that although murderers do *deserve* to die, we *ought not* to execute them.

47. See BEDAU, *supra* note 3, at 30–32.

48. See in particular the liberal theories of constitutional government variously formulated by H. L. A. HART, THE CONCEPT OF LAW (1961); JOHN RAWLS, *supra* note 35, and his POLITICAL LIBERALISM (1993); BRUCE ACKERMAN, SOCIAL JUSTICE IN THE LIBERAL STATE (1980); MICHAEL J. SANDEL, LIBERALISM AND THE LIMITS OF JUSTICE (1982); RONALD DWORKIN, LAW'S EMPIRE (1986), and his FREEDOM'S LAW: THE MORAL READING OF THE AMERICAN CONSTITUTION (1996); BRIAN BARRY, THEORIES OF JUSTICE (1989), and JUSTICE AS IMPARTIALITY (1995).

49. *See in general* HENBERG, *supra* note 8.

50. Ernest van den Haag, for one, accepts the distinction between retribution and revenge, and argues that both are legitimate; *see* his *The Death Penalty Once More*, U.C. DAVIS L. REV. 957 (1985), *reprinted in* BEDAU, *supra* note 3.

51. For representative views on the role for retributive considerations in nonretributive theories of punishment, *see* H. L. A. HART, PUNISHMENT AND RESPONSIBILITY, *supra* note 36, at 230–37; NIGEL WALKER, WHY PUNISH? 67–118 (1991); JOHN BRAITHWAITE & PHILIP PETTIT, NOT JUST DESERTS: A REPUBLICAN THEORY OF CRIMINAL JUSTICE 156–201 (1990); NICOLA LACEY, STATE PUNISHMENT: POLITICAL PRINCIPLES AND COMMUNITY VALUES 25–27, 53–56 (1988); C. L. TEN, CRIME, GUILT, AND PUNISHMENT: A PHILOSOPHICAL INTRODUCTION 38–65, 150–60 (1987); R. A. DUFF, TRIALS AND PUNISHMENTS 87–204 (1986).

52. Thus, a recent defense of retribution in punishment fails to make this distinction, with the result that we do not know what the author thinks is the appropriate deserved punishment for any given crime or offender; *see* Michael S. Moore, *The Moral Worth of Retribution, reprinted in* PHILOSOPHY OF LAW 632–54 (Joel Feinberg & Hyman Gross eds., 5th ed. 1995).

53. I would say the same of the "expressive function" of punishment, according to which punishment by its nature "expresses" condemnation of the criminal act. It is plausible to assume that the more severe the punishment, the more severe the condemnation warranted, and thus if murder (especially the worst murders) is the gravest crime, then it warrants the strongest condemnation, which only death can provide. Insofar as this is true, it is only because lesser crimes that now are punished by life imprisonment ("Three strikes and you're out!") make it impossible to "express" the greater condemnation appropriate for murder by life imprisonment. (I am indebted to Michael Davis for bringing this point forcefully to my attention.) Second, cruelty in punishment "expresses" other things besides condemnation of crime; it testifies to the willingness of officials to carry out death sentences on prisoners safely in their custody. It is by no means obvious that the greater condemnation of murder conveyed by execution cancels or supersedes the other messages that executions "express."

54. Two detailed but completely different versions of a retributive penalty schedule are to be found in ANDREW VON HIRSCH, DOING JUSTICE: THE CHOICE OF PUNISHMENTS (1976), and in Michael Davis, *How to Make the Punishment Fit the Crime*, 93 ETHICS 726 (1983), *revised and reprinted in* his TO MAKE THE PUNISHMENT FIT THE CRIME: ESSAYS IN THE THEORY OF CRIMINAL JUSTICE (1992). Elsewhere I have criticized von Hirsch's theory; *see* Bedau, *Retribution and the Theory of Punishment, supra* note 39, at 613–15, and my *Classification-Based Sentencing: Some Conceptual and Ethical Problems*, 10 NEW ENG. J. ON CRIM. & CIVIL CONFINEMENT 1 (1984). For another attempt at a retributive matching of punishments to crimes, *see* GEORGE SHER, DESERT 69–90 (1987).

Phillip Montague, in his PUNISHMENT AS SOCIETAL DEFENSE (1995), does not present and defend a retributive penalty schedule; but he does defend the death penalty by invoking a principle he believes is required to justify individuals in using lethal self-defense. However, his argument relying on this principle (42, 135) equally well justifies the use of torture, maiming, decapitation, or any other brutal form of punishment. Montague does not defend this alarming consequence, perhaps because he fails to see that it follows from his argument, thus providing us with another example of what happens in a theory of punishment when no upper bound to cruelty or savagery in modes of punishment is recognized.

For other defenses of the death penalty on retributive grounds that fail to do so within the framework of any comprehensive penalty schedule, *see* TOM SORELL, MORAL THEORY AND CAPITAL PUNISHMENT (1987), and IGOR PRIMORATZ, JUSTIFYING LEGAL PUNISHMENT (1989).

55. The problem was identified and discussed years ago by CHARLES L. BLACK, JR., CAPITAL PUNISHMENT: THE INEVITABILITY OF CAPRICE AND MISTAKE, 115–21 (2d ed. 1981). For a recent discussion of the vicissitudes in trying to predict future dangerousness, *see* Robert Menzies et al., *The Dimensions of Dangerousness: Assessing Forensic Predictions about Violence*, 18 LAW AND HUMAN BEHAVIOR 1–28 (1994).

56. *See* Kansas v. Hendricks, 95–1649, decided on June 24, 1997, upholding state statutes that detain predatory sex offenders beyond the expiration of their prison sentences; N. Y. TIMES, June 25, 1997, at A20.

57. On the distinction between the right and the good, and the priority of the former, *see* RAWLS, *supra* note 35, at 30–32, 446–52.

58. On relative costs, see RICHARD C. DIETER, MILLIONS MISSPENT: WHAT POLITICIANS DON'T SAY ABOUT THE HIGH COST OF THE DEATH PENALTY (rev. ed. 1994), *reprinted in part in* BEDAU, *supra* note 3.

59. *See in general* GILLIGAN, *supra* note 12.

60. ALBERT CAMUS, NEITHER VICTIMS NOR EXECUTIONERS (1946; trans. Dwight McDonald, 1986).

ACKNOWLEDGMENTS

In addition to expressing my appreciation to the several audiences before whom I presented the original versions of all but one of the chapters in this book for their patience and stimulation, I want to single out six persons, each of whom made a distinctive contribution to the book. I start with William Frohlich, director of Northeastern University Press, because of his support from the very start for this venture. Ann Twombly and Deborah Kops were, as usual, an outstanding production team; without them there would be no book. Megan Kelly provided indispensable help in preparing the manuscript. Michael L. Radelet generously allowed me to reprint here a revised version of an article that, as the record shows, we co-authored and he drafted in the first instance. Last but far from least I am indebted to Constance E. Putnam for her willingness to put aside her own work to help me with mine. The reader has much for which to be grateful to her, as do I. The flaws, such as they are, that remain—factual errors, omissions, poor judgment, and worse—are all mine.

Hugo Adam Bedau
Concord, Massachusetts

Permission to reprint revised versions of essays initially published elsewhere is gratefully acknowledged, as follows: Chapter 1, originally titled "The Death Penalty in America: Yesterday and Today," *Dickenson Law Review* 95 (1991): 759–72; Chapter 2, originally titled "American Populism and the Death Penalty," *Howard Journal of Criminal Justice* 33 (Nov. 1994): 289–303, © 1998 Basil Blackwell; Chapter 3, originally titled "The Execution of the Innocent," (and co-authored with Michael L. Radelet), *Law and Contemporary Problems* 61 (Autumn 1998): 105–24;

Chapter 4, originally titled "The Decline of Executive Clemency in Capital Cases," *New York University Review of Law and Social Change* 18 (1990–91): 255–72; Chapter 5, originally titled "Imprisonment vs. Death: Does Avoiding Schwarzschild's Paradox Lead to Sheleff's Dilemma?" *Albany Law Review* 54 (1990): 481–96; Chapter 6, originally titled "The Eighth Amendment, Human Dignity and the Death Penalty," in *The Constitution of Rights: Human Dignity and American Values*, ed. Michael J. Meyer and William A. Parent (Ithaca, N. Y.: Cornell University Press, 1992), 145–77, used by permission of Cornell University Press; Chapter 7, originally titled "Interpreting the Eighth Amendment: Principled versus Populist Strategies," *Thomas M. Cooley Law Review* 13 (1996): 789–814; Chapter 8, originally titled "How to Argue About the Death Penalty," *Israel Law Review* 25 (1991): 466–80; Chapter 9, originally titled "Abolishing the Death Penalty Even for the Worst Murderers," in *The Killing State: Capital Punishment in Law, Politics, and Culture*, ed. Austin Sarat (New York: Oxford University Press, 1999), 40–59.

INDEX